THE FORGIVENESS FACTOR

THE
Forgiveness Factor:
Stories of Hope in a World of Conflict

MICHAEL HENDERSON

Grosvenor Books, USA
Grosvenor Books, London

Grosvenor Books USA
Grosvenor Books, London

© 1996 by Grosvenor Books.
All rights reserved.

Printed in the United States of America.

Library of Congress Cataloging-in-Publication Data

Henderson, Michael.
    The forgiveness factor : stories of hope in a world
of conflict / Michael Henderson
        p. cm.
        Includes bibliographical references and an
index.
        ISBN 1-85239-024-7
        1. History, Modern—1945– 2. Ethnic rela-
tions—Moral and ethical aspects. 3. Pacific settlement of international disputes. 4. Diplomatic negotiations in international disputes. 5. Forgiveness. I.
Title.
        D842.H46 1996
        909.82-dc20   96-24605
                                                 CIP

Available from:

Grosvenor Books
3735 Cherry
Avenue NE
Salem, OR 97303
USA

Grosvenor Books
12 Palace Street
London,
SW1E 5JF
UK

Grosvenor Books
226 Kooyong Road
Toorak, VIC 3142
Australia

Grosvenor Books
P O Box 1834
Wellington
New Zealand

MRA Books
Suite 500
251 Bank Street
Ottawa, Ontario
K2P 1X3
Canada

Dedicated to Lawson and Mary Wood,
without whose care for our family
this book might never
have been written.

ABOUT THE AUTHOR

Born in England, Michael Henderson is a freelance journalist and radio commentator now living in Oregon. He is a recipient of national and local awards for his radio commentaries and newspaper columns.

Books by the author

FROM INDIA WITH HOPE

EXPERIMENT WITH UNTRUTH

A DIFFERENT ACCENT

ON HISTORY'S COATTAILS

HOPE FOR A CHANGE

ALL HER PATHS ARE PEACE

CONTENTS

FOREWORD

Rajmohan Gandhi

Sometimes history, selective history, gets us by the throat, threatening revenge and breathing new life into a chain of oppression and retaliation. Here, however, in this book on the possibility and power of forgiveness, courtesy of Michael Henderson, we have a selection of facts from the recent past that do the exact opposite: They kindle the hope that we may yet catch history's hand and guide it along calmer, safer pathways.

I marvel at the array of Henderson's evidence of reconciliation between bitterly divided groups. What is the invisible spark that, seemingly sudden at times, unites humans who had vowed death and humiliation to each other? Is it composed of forgiveness offered or asked? Of pity for survivors? Of a willingness to pause and reflect? Of an unexpected glimpse of the enemy in oneself, or of oneself in the enemy? Of an abrupt awareness that greatness was designed for us? Of an unexpected recollection of a long-forgotten mercy we had not merited? Is it a mystery linked to the Grace of God?

Henderson does not spell out his answers. Neither does he seek to reduce the real-life episodes in this book to a set of rules or steps. Reflecting readers may arrive at different conclusions. I think, however, that most will link the episodes to current headlines, and some at least may wish to see the spirit informing the episodes invoked over today's divides.

Michael Henderson's standing as a monitor of our times with an eagle eye for the gallant act is almost unique: I find it hard to

Rajmohan Gandhi is an author, research professor at the Centre for Policy Research, New Delhi, and a former senator.

think of others who have shown his perseverance over the decades—come wind, come weather—in spotting shoots of hope and describing these shoots, as well as the soil against which they struggle, to the large numbers who read, hear, or view him.

To be associated with his latest book is a privilege. It is also how I felt in 1977 when, in responding to my request, Henderson wrote *Experiment With Untruth,* a scrutiny of India under the 1975–77 Emergency declared by Mrs. Indira Gandhi. That valuable book illuminated, for the world and for Indians, a dark phase in a country that prizes democratic rights. In the years that followed, Henderson wrote regularly for the weekly *Himmat* that I was editing in Bombay, and he and I have found ourselves working together for reconciliation in different parts of the world.

I also feel moved as I pen these lines because of Henderson's English origins, which in his speech and demeanour are as unmistakable now, after the quarter century he has spent in the United States, as they were when I first met him in Germany almost forty years ago.

I cannot for long be with a Briton—whether physically or in the mind—without remembering that for about two hundred years Britain ruled over India. This rule did not commence at the invitation of Indians; neither did they ask for its continuance.

If, in the process, Britain did several useful and indeed remarkable things in India, it did not remove either the resentment that Indians felt at being held against their will, or the humiliation at being held by relatively small numbers of aliens. The fact of independence in 1947 did not fully dissolve these feelings.

Recently I was in the city of Kanpur in the North Indian province of Uttar Pradesh. In Kanpur had occurred some of the most painful killings of 1857, the year of the mutiny by Indian soldiers employed by the British.

Many perished in the violence, women and children as well as men, whites as well as Indians. The Mutiny, as the British called it, or the First War of Independence, as some Indians think of it, was effectively suppressed. In Kanpur I sought out some of the graves of 1857's victims. One epitaph I lingered with was to Judge Thornhill, his wife, and two children. It said: "Though he slay me, yet will I trust him."

In contrast with several of 1857's British victims, few of the Indians killed that year appear in diaries, letters, or epitaphs. Though each had a face, a name, hopes, a personality, and loved ones, these are now beyond recall. All we have are the numbers of Indians hanged, shot, and bayoneted in that year.

Born twelve years later, my grandfather Mohandas Gandhi—the Mahatma—led a nonviolent struggle that sought India's freedom without having to hurt a single Briton. The result was cordiality in independent India's relations with Britain, but it cannot be claimed that Britons and Indians have together acknowledged the past, or wholly agreed on it.

Why does grief trigger in one the emotion of revenge, and pity in another? Every episode related in this book by Henderson sparks such a question. We edge back in our chairs, stare at the horizon, wonder about the workings of a heart that decides to forgive, and ask if our heart is similarly capable.

We also ask other questions, and wonder whether, in practice, trust is likely between whites and blacks in the United States. Between Hutus and Tutsis, Indians and Pakistanis, Arabs and Israelis. Between the world of the West and the world of Islam.

These are formidable questions, yet we can, it seems to me, draw a little confidence from democracy's triumphs over totalitarianism in the last six decades. A great price was paid for these triumphs, and there were long spells of waiting and suspense, yet in the twentieth century history has more often than not seemed to side with decency.

Nevertheless, to this day, thick walls of blame and suspicion segment our global village. Vast and detailed information is at our fingertips; we touch a button and the world emerges on the TV screen; but evoking friendliness from the ethnic Other—or even an estranged family member—seems as hard as ever.

Thus, though we are awed by it, the Information Highway will not heal history's wounds. There is a limit to what facts can achieve; as a religious fundamentalist friend said recently to me, "Never mind the evidence, I will only believe what I want to believe." All the same, Henderson's history suggests that men and women may be drawn to a Reconciliation Highway.

May these narratives of courage and faith be widely read! I think they will inspire at least some acts of bridge-building.

New Delhi, May 25, 1996

FOREWORD

Joseph V. Montville

SCIENCE AND FAITH COME TOGETHER

This book is easy to read and full of stories of self-searching, modesty, quiet courage, and unacknowledged successes in resolving conflict. The protagonists are real people, and the tales are deeply human and appealing. The men and women described in *The Forgiveness Factor* qualify as spiritually motivated, sympathetic people who, unlike third-party outsiders, are often full-fledged members of one ethnic group in conflict with another. Their capacity for personal transformation and the spiritual qualities they reflect to their antagonists give them a special moral authority that both impresses opponents and reduces their defensiveness as solutions to conflicts are sought.

It would be a mistake, however, to regard this work as a well-meaning—and therefore naive and inconsequential—collection of anecdotes about a group of admirable souls whom the power brokers of the real world would summarily dismiss if they noticed them at all.

The stories recounted in this panorama are those of morally compelled actors and their effects in various parts of the world over fifty years since the establishment of Mountain House in Caux, Switzerland, in 1946. Their experiences at this center of reconciliation and change, owned and run by the Swiss Foundation for Moral Re-Armament, are now recognized as raw data for a rigorous new theory of personal and political conflict resolu-

---

Joseph V. Montville is a director of the Program on Preventive Diplomacy at the Center for Strategic and International Studies in Washington, D.C. A retired foreign service officer, he is a leading architect and practitioner of track-two, or nonofficial, diplomacy.

tion that had its origin in spiritual experience and is being studied at diverse secular research institutions. For example, Stanford University's Center for International Security and Arms Control, the Center for Strategic and International Studies (CSIS) in Washington, D.C., Harvard's Center for International Affairs, and the Council on Foreign Relations in New York are all working to expand the field of ethnic and sectarian conflict analysis and resolution. Similar research is being conducted in Europe with Germany, Sweden, the Netherlands, and the United Kingdom in the lead; in the Middle East, with Israel and Lebanon in the forefront; in Asia, with India and Japan paving the way; and in South Africa.

As if to underscore the irony of science's validation of the power of faith and spirit in healing human conflict, the trail leading to the powerful evidence in this book started in the late 1970s with an alliance between me, in my capacity as an American career diplomat, and the Committee on Psychiatry and Foreign Affairs of the American Psychiatric Association. The clinicians wanted to apply their knowledge and therapeutic skills to discovering a way out of the Arab-Israeli impasse. As a Middle East area specialist, I welcomed and actively supported their goal.

Some three years into the process our group of American doctors and diplomats found themselves with Israelis, Egyptians, and Palestinians at Mountain House. The center was hosted by Moral Re-Armament volunteers who were ready to support the scientific dialogue process in the service of peace building in the Middle East. The physicians and public servants had little difficulty understanding the basic tenet of Moral Re-Armament: Before change for the better can occur in nations, there must be change in individuals; moreover, those individuals must start the change process in themselves. For this transformation to happen, people in conflict need to listen to and hear each other. This process is best helped by trusted third parties convening the adversaries in safe and dignified surroundings. Caux is such a place. I am glad that through this book more people can come to know about its work spanning fifty years.

The critically important quality of trust in any peace process is described well in CSIS's *Religion, the Missing Dimension of Statecraft.*

Douglas Johnston, coeditor with Cynthia Sampson of the book, reprinted a memorandum I had given him summarizing what I believed the message to be. I repeat it here because it applies equally to this book:

> If one single quality has to be chosen to account for the influence that religiously identified third parties have, it would be their ability to inspire trust. One might think that is an obvious answer and, indeed, an easy quality to find in, say, any gentleman or lady, or well-bred lawyer or diplomat. But ethnic or sectarian conflict has a special aspect in that people have endured aggression and loss simply because of their membership in an identity group. They are dehumanized, despised, raped, pillaged, and murdered for no other reason than who they are, not for anything they have done.
>
> Until these people have suffered aggression and loss, they probably have a sense of fairness and predictability in life that allows them to get on without any particular daily foreboding. After their attack and loss, or the unreconciled and unmourned loss of their forebears, they feel distinctly distrustful of all outsiders. Their lessons in life have been that they can be killed because of their ethnic identity and, therefore, only members of their ethnic group can be trusted (and even some of them are suspect).
>
> Into the lives of these victimized people come religious outsiders, who in varying ways convey a sense of understanding and empathy for their fears and who have established reputations for honesty, discretion, and integrity. They are disinterested in the conflict except for their sadness over the human issues associated with it. And even the spiritually motivated third parties have to work "on site" with their new friends to prove through daily interaction that their reputations are justified and that they can be trusted to care about the life and death and future of the group they hope to help.

THE PSYCHOLOGY OF RECONCILIATION

In keeping with the theme of this foreword—that this book's accounts should be read as additional scientific data for a rigorous "secular" theory and practice of political conflict resolution—I offer a summary of the individual and group psychological and political processes that I believe occur in genuine reconciliation.

Traditional concepts of diplomacy and peacemaking rarely take into consideration the psychological influence on individuals, groups, and nations of traumatic or violent attack and grievous loss. Yet most political conflicts have had episodes of violence, open warfare, or even genocide. Certain psychological effects of political traumatic loss endure for years, generations, and centuries. Modern experience shows that time does not heal wounds. Only healing heals wounds.

Almost all longstanding ethnic and sectarian conflicts are characterized by recent or historic violence and by devastating loss of life, human physical capacity, property, and often territory. Equally important from a peacemaker's point of view is the victim or victim group's loss of a sense of confidence in the future and a capacity to trust; especially to trust the authors of their loss, their representatives, or their descendants in any negotiation or interaction. Victims believe that they have lost control over forces threatening their lives and that they are perpetually vulnerable to new attack.

The fear of new attack in the psychology of victims is sustained by the following facts: First, the aggressors or their descendants have never acknowledged that the original act or acts of aggression were unjust. Second, the aggressors or their descendants have not expressed regret or remorse for the acts. Finally, they have never genuinely apologized or asked forgiveness of the victim group or nation for their aggression.

Joseph V. Montville

THE HEALING PROCESS

A politically, but not morally, neutral third party can play a valuable role in launching a healing process. *Politically neutral* means the third party has no political interest in the outcome of the process. *Moral interest* means that the third party shows a sense of justice and moral values and is instinctively sympathetic to victims of injustice. Although the third party could be an official, track-one diplomat, most experience indicates that the special qualities of commitment to principle and interests greater than the self are found more often mostly in the unofficial, track-two diplomats, the type found so frequently in this book.

A qualified third party, which can also be a third-party team, helps to establish an atmosphere of safety and respect for all parties in a problem-solving workshop or dialogue process. It is essential for victims to feel safe so that they can confront their own losses without fear of the situation getting out of control emotionally. The psychologically sensitive third party provides that sense of safety.

A detailed, personalized description by the victim or representative of a victimized group of the traumatic event or events that caused the loss is a first step in the healing process. This can be begun by the third party by inviting the sides to take a walk through the history of the relationship or simply asking each side, "Tell us who you are." The answers almost inevitably include presentation of historic loss.

The interactive part of the healing process begins when the aggressors acknowledge the tragedy and injustice of recent or historic losses. From the psychological perspective acknowledgment has the effect of telling the victim group that the aggressors or their successors recognize that the aggression was unjust and the victim group's losses were terrible and unjustifiable violations of their basic human rights, even if the aggressors do not explicitly use such words. When the acknowledgment is sincere, complete, and detailed, the victim group can begin to believe that it is possible to trust the good faith of the aggressors in current negotiations and future relationships.

Explicit and sincere expressions of remorse or contrition by the aggressors can have a profound healing effect on the victim group. If such expressions are accompanied by a formal apology and request for forgiveness, the healing process will be under way. Where the aggressor's acknowledgment, contrition, apology, and request for forgiveness are sincere, there may or may not be an explicit grant of forgiveness to the aggressors by the victim group. This does not mean that the sincere expressions by the aggressor have not had an effect. It may mean that the victims will need time to absorb emotionally the impact of the act. There is also the psychological possibility that the victim group will need time to give up its identity of victimhood, which can provide a perverse kind of orderliness and predictability in a cruel world.

The challenge of peace may take time for testing before it begins to feel safe emotionally. Nevertheless, if a dialogue process can produce a sincere (if imperfect) acknowledgment-contrition-forgiveness transaction, then a healing process in the political and human relationship of the two peoples will have been launched and will be reflected in concrete, practical ways.

As you, the reader, move through this book, you will see illustrations of some of the key elements of the healing process.

The quiet heroes and heroines in these pages, through their lives and through connection to a network of people associated with Moral Re-Armament, represent the vanguard in the enduring struggle between commitment to principle and human potential for good, on the one hand, and the still-dominant cynicism of contemporary politics, diplomacy, and, quite often, business, on the other.

I believe strongly that the values and spiritual qualities revealed in these chapters will ultimately prevail in the contest and that scientific knowledge of human needs will confirm the power of spiritual conviction to shape an entirely new international culture of preventive diplomacy and conflict resolution initiative.

Mahatma Gandhi, whose grandson kindly wrote a foreword to this book, once heard that a British administrator had apologized for his arrogance to the Indians with whom he was working. For some reason the Mahatma thought this was out of character! He had the incident investigated and found that the administrator's apology had not only taken place but was resulting in fruitful teamwork between Indians and British.

Gandhi commented afterwards that politics had become like a great game of chess. We know the value of the pieces. We know the moves each one is permitted to make. But when one player's motive is changed, as had happened with the British administrator, the chess board is upset and everyone can start over.

Forgiveness is like that.

I have just been in South Africa, a nation that is starting again, courageously facing up to the inhumanity of the apartheid years and building a new equality between the races. A Truth and Reconciliation Commission established by parliament is trying to close the book on the past, with the realization that first you must know what the book says. But even as painful abuses of authority and flagrant trampling of human rights are being exposed, Archbishop Desmond Tutu, who heads the commission, can say, "One lesson we should be able to teach the world, and that we should be able to teach the people of Bosnia, Rwanda, and Burundi, is that we are ready to forgive."

Is forgiveness—both asking and offering—a realistic philosophy between nations and between individuals? Given the track record of this century, the cruelty and senseless killing, the holocaust and genocide, one's skepticism about its possibility and efficacy is justified. The stories in this book, however, show that forgiveness, like hatred, knows no national boundaries and has the power to break vicious cycles of hatred and revenge.

The book is written now because the future of many nations could be vitally affected by the issues raised between its pages; the nations include Ireland (I have both an English and Irish passport) where my family suffered and contributed to suffering during "the troubles" in this century and earlier. It is written now because Mountain House, a conference center in Caux, Switzerland, is marking its fiftieth anniversary as a place where people can come to seek change and reconciliation. I first visited Caux as a youth of fifteen. As a family we had experienced five years of separation during World War II and sought ways to find unity and to learn how the truths of our faith could be brought to bear on the world scene. And the book is written now because, over the close to fifty years since then, I have seen abundant evidence that the forgiveness factor has upset many a chessboard around the world.

Mountain House itself was founded by a network of people who go by the name of Moral Re-Armament, or MRA. Younger readers may think the name suggests the moral majority or military weaponry, not knowing that MRA was conceived as a program of moral and spiritual armament for a world rearming frantically before what became World War II. On hearing of MRA, on the other hand, some of our older readers may be tempted to ask, "Are they still around?"

All over the world people and organizations, of all kinds on all continents, are working to build mutual respect and further a spirit of forgiveness. Some of these efforts have been helped forward by the spirit of Caux and the concept of Moral Re-Armament.

This book, however, is not so much a celebration of the achievements of one particular group of people as it is an attempt to get at truths that can be valid for everyone. It is about people departing from predictable ways, contributing to solutions where they themselves were sometimes seen by some as the problem in the first place.

Preface

Over the years, I have gotten to know, see at work, and talk with many of the men and women in this book, including Frank Buchman, the initiator of MRA. Buchman believed that if you want to put right what is wrong with the world, the appropriate place to begin is with yourself—in other words, that it is changed men and women who are the raw material for a changed world. I offer their stories in the hope that those who are not engaged in the tasks described will become so, and those already working in the field will find the information and encouragement that makes it possible to persevere.

My firsthand experience with many of the events described were a major resource for my writing. I have, indeed, discussed many of the people in my book in my weekly radio show over the past fifteen years. Back numbers of MRA publications in Britain and the United States, including the magazines *New World News* and *For a Change*, have been further repositories of information. Material was also available from the archives at Mountain House, various books published about the center, and two well-researched academic dissertations, "The Moral Re-Armament Movement and Post-war European Recovery" by David J. Price at London University and "Zur Bedeutung der Moral für die Politik: Eine Untersuchung der Arbeit der Moralis-chen Aufrüstung an drei Fallbeispielen" by Franz Johann Vock at Salzburg University.

In closing, I would like to thank everyone who helped me with this book, those who researched information, corrected detail, provided perspective and, in doing so, often interrupted their own busy schedules. They include many of the people whose stories appear in these pages. Some of those who were of greatest assistance are mentioned in the chapter notes. A particular word of gratitude must go to Steve Kent, Elizabeth Locke, Hugh Nowell, Erika Hetzner, Gordon Wise, Shirley Sirota Rosenberg and her editorial staff at SSR, Incorporated, graphic designer Stephen Kraft, and Dick Ruffin.

M.H.

SECTION ONE

Healing the Postwar World

1

Caux: Forming
a world conscience

It is there that a thousand and one links
have been forged in a kind of parallel diplomacy,
apparently unstructured, which counts on the
human heart rather than on the weight of
arms to resolve conflicts and bring
the world closer together.

LE MONDE

MOUNTAIN HOUSE

In the summer months, hang-gliders with their gaily colored
canopies are launched from the Rochers de Naye towering
above and drift lazily down past the bedrooms of Mountain
House in the Swiss village of Caux. In the winter skiers race
down the slopes above the building, while skaters waltz to
canned music just up beyond the Catholic and Protestant
chapels. Below stretches a vista as awe inspiring as any in the
world, with Lake Geneva and its paddle steamers and sailboats,
the Grammont and French Alps behind, and the snow-capped
ridge of the 12,000-foot Dents du Midi dominating the Rhone
valley to the east. It is no wonder that a luxury hotel, the Caux
Palace, was built here at the turn of the century; it's no wonder,
too, that the local authorities were pleased when it was not
demolished in 1946 as planned. Instead, it was turned into
Mountain House, a center for change and reconciliation: one
more Swiss contribution, like the Red Cross, to world peace. It

3

is a center that, when celebrating fifty years of service, gave its jubilee conference the theme, "Healing the past, forging the future."

Since 1946 some two hundred and fifty thousand people have come for conferences at Mountain House. Its work to overcome hatred, to end long-standing conflicts, to sometimes host rival groups looking for solutions, has led to its being nominated for the Nobel peace prize in 1996. Speaking there on the fortieth anniversary in 1986, Austrian Franz Cardinal König said, "Since the end of the Second World War, Caux has been a place where people of different races, political opinions, and classes have come together, often from seats of conflict that were threatening the peace of the whole world. Here the idea of reconciliation and peace has grown, in a world where the fronts have hardened and the tensions increased. Again and again a way has been found, a breakthrough has happened. I am convinced that the spirit of God is at work here. Today there are many conflicts in which simple, unofficial dialogue has a greater chance than any official mediation."

The Caux Palace Hotel, built as a luxury hotel in 1902, had, as a result of the First World War and the Depression, never been a success financially. In 1945 it was a home for interned Allied prisoners of war who had escaped from Italy, Italian refugees, and Jewish exiles from Hungary—all crammed six and eight to a room. A contemporary account describes what met the eyes of a group of Swiss as they entered the building: "This hotel had seen the soft and easy living of the pre-war years which had made it necessary in time of war to house 1200 refugees, whose hopelessness and bitterness towards their fellows and the future could be seen in the eight hundred door handles and locks wantonly destroyed, in the two hundred broken chairs, in the sickening dirt and the state of the mattresses and bedding."[1]

These Swiss had just agreed, out of great sacrifice, to buy the hotel as a neutral setting where former enemies could meet and be reconciled. They were inspired to do so by their association with an American, Frank Buchman, the initiator of Moral Re-

Armament (MRA). They were not lacking in hubris: "2.30 P.M. June 1st, 1946. At this hour began an event more important even for the future of the world than H-hour on D-Day when the liberating armies of the democracies launched their long awaited attack on the shores of Nazi-dominated Europe." But they were awed by the size of the immediate challenge:

> We had six weeks in which to transform this cold, gaunt giant of a place into a home to welcome a family of three hundred and more. We had to prepare two hundred bedrooms from top to bottom, 600 mattresses and beds. Many of the mattresses needed entirely redoing. There are 15,000 windows, several miles of corridors, acres of parquet flooring and all the hundred and one things that make a home a home. Our biggest headache was the kitchen, a black hole of Calcutta from the field kitchens which had belched their sooty smoke on walls and ceilings. How to turn it from one which fed 300 to one that would feed 800. Like the statesmen of Europe today, we faced a humanly impossible task.[2]

From all around Switzerland and Europe, volunteers came to help. They included many Allied ex-servicemen and women who saw this center as the embodiment of the kind of world they had fought for and who came in a spirit of reaching out to former enemies. By July 8 the first meal for one hundred fifty was served—prepared by eight cooks from five nations who, lacking a common language, had drawn pictures of the vegetables they proposed serving. By the end of that month, Mountain House was ready for the first conference. The bank had received the first installment of 450,000 Swiss francs, as stipulated by the contract—collected through gifts from ninety-five Swiss families.

It was the fulfillment of a thought that Swiss diplomat Philippe Mottu had had three years earlier: If Switzerland were spared by the war, its task would be to make available a place where Europeans, torn apart by hatred, suffering, and resentment, could come together. That place was Caux.* Switzerland's wartime commander-in-chief, General Henri Guisan, said that his country had tried its best to assuage the misery and suffering caused by war. Now, through Caux, it was being given a chance "to bring to Europe the secret of a living democracy."†

That summer of 1946, three thousand people from thirty-four countries attended. Swiss newspaper headlines echoed the themes of the sessions: "Enemies of yesterday can be friends tomorrow," "German-French conversation in Caux," "Class war or teamwork?" "Do what is right not what seems useful." The correspondent for *Neue Zürcher Zeitung,* the leading German-language daily, had a glimpse of the potential: "Caux has every chance of becoming a world center of a very outstanding kind."

Today the crenellated towers of the buildings, believed by some to be the model for Walt Disney's Snow White castle, look much as they did nearly a hundred years ago when the building was constructed. The interior, however, with meticulous Swiss attention to detail, has been regularly refurbished and modernized. Many families have contributed their best furnishings and international artists their paintings. The main dining room wall, for instance, is a fresco, "Living streams of water," by Finland's master Lennart Segeståle. The ballroom of the old Caux Palace has been transformed into an intimate theater.

At the first conferences fifty years ago a succession of translators would interpret speeches from the platform, usually in a few West European languages. Now a donated modern translation system is in place, and the interpreting through headphones will likely be in Russian or Serbo-Croat, Chinese or Korean, Swahili or Khmer. After World War II the emphasis may have been on reconciliation.

---

*In November 1985 Mottu described the whole development at a symposium organized by the Geneva University Institute of European studies on the theme, "Switzerland and Europe: 1945–50."

†General Guisan came to Caux three times in 1947. This is from a message sent by the general to Caux in June 1948 on the occasion of the 10th anniversary of MRA and the 70th birthday of Buchman.

In the nineties it is often on dealing with the hatreds that have been given free rein since the end of the Cold War and on how to bring to an end some of the century's longest-lasting conflicts. The dress of the participants and the conduct of meetings are, of course, more informal today. The large conference halls and smaller breakout rooms are ideal for modern conference requirements. But even the far-seeing Swiss must have had some doubts about what they were taking on in 1946.

ENCOUNTERS AT CAUX

For those who had been through the six years of World War II, some of whom had been in concentration camps and prison camps, the prospect of a visit to orderly Switzerland and decent meals was an alluring one. Fifty years later the tranquil setting was just as refreshing for Russians coming out of their ideological hell, or Hutu and Tutsi from the killing jungles of Burundi, or those Croatians, Bosnians, and Serbs who managed to get out of former Yugoslavia to attend.

In 1994 Russian philosopher Grigory Pomerants wrote in the Moscow paper *Novoye Vremya,* "The first impression is of the overwhelming beauty of Mountain House. The second is of the people who in no way ruin the beauty." In the Caucasus or in the Crimea, he continued, there are mountains, valleys, and lakes equal to those in Switzerland. But the people spoil the beauty with noise and dirt. In Switzerland he noted an absence of litter, clean and quiet cars, no drunks, and the custom of saying, "*Bonjour, monsieur*" or "*Bonjour, madame.*"

> Maybe it's only a custom. But a very good custom. In it is the age-old respect for another person, the sense of responsibility to others. And supported by these customs the special spirit of Mountain House has been created, infusing customary politeness with sincere goodwill. I don't see how to avoid this old-fashioned word.[3]

The Swiss might perhaps feel that the Russian thinker was being a little overgenerous to their country but there is no doubt of the effect of Caux on the first-time visitor. Their countries' flags fluttering from poles outside the building often greet them. The first major Japanese group, for instance, was moved to see the rising sun emblem flying when it was forbidden back home. Cypriots were later honored by their own flag, the country's first, sent by Archbishop Makarios in gratitude for the role of Caux in helping their island gain independence.[4] And South Africans of all races gathered in 1995 when their new national flag was raised at Caux.

The first large German group after the war was welcomed to Mountain House by a French chorus singing in German; Swedish Count Folke Bernadotte, one of the early UN peace-makers, by a Swedish chorus; French Foreign Minister Robert Schuman was serenaded by a group of international singers. Prime ministers as well as cabinet ministers and others who have gone on to lead their countries, captains of industry and trade union leaders, and religious figures from Billy Graham to the Dalai Lama, from Russian orthodox priests to rabbis and imams, have passed through its doors.

NATIONAL DELEGATIONS

According to historian Robin Mowat, the new center "proved a magnet for many of Europe's postwar leaders from all walks of life"[5] when it opened. Journalist David Price wrote that "Caux, throughout the 1950s, was perhaps the most important European forum for reconciliation." This was particularly so for France and Germany. In the first four years, more than five thousand people came to Caux from those two countries alone. The interaction of Germans and French there and their work on their return to their countries had a powerful effect. In its fifty years of existence, the role of Mountain House as a supplement to official diplomacy is seen most dramatically in the way it has helped undergird efforts at the political and economic level to build unity at the heart of Europe. According to some observers, what the Marshall Plan achieved on the economic level in assisting the recovery of Europe, Caux helped achieve on the moral and spiritual level. Indeed, Paul Hoffman, the plan's administrator, described Caux's work as "the ideological counterpart of the Marshall Plan."

French Catholic philosopher Gabriel Marcel believed that what he saw at Caux was a "real world conscience" being formed for the first time. Many there had what he called "decisive encounters." He wrote, "I know of no other place where you come into such clear touch with the only freedom which is worthwhile, the freedom of the children of God." A French member of parliament, Jean-Marie Daillet, said at Caux in 1995, "I experience here a kind of face to face with the whole world, with myself, with God."

Hundreds of such encounters set men and women on new roads. A German cabinet minister, Heinrich Hellwege, struck up a friendship in Caux with Danish Foreign Minister Ole Bjorn Kraft. In 1955, thanks to the trust between them, they were able to have private conversations that led to a settlement of the Schleswig-Holstein border dispute. Four young men from Costa Rica came in 1950, and each in turn became the country's president. One of them, Alberto Monge, speaking at the opening of a Central American conference in San Jose in 1984, said that in Caux they had received "the sense of responsibility which led us to found and create a political movement a year later which is still continuing, the only political force which has taken the shape of a democratic political party."

In 1953 Australian politician Kim Beazley, Sr., made a commitment while in Caux to champion the rights of Aborigines throughout his parliamentary career. "I had to admit that what I saw at Caux was far more significant for the peace and sanity of the world than anything being done at that time in Australian politics." For twenty-three years he was in the political opposition; yet it was from this position that he achieved great gains for the country. When awarded an honorary doctorate by Australian

National University, the citation pointed out that his two great achievements—the healing of the ulcer of sectarian bitterness as minister of education and the enhancement of the dignity of the Aborigine people—came because he had worked irrespective of political party gain.

In Caux Maori leader Canon Wi Te Tau Huata, chaplain to the Maori queen from New Zealand, faced up to his "cancer of bitterness" toward Catholics resulting from his son's marriage to a Catholic woman and toward Germans against whom he had fought in World War II. He was moved when a German woman said she was sorry for her people's treatment of the Jews. "By honestly accepting blame and asking forgiveness," he said, "she made me see that hate and faith could not exist side by side in the same heart."

The canon went from Caux to Rome where he met the pope. Later he was a guest of honor at a reunion of the Afrika Korps in Germany. Seated beside Field Marshal Rommel's widow, Lucie-Marie, and their son, Manfred, he was asked to speak. "This is a time for brotherhood," he told seven thousand German veterans, "a time for reconciliation, a time for cleansing." General Siegfried Westphal, Rommel's successor as commander of the Afrika Korps, responded, "Your greatness is not only in battle but also in your heart by accepting our invitation of goodwill."

Over the years U.S. congressional delegations and U.S. ambassadors have visited Caux. Then-chairman of the Senate Foreign Relations Committee Alexander Wiley told his colleagues in 1954, "Those of us who are among the many members of the House and Senate who have visited Caux, are convinced that more information and answers on the current world situation can be found there than at any place we know."[6]

In 1960 Chief Walking Buffalo of the Stoney Indians spoke at a conference. (His granddaughter, Clarice Kootenay, also spoke there in 1995.) With her at the time was Mohawk Grand Chief Joe Norton. Marian Anderson, the great American singer, said, "The inspiring days I spent here at this beautiful and sacred spot will remain a treasured memory. I never knew that there was a vast army of people of so many races pledged to put right what is wrong in the world."

Not everyone is always prepared to be confronted by people with whom they differ. Nor is it always wise for them to be so. In 1968 a group of Czechs were in the house, also the exiled King Michael and Queen Anne of Romania. Suddenly a senior Soviet journalist arrived. The house was fortunately large enough for them not to meet each other. The journalist returned to Moscow to write an article belittling what he had seen. In the 1990s all were back in Caux. The Romanians where able to meet openly with their people, the Czechs and the Russians had moving reconciliations—and the Russian journalist now comes regularly, interprets for other Russians, and writes honest accounts for the newspapers.

INTERPERSONAL RELATIONS

The experiences at Caux reveal the surprising link between the global and the intimate, the integral connection between the personal and the national. Oscar Alaniz, from Uruguay, for instance, a civil servant with the Organization of American States, asked himself what an ordinary person like himself could do. After his wife's visit to Caux in 1981, a change occurred in their relationship. Through honesty and sincere repentance the gap between them disappeared. Would it not be possible, he wondered, to do the same for the nation? Unexpectedly, a politically neutral friend was named minister of education. He invited the collaboration of Oscar, who became deputy director-general in the ministry of education. Together and through democratic processes they introduced measures to improve national education that the military had thought impossible. "In times of meditation together," he said, "God inspired us and led us through the crisis we were facing." Soon his home was being used as a place where leaders of the different democratic groups would come for frank dialogue on the way to move the country from military rule to democracy. One meeting in his home with political leaders of all

11

backgrounds included the president. "Seeking inspiration in silence," a rough agreement was drawn up which the minister presented to the military and political leaders in turn. Later the military and political leaders came to a complete agreement in the Naval Club of Uruguay. "I was in Caux in August 1984," he said, "when I received a copy of our newspaper, *Oficial;* to the joy of the Uruguayan people, it announced the date of the first democratic elections."[7]

THE ATMOSPHERE AT CAUX

What do those coming to Caux find besides the imposing buildings and a restful setting with miles of woods all around to enjoy and the chance to meet people they might not meet elsewhere? Many coming up from UN conferences at the other end of the lake in Geneva speak of the absence of blame in the public utterances and the private exchanges with each person seeking the process of reconciliation. The Swiss paper *Der Bund* wrote in May 1954 about a conflict being dealt with by the UN, "At best all that can come out of Geneva is a compromise which can dam up bloody passions for a while without curing the fundamental differences. In Caux, on the other hand, there is ever rising the spiritual building that does not just appease hate, but actually overcomes it."

The emphasis at Caux is not on theory but on the exchange of experience, which often continues over meals or walks. The anecdotal approach has proved over time to foster an atmosphere of reflection. All have the opportunity to take time in quiet daily for God to give them fresh illumination. This is a practice encouraged both for those who believe in God and for those who may attribute any inspiration that comes to what some call the inner voice. Most sessions at the conference are also away from the glare of publicity.

The presence of people from throughout the world at Caux provides a different perspective on both history and the present. People begin to take to their hearts the suffering of those from countries that may have previously seemed remote. At a 1995 meeting a young Bosnian spoke "for those in the front lines who can't speak to you" of "forgiveness without barriers" that springs from love. He had been in the fighting and lost close friends, but he went on, "We must not hate and imitate the hate of others. Revenge is against God." Four Somalians from different corners of their country spoke and then sang together.

Some people's experiences go further back in time. On the anniversary of the Warsaw Pact invasion of Czechoslovakia, a Polish police officer apologized for his part in putting an end to the Prague Spring. A rabbi from Israel who refused to serve with the Israeli army when it invaded Lebanon said, "The closest thing we have to God is the spark of life in each one [of us], and if we deny others equality, we deny God." A Polish couple, the Stepans, now living in London, spoke of their deportation during World War II to Siberia and their suffering at the hands of Russians. Olgierd Stepan, an architect and leading Catholic layman, told how his father was arrested by Soviet soldiers, one of them weeping at what he was being forced to do. He had never seen his father again. Yet he owed his survival in Siberia to the kindness and bravery of other Russians. "We must separate the people from the satanic system under which they also suffered," he said.

An American orthodox rabbi, Dr. Marc Gopin, remembers the critical backdrop provided by Caux for his exchanges with young Muslims and what he calls "the commitment to informal meetings, networking relationships, and introductions, and a strong level of attention to civility." His experience at Caux helped him see how to integrate the deepest elements of his Jewish culture with conflict resolution strategy and to use Judaism as a bridge between secular and religious, Jews and non-Jews.

He relates that one summer some Jews at Caux were about to say the Friday night *kiddush* (Sabbath sanctification chant) and wanted to invite some of the Muslims present to observe or participate with them. But it occurred to them that alcoholic wine would be a problem for them, so they found some grape juice, and the Muslims joined them. These same Muslims, Rabbi Gopin recalls, were clearly angry at Israelis because of what they perceived as the humiliation of Palestinians since 1967. As Gopin watched them he thought, "Who is honored? He who honors all human beings." And so, as a rabbi, he went out of his way to honor these young Muslims in very practical ways for many days. "By the end they, astonished by my behavior, completely transformed their attitudes toward Jews. A real love developed, and they were eager to return to their country and encourage a different attitude toward Jews. This was before Oslo, where the present peace process began." Gopin wrote:

> Caux alerted me to a biblical method of conflict resolution. Exodus 23:5 teaches that it is a *mitsvah* (good religious deed) to help your enemy when he is struggling under his burden. And rabbinic Judaism taught over a period of many centuries that shared work is designed to actually confuse the enemy, wake him up from his safe assumptions that the other person is evil. In creating that confusion the *mitsvah* creates the possibility of change inside someone's heart, forcing him to re-evaluate his feelings, moving him to repent of his hatred and forgive. I have thought about that text for years now, and since Caux I have thought about the work details, and how the Muslim students and I shared the kitchen duty, and how this did so much to create a bond. The shared work, the leveling of social distinctions, the shared new experience that leaves behind old stereotypes and prejudices as we shared a new task and challenge together, the deflection of conversation away from—temporarily—the hard issues, and towards filling the salt shakers. All of these things helped to transform the relationship of enemies.[8]

CONTRIBUTING IN KIND AND IN SPIRIT

Everyone who attends Caux conferences is encouraged to help with the practical running of the house, which as Rabbi Gopin points out, often provides the relaxed setting needed for deep

friendships to develop. In its early years Mountain House sometimes provoked cartoons in newspapers showing national or
international leaders washing dishes together in Caux. At one
point, those arranging the conferences at Mountain House were
worried that Italian parliamentarians were reluctant to come to
Caux because of this image. A Nigerian woman joked that she
comes to Caux because it is the only place in the world where
she finds Nigerian men in the kitchen. Caux offers not the luxury
of a five-star hotel but instead the extra mile that comes from
volunteers who care. In an article August 31, 1947, the Philadelphia *Sunday Bulletin* called them "one of the most remarkable
hotel staffs ever assembled."

Participants are invited to contribute according to their means
and to help others who may not be able to cover the cost of their
stay. Gifts are provided in kind. Early in the history of Mountain
House there was a rail line to the front door on which wagon
loads of coal would come from the Ruhr to heat the buildings. A
Thai prime minister, Field Marshal Pibul Songgram, once sent ten
tons of rice for Asian delegates at Caux. Today's gifts range from
regular supplies of fish from Norway to fruit from Switzerland.

French parliament member Georges Mesmin says that political
figures who come to Caux find three things:

• A respect for all opinions: "Despite certain remarks which
could be hurtful, people have not become angry. We have listened to everyone, and we have all benefited."

• An openness to others and to forgiveness even when one
thinks another is wrong: "We politicians are inclined to battle at
the level of personalities. One thing we slowly learn at Caux is to
distinguish between the battle of ideas and the battle with a person who is an adversary now but who tomorrow could become a
friend."

• An atmosphere of friendship. "In this building you make
friends who want nothing from you. Here we have a vision of a
world of goodwill, a world where one cares for the real interests
of others and not one's own. It is a well of living unselfishness."[9]

In 1994 an interfaith panel comprising two Jews, two Christians, and two Muslims discussed the topic, "The Holy Land and the People of the Book." One Israeli said it was the first time in his life that he was in a minority situation in which he felt totally welcome and included. A rabbi and an imam embraced each other as they left the conference. At one session called "Healing the wounds of history," Vytautas Landsbergis, the former president of Lithuania who had led his country to restored independence, spoke at Caux of the need for reconciliation founded on justice. On his return home he told his parliament that this perspective of change and reconciliation was very necessary for Lithuania's relations with Poland.[10]

In 1995 twenty-five Jamaicans led by Governor General Sir Howard Cooke, and fifty-two Cambodians including cabinet ministers and the Supreme Patriarch, the Venerable Maha Ghosananda, as well as some of the first Chinese to come officially from Beijing, and the first representative from North Vietnam, spent time at Caux. A group of Somalis from different allegiances felt this was the place where their countrymen and women could come together. One Somali, Ahmed Hussen Egal, a former guerrilla fighter, said, "Last summer the UN troops had not yet left Somalia. All of us expected that the war would start again at the moment they withdrew from our country. But, to our astonishment, that didn't happen. Personally I even dare to believe that what happened to us here at Caux last summer played its part in this development."[11]

Notes

1. Letter signed by Philippe and Hélène Mottu, Elspeth Spoerry, Kärstin Rääf, and Theo Metcalfe.

2. Ibid.

3. Moscow *New Times* No. 45, November 1994.

4. This role is described in Dommel, *Histoire Economie et Societé*, third quarter 1995.

5. Mowat, *Decline and Renewal*.

6. *New World News,* summer 1954.

7. Told by Alaniz at Caux and at a conference, "Making a world of difference," at Georgetown University, June 15–23, 1985.

8. Gopin, "Hope from the Middle East," *Breakthroughs,* January/February 1986.

9. *New World News,* September 15, 1979.

10. Reported in *Lietuvos Aidas,* Vilnius, September 22, 1994.

11. Caux archives.

2

Bridges over the Rhine

*The rapid Franco-German reconciliation
after 1945 is one of the greatest achievements
of modern statecraft.*
EDWARD LUTTWAK
U.S. MILITARY STRATEGIST

THE FIRST GERMAN SPEAKER IN
AN AMERICAN SYNAGOGUE

It was only at breakfast time that German Member of Parliament
Peter Petersen was told by his host, a Jewish member of Congress, that he was expected to speak shortly in a New York synagogue.[1] Peter was shocked. Without even asking his overnight
guest, Congressman Jim Scheuer, whom Peter had met and
talked with at an international conference, had informed his
rabbi that Peter would speak. What should he speak about, Peter
asked. Oh, whatever he liked, responded Jim; he was sure that
everything they had discussed about policies toward Israel would
be of great interest. No German had ever spoken in the synagogue, so the public would be very attentive.

Half an hour after breakfast they arrived at the synagogue,
where they were greeted by some of Jim's Democratic Party
friends. With apologies to Peter, they warned Jim of the possible
political consequences if he deliberately brought in a German in
this way. The rabbi, however, welcomed them warmly and
escorted them to the front, greeted those present, and turned

the proceedings over to Jim. Peter had naturally expected his host to smooth the way for him a little, explaining why he had invited him. But Jim said simply that they had expected a talk today from their representative about developments in Washington; he was instead asking his friend, Peter Petersen, to speak to them. "He is a German and a member of the German Parliament," he said. "Come on, Peter!" The hall was dead quiet.

Peter knew he could not deliver his normal political speech. "Ladies and gentlemen," he told the four hundred Jews, "if I appear before you today as a German and look as I do and have just about the right age, then you will have a question at the back of your minds that will drown out anything I could tell you about the German perspective on Israel. Therefore, permit me to answer that question first."

Peter says that after these first words he could feel the tension in the hall. He went on. "I grew up as an enthusiastic Hitler Youth boy." At the back of the hall a man jumped up and interrupted, "So you admit it?" Peter responded, "Would you rather have someone here who lied—who acted as if he had never heard of Hitler? I was 17 years old when the war ended." Shaking, the man sat down.

Then Peter went on. At that time, the war's end and the collapse of the Third Reich meant only one thing for him and his friends: The Americans and the Russians had more planes and bombs. Many of his friends had been killed, and Peter himself had been wounded only two weeks before the end of the war when he had tried to knock out a Canadian tank. He had regarded the news of what had gone on in the concentration camps as Allied propaganda; it was something he felt Germans would never do. His father, however, had brought home a Jewish man who had been in a concentration camp for eight years. After learning what the man had lived through, Peter had had a sleepless night. It was clear that this would always be on the country's conscience. He wanted to run away—to emigrate, to get away from being a German. But his father helped him to see that he could not and must not run away from himself.

19

It took time, Peter said, to move beyond his self-pity and self-righteousness. The illumination came after he suddenly remembered an incident in 1944, when he had been a soldier in Silesia. There he had seen a group of people in terrible shape, heavily guarded by the SS, being herded from one cattle car to another. He had asked his lieutenant who they were, and the officer had replied, "Oh, don't worry, they're just Poles and Jews."

"The terrible thing was that I did not worry," said Peter, "because that reason was good enough for me. And I realized the moral insensitivity in me that made Hitler possible was as much part of me as it was of these SS people. Only by the grace of God was I not in the SS." After a private talk about this with a friend, he found forgiveness and became free—free as an individual, free as a German, and free, as he told his Jewish audience, to speak to them. "So, ladies and gentlemen, I am now ready for your questions."

At that moment another man stood up. He was older than Peter, and his wife sat beside him, crying. "One moment," he told the congregation, "before we talk about policies, I'd like to tell you a story. We have a son who lives in Peru. Six months ago he wrote us that he was going to marry a woman from Cologne." Turning directly to Peter, he went on. "You must understand, he said. "I got out just in the nick of time in 1938 from Wuppertal. I sent the boy extracts from my diary but to no avail, and I told him that if he did not part from this woman, if he did this to our family, he would no longer be our son. But now—I have just spoken to my wife—we are going to phone him right away and invite him and his fiancée to our home."

Peter Petersen had been one of the first Germans after World War II to come to Caux. They came disillusioned: "We were all in the same boat: Our world had collapsed, values, élite, concepts, national anthem, flag. Everything had been thrown overboard as it had twice before in this country in this century. There was therefore a crisis of identity." It was at Caux that Peter and many other Germans found a depth of honesty that changed their lives, where he discovered that he did not have to suppress the past but could use it to bring healing to the present. It was there that French men and women reached out to them and built "bridges over the Rhine."

AN UNLIKELY COMING TOGETHER

With the world's present preoccupation with the former Yugoslavia, Rwanda, and other immediate trouble spots, it is easy to overlook the strides made in Europe in bringing people together. The reconciliation, particularly of France and Germany, if thought about at all today is taken for granted.

If a European Rip van Winkle had been asleep since 1945 and awoke today, he would be amazed. He would know that the two countries had been regarded as archenemies. He would be aware that few relationships in history have been as bitter and as costly to the world. Ever since the division of Charlemagne's empire one thousand years before, a heritage of bitterness and revenge in both nations had thrown the world into one catastrophe after another. Germany and France had fought three wars against each other in seventy years. Yet now, by some miracle, the latter-day Rip van Winkle would see them working together. Thirteen hundred cities and towns in the two countries are "twinned." There are no customs barriers, no passports have to be shown at the borders between the two countries, and even some military units are integrated. There is also a bilingual TV channel. With a little research Rip would discover that, in the previous twenty years, five million young German and young French men and women have participated in 150,000 projects in *Deutsch-Französisches Jugendwerk,* probably the largest youth-exchange program ever undertaken by two nations. And perhaps even more significant for the future, teachers of history in both countries are harmonizing what is taught to their young people. The head of the French historical archives has even asked a German historian to write the first volume of a new history of France.

That this unity could have come about should not be taken for granted. In 1945, in the view of military strategist Edward

Luttwak, "any attempt to effect a reconciliation between the two peoples was seemingly premature to the point of absurdity." There were some in Allied capitals with vindictive spirits—some who advocated the stripping of German industries, the pastoralization of the country, and even the resettling of people. At the same time there were also far-seers such as Winston Churchill, who believed that the first step in the re-creation of the European family must be a partnership between France and Germany. "There can be no revival of Europe," he said in Zurich in 1946, "without a spiritually great France and a spiritually great Germany."

Another visionary was the French and international civil servant Jean Monnet, whose creative ideas were later to emerge as the Schuman Plan.* Monnet came out of World War II with the deep conviction that the creation of one European economic unit was the best protection against another war between European nations. Unlike the vindictiveness expressed by the victors after World War I in the form of the overly harsh provisions of the Versailles Treaty, this time a generous spirit prevailed among the victors. This spirit led to the astonishingly rapid Franco-German reconciliation in which Caux was to have a part.

Philippe Mottu, the Swiss diplomat who was one of the founders of Caux, described how it began with the arrival of Frank Buchman: "On the day he arrived in Caux in July 1946, Buchman confronted us with a challenge. After meeting all those who had worked so devotedly to get Mountain House ready, he suddenly asked, 'Where are the Germans?' And he added, 'Some of you think that Germany has got to change; and that is true. But you will never be able to rebuild Europe without Germany.'" His compassion for the countries that had suffered at the hands of Nazi Germany, and his understanding of Germany's own suffering in defeat, were matched by his realism.

---

*This plan for the integration of the French and German coal and steel industries was named after the French leader who saw it through to fruition, Robert Schuman.

The material and moral ruins of six years of war formed the background to the first conference; national hatreds, class war, and personal vendettas were poisoning the atmosphere of Europe. "Neither international conferences nor grudging concessions could heal these wounds," Mottu said. "The peace for which Europe had so ardently longed was tragically incomplete, for there was no peace in people's hearts." In Germany there was a vacuum that would be flooded by forces of anarchy and materialism unless the Germans were offered a better concept.

At Buchman's insistence approaches were made to the occupation authorities to permit a selected group of Germans to visit Caux the following year. A preliminary list of 150 names was drawn up with the help of Dr. Hans Schönfeld, a German representative on the Ecumenical Council at Geneva and one of the few survivors of the 1944 plot against Hitler. In the same week that General George Marshall, then U.S. secretary of state, announced his plan for the reconstruction of Europe—later known as the "Marshall Plan"—his aid was also sought on this project. With the help of Robert Patterson, the U.S. Secretary of War; Lord Pakenham, the Minister in the British cabinet responsible for German affairs; and General Lucius Clay and General Brian Robertson, two military commanders in the U.S. and British zones of Germany, the first large German delegation was able to leave the country.

THE GERMANS ARRIVE AT CAUX

With the cooperation of the Swiss authorities the Germans arrived in Caux in the summer of 1947. The group included survivors of Nazi concentration camps, widows of officers executed after the 1944 attempt on Hitler's life, and German personalities who were working with the Allies in the administration of Germany. Among them were three minister-presidents of West German Länder (states) and two future chancellors of the Federal German Republic. Dr. Hans Ehard, minister-president of Bavaria, told the international audience, "It is a unique experience for Germans to find themselves received into a circle of so many different nations on a level of complete equality and in an atmosphere where they have every freedom to speak without previously set limitations on what they shall say and on what they shall remain silent, and where one can be sure that one will not be met by that hatred which is so strong in the world today."

The lord mayor of Essen, Gustav Heinemann, later president of the Federal Republic, saw the conference as "the living example of the fact that all are equal in the sight of God." Dr. Hans Lukaschek, a founder of the Christian Democratic Union and later federal minister of refugee affairs, said, "The thing that impressed me was the tremendous love with which we were accepted and welcomed." His visits to Caux encouraged him to look at every refugee not as another mouth to feed but as an asset for the rebuilding of Germany. In his autobiography, *Against Two Evils: 1931–45,* Hans von Herwarth, the first Federal German ambassador to Britain, said that most of the German personalities who were involved in the reconstruction of western Germany took part in Caux or its outreach: "At Caux we found democracy at work, and in the light of what we saw, we faced ourselves and our nation. It was personal and national repentance. Many of us Germans who were anti-Nazi made the mistake of putting the whole blame on Hitler. We learned at Caux that we, too, were responsible."

The Hamburg *Freie Presse* wrote, "Here, for the first time, the question of the collective guilt of the past has been replaced by the more decisive question of collective responsibility for the future. Here in Caux, for the first time, Germany has been given a platform from which she can speak to the world as an equal." And at the end of that summer conference, the *New York Times* on September 8, 1942, headlined its report on the meeting, "New hope held out to German people."

Between 1948 and 1952, more than three thousand Germans attended Caux conference sessions. Among them were most of the minister-presidents and leaders in industry and education.

The personal trust built between hundreds and thousands of men and women, opinion formers at all levels and occupations, "gave a decisive impetus to European unity at a crucial time." By 1951, according to a report in the *New York Times* on January 7, Dr. Hermann Katzenberger, secretary of the Bundesrat, the upper house of the German Parliament, could say that half the German cabinet were firm MRA believers.

At Caux the Germans, like everyone else, had the chance to meet those from their own country and from other countries not only in meetings and at meals but in walks and in taking on the duties of the house together. The *Essener Allgemeine Zeitung* wrote on May 31, 1950, "That cabinet ministers wash dishes when they visit Caux is not the decisive fact. After all, they could do that just as well at home. What makes these days at Caux really worthwhile is the fact that they come to feel they are human beings. The essence of the movement is not that each should make a pronouncement that 'things have got to improve'—everybody in the world is unanimous on that point—but that each one says, 'I must become better if things are to improve.' "*

THE FRENCH JOIN IN THE DIALOGUE

That "spirit of Caux" was helped immeasurably by French participants and their willingness to see their country's part in the

---

*In *Religion, the Missing Dimension of Statecraft*, Luttwak describes what happened when the Germans arrived:

> Often German participants would give vent to expressions of self-pity upon their first arrival at Caux, recounting their own sufferings and those of their families as if they were unique, and with no apparent recognition that others had suffered far more at German hands. Later, having absorbed the "spirit of Caux," the tone and content of the declarations would change drastically, combining expressions of intense gratitude for being received as equals and even as friends by the other participants, avowals of guilt and repentance, repudiations of past belief in Hitler and his ideology, and promise that Germans would never again be guilty of aggression.

European tragedy. Some two thousand French men and women attended sessions at Caux in those first five years. They, too, included cabinet ministers, members of parliament, men and women from both sides of industry, teachers, clergy, and journalists. The French paper, *L'Aube,* reported that Franco-German relations were dealt with in Caux "frankly and courageously." Joseph Wasmer, for instance, a member of parliament and wartime resistance leader from Alsace, asked forgiveness for his hatred of the German people: "I hated the Germans with everything in my power for what they did to my friends and my country. I rejoiced to see Berlin in flames. At Caux this hatred has left my heart. I ask forgiveness from the Germans. I want to make restitution to them." Madame Suzanne Herrenschmidt from Alsace whose family for forty-six years had made it a point of honor that a German should never cross the threshold of their home, said, "With the help of the Germans, I want to build bridges between their country and mine." Her father, husband, and four sons had all fought against the Germans. She returned to Alsace ready to welcome Germans into her home.

One who made the deepest impression on many Germans, including Petersen, was Irène Laure, executive member of the French Socialist Party, a former resistance figure whose son had been tortured by the Gestapo. Petersen and other Germans knew of her reputation; some were even primed to answer back if she talked about German atrocities. But as Peter remembers, "It was so different."

Irène Laure had come to Caux without realizing that there would be Germans there, unaware too that some Germans had paid dearly for their opposition to national socialism. Although she had been an ardent internationalist, when she encountered Germans at Caux, she wanted to leave. She went to her room and then, as she puts it, "a miracle happened." Later, speaking from the platform, she said, "I have so hated Germany that I wanted to see her erased from the map of Europe. But I have seen here that my hatred is wrong. I am sorry and I wish to ask the forgiveness of all Germans present." When a German woman came up from the hall and took her hand, Irène Laure said it was "like 100 kilos being lifted from my shoulders."

Responding to Irène Laure, Madleen Pechel from Berlin said, "I shall take Madame Laure's words to the women of Germany. Many times tears of joy have come to me at Caux. I do not think from 1934 to 1947 I have ever laughed with such a full and open heart as in the last eighteen days, here among people who would have every right to hate us Germans."

Frau Pechel had been with her husband, Rudolf, in a Nazi concentration camp, where she had lost her hearing. Rudolf Pechel was the publisher of a literary monthly, *Deutsche Rundschau*. He wrote later that the significance of Caux for Germany lay in the fact that Germans could meet there with responsible people from other countries—especially from countries that had suffered under the national socialist regime—and talk in an atmosphere of mutual trust. "Even the most delicate and difficult questions between us could be touched. Caux showed us that we in serious and inexorable examination of conscience could put ourselves in order, and that in our readiness to recognize our mistakes had something to give other people and nations."

For Peter, Madame Laure's words were a turning point: "I was dumbfounded. For several nights it was impossible to sleep. All my past rose up in revolt against the courage of the woman. But we knew, my friends and I, that she had shown us the only way open to Germany if we wanted to join in the reconstruction of Europe."

In *The Psychodynamics of International Relationships* Joseph Montville singles out the change in Irène Laure at Caux as "perhaps the signature event in terms of psychological breakthroughs in the Franco-German conflict" and "one of the most dramatic examples of the power of a simple appeal for forgiveness."

A BRITISH ADMIRAL APOLOGIZES

The reconciliations that took place after World War II were not only between the French and the Germans. And the readiness of those from other nations to be generous to their wartime opponents played its part in creating a new openness among all. British Admiral O.W. (Bill) Phillips had come to Caux prepared to let bygones be bygones—not difficult, a friend told him, if you are on the winning side. At the time there were several former German generals at Caux, including General Hans Speidel, later to command NATO ground forces. The admiral's friend, Reg Hale, told the story:

I'm fed up with these damn fellows!" Bill exploded to me. "You know, Reg, I think if I was one of them and my country had done such terrible wrongs, I'd . . . well, I'd jolly well apologize." He pondered on this for a while and then said, "For instance, if Britain had ever done anything wrong, I don't think I'd hesitate to apologize for it." Of course, put that way it sounded silly. So he added, "I suppose Britain has done some wrong things, but for the life of me I can't think what they are." I didn't say anything; a wiser voice than mine was talking to him. "Come to think of it," the admiral went on quietly, "After the First World War, what did I do? What did England do? We went home and got on with our own careers and pleasures and never gave a thought to helping the Germans. Not very good neighbors, really. You remember how Germany went through hell after the war . . . devaluation of the mark and so on. Then they got off the track with this Hitler fellow and we had to knock them down again. Maybe if we had been better neighbors to them in the 1920s it would never have happened."

Admiral Phillips had been asked to address the assembly and he asked me to help him with his speech. We read it over. It was awful! Typical of the skipper's pep talk to the lower deck. But in the last paragraph he expressed some of these thoughts about the Germans. I fastened hopefully on this paragraph and urged him to expand it. Each time he recast the speech this section got bigger and the "pep talk" smaller until it was about fifty-fifty. However, as I watched Bill join the other speakers on the platform I had some misgivings. The meeting ran its course and as Bill waited his turn he sat facing the grim trio of generals. All other thoughts fled his mind except sorrow for the way he and his people had failed men like these when we might have helped. When his name was called the words tumbled out unrehearsed, fragments, but from his heart. Then he stepped off the platform, said "I'm damn sorry" and stuck out his hand. It was an astonishing spectacle. The armor plate seemed to fall from the Germans. They almost lynched Bill, shaking his hand. "Trouble was there were three of them and I'd only got two hands," Bill reported afterwards."[2]

Present in the hall that day was General Ivar Holmquist, wartime commander-in-chief of the Swedish army. "This was one of the greatest moments of my long life," he commented.[3]

The German generals were also stirred by the British officer's words. "I have been deeply moved as a German soldier by the complete equality accorded me by the admiral," said General Friedrich Hossbach. To General Martin Gareis the admiral's simple statement was like an electric shock. It opened a door in his mind, and he suddenly realized that he would have to identify himself with the things Germany had done, however small a part he himself had played in it. "I realize now," he said, "that, instead of pointing the finger at other nations, I must first see my own country's terrible failure and my part in it, and change." He said he would commit himself "to build a bridge between nations who have fought each other for centuries."

VISITING POSTWAR GERMANY

In 1948 Irène Laure and her husband and son, accompanied by Peter Petersen and others, set off for Germany. For two months they toured the western zones, speaking in eleven of twelve Land parliaments. Irène reported that, upon hearing her speak, "Generals and other officers, politicians, and young former Nazis apologized to me." Konrad Adenauer, future Federal German chancellor, had been at Caux that summer with eleven of his family. He said that as a result, one son was studying better and his secretaries were working better. He arrived skeptical but by the second day had become convinced of "the greatness of the work being done at Caux." He joined other German personalities in inviting Frank Buchman to come to Germany with a large team.

Two hundred sixty people from thirty countries accepted the German invitation and traveled from Caux by bus in October 1948. It was the largest civilian cavalcade to visit Germany since the end of the war. They included the cast of a musical, *The Good Road*, which presented the ideas of "inspired democracy." Many of the international group were veterans who contributed their war demobilization gratuities to the venture. One U.S. soldier commented, "This time I was in Germany by invitation."

The group included some who had lost many members of their families in German concentration camps. One French-woman, Clare Weiss, said, "I saw a signpost saying, 'Dachau,' where four of my grandmother's family were killed. I wished I could forget. Then I thought: 'France does not really want to forget, and you are part of it. Ask forgiveness for feeling so supe-rior and resentful, and be concerned with what Germany can become.' And my hatred went. It was a miracle."

A Frenchman, Count Armand de Malherbe, had been twice condemned to be shot by the Nazis. However, his hatred of the German nation, he said, came principally from the way he had been brought up. He knew intellectually that friendship between the two countries was essential. But it was not until he accepted personal responsibility for the feelings his nation bore toward the German nation that reconciliation became more than a good idea. It became a reality when he began to make friends with Germans and asked his God for a deep love for them. "Then a miracle happened—and I can now greet German men and women as my family and friends."

After sixteen performances in fifteen days in five cities for twenty thousand people, the large international musical returned to Caux. But by invitation of the cabinet of North Rhine West-phalia, a team of people stayed on. They were soon joined by a German cast from a play that had been performed at Caux, *The*

Forgotten Factor, which would be seen over the next two years by 120,000 people in the Ruhr. The play encouraged teamwork between management and labor. German cities provided invitation committees, transportation, and accommodations. During that 1948 winter these hundred foreigners, mostly under the age of thirty, stayed in the Ruhr, sharing the rough conditions and little food of the period, living in the homes of the people, and having vigorous ideological discussions.

A German historian, Dr. Gabriele Müller-List, described the aims of these visits to postwar Germany as she saw it:

- Propagation of a Christian ideology in the midst of the general disillusionment of the times.
- Dismantling of class differences and the aggressiveness between employers and trade unionists and workers through change in individual and common conversations.
- Reconciliation of Germany with its wartime opponents.
- West European teamwork and the integration of Germany.[4]

FORGING MORAL AND ECONOMIC LINKS

According to Joseph Montville, three steps are needed in any kind of conflict resolution between enemies who have been at war with one another: humanize relations among adversaries, improve the public environment for peacemaking, and build cooperative economic development schemes. Those taking responsibility at Caux might not have formulated their intentions so precisely, but the initiatives at Caux and the subsequent friendships developed in France and Germany helped this process forward. Beginning with those first years the French and Germans who had been at Caux in the thousands (including several hundred media people) began to have an effect in their countries, privately as well as publicly through the press and radio.

Buchman's biographer, Garth Lean, reports on the leadership of Caux-influenced Germans in bringing about changes that "played some part in creating preconditions for the German 'economic miracle.'" On an eminently practical level Mayor Gustav

31

Heinemann could say that since the ideas of Caux had taken hold in Germany, "We have more volunteers for rubble removal and reconstruction than we have been able to employ." The work in German industry provided a natural link to the parallel work being done in France, which had caught the attention of French statesman Robert Schuman. In 1949 George Villiers, president of the French Employers Federation, represented Schuman at Caux. There he got to know Hans Böckler, president of the German Trades Union Congress, who is regarded as one of the architects of the new Germany. Böckler said to Villiers, "We ought to be enemies on two counts—I am a German, you are French; you are the head of the employers, I am a trade union leader." Villiers replied, "Yes, and there's a third count. Your countrymen condemned me to death; I was in a political concentration camp; I saw most of my comrades die around me. But that is all past. We must forget it. And personally, I would like to shake your hand." Afterwards, Villiers announced that he had lost his bitterness and would throw his weight behind the "moral and economic union" of France and Germany.

In 1948 in Koblenz, Schuman had renewed his friendship with Konrad Adenauer—a friendship that would play an important part in subsequent developments between France and Germany.[5] In 1949, hearing from another French industrialist about the change of heart taking place in industrial circles in the north of France, Schuman asked to meet Frank Buchman. When they met that October, Schuman told Buchman he did not know whom he could trust among the German leaders apart from Adenauer. Buchman gave him a list of a dozen Germans who had been at Caux. Later Schuman said that Buchman had helped him to continue with the Germans when the going was difficult.

In December 1949 Buchman met with President Theodor Heuss and Chancellor Adenauer in Bonn. Adenauer thanked Buchman for what he had done for Germany and wanted to hear Schuman's views on what relations ought to exist between the two countries. A month later, in January 1950, Schuman came to Bonn on his first official visit. In February Schuman wrote the foreword to the French edition of Buchman's collected speeches, *Remaking the World*. In it he described Buchman's work as a "philosophy of life applied in action":

> To begin by creating a moral climate in which true brotherly unity can flourish, over-arching all that today tears the world apart—that is the immediate goal. To provide teams of trained men, ready for the service of the state, apostles of reconciliation and builders of a new world, that is the beginning of a far-reaching transformation of society in which, during fifteen war-ravaged years, the first steps have already been made. It is not a question of changing policy; it is a question of changing men. Democracy and her freedoms can be saved only by the quality of the men who speak in her name.

Meanwhile Jean Monnet and a team of dedicated experts had been working secretly on plans for the creation of the European coal and steel community. This "Schuman Plan" was accepted by the French government on May 9, 1950. That morning Schuman sent a personal message to Adenauer in which he said, "World peace cannot be preserved without efforts in proportion to the dangers threatening us. Europe cannot be made in a single day. It will be built by means of a series of concrete achievements which will create a real solidarity. That requires the elimination of the age-old opposition between France and Germany, and a pooling of resources and production will make war between the two countries not merely unthinkable but actually impossible."

In 1950, however, relations between the two countries were, as Adenauer wrote, "in danger of hardening in mistrust and reserve." At issue was the unsolved problem of the Saar, a territory on the border between France and Germany. It had been a separate state under the League of Nations, but as a result of a 1935 plebiscite had become German. Then at the end of World War II the Saar came under French control. Members of Adenauer's cabinet, led by Theodor Oberländer, contested the amity presumed by the agreement because of the French refusal to return the Saar. Men and women from Caux intervened directly at a critical juncture. An unofficial meeting was arranged between Schuman and Oberländer on the neutral ground of Luxembourg. Schuman expressed compassion for Oberländer's personal grief as a refugee from the lost territories of Germany and promised that the Saar issue would be settled democratically, thus necessarily in Germany's favor, and Oberländer abandoned his opposition to the Schuman Plan.

In that spring of 1950 Adenauer encouraged Buchman's decision to hold a major demonstration in the heart of the Ruhr in Gelsenkirchen. The most dramatic speakers were a group of German trade union leaders who spoke of finding through Caux and Moral Re-Armament what they called an ideology superior to class war. In fact, through their efforts and those of other members of the Communist Party, more than forty leaders of the party had either resigned or been expelled. Hubert Stein, an executive member of the miner's union, said that Communist representation in the Ruhr works councils had dropped from 72 percent to 29 percent. The Communist Party forbade its members to go to Caux, conceding that a Communist who speaks with a man from Caux "becomes a man from Caux."

With all that was happening to undergird the coming together of France and Germany at the official level, it is perhaps not surprising that both countries decided to award decorations to Buchman. Six weeks after the essentials of the Schuman Plan had been agreed upon by both governments and a week after the Gelsenkirchen meeting, Schuman sent Senator Eugenie Eboué to the Ruhr to present Buchman with France's Legion of Honor. Eboué, from Guadeloupe, had found her own answer to her hatred of Germans through Caux.

In 1951, two months after signing the treaty creating the European Coal and Steel Community, Chancellor Adenauer stated, "The nations of the world will only have stable relations with one another when they have been inwardly prepared for them. During these last months we have witnessed the success of difficult negotiations and the signing of important international agreements. Moral Re-Armament has played an unseen but effective role in reducing the differences of opinion between the negotiating parties and has guided them toward a peaceful agreement by helping them to seek the common good."[6]

In 1952 the German government decorated Buchman with the Grand Cross of the Order of Merit. Speaking at Caux on September 15, 1953, Helmuth Burckhardt, chairman of the Advisory Council of the Coal-Steel Pool's High Authority, said that this organization had sprung in large measure from the ideas and philosophy of Caux.

Henri Rieben, director of the Jean Monnet Institute in Lausanne, Switzerland, sees Buchman and Monnet as "kindred spirits." He says that Buchman had "geo-political diagnosis plus inspiration" and did on a spiritual level what Monnet did on a political level. After studying the subject at length, Edward Luttwak wrote, "MRA did not invent the Schuman Plan but it facilitated its realization from the start. That is no small achievement given the vast importance of every delay—and every acceleration—of the process of Franco-German reconciliation during those crucial, formative years."[7]

In subsequent years the close ties between the two countries have been further solidified at both the grassroots level and the top. In September 1958 Adenauer and President Charles de Gaulle met at the French president's home. In their joint statement they said, "The longtime French-German hostility is finished once and for all." They called on French and Germans "to live in agreement and work side by side" in solving the problems of the world. The *New York Herald Tribune* called it "a very profound international alteration . . . a corner-stone of a united, free Europe, a major element in a united free world."*

After Buchman's death, the German government *Bulletin* wrote that although Hitler had banned his MRA movement from Germany, through Caux Buchman had brought Germany

---

*The *New York Herald Tribune* headline June 4, 1951, was: "Moral Re-Armament is credited for role in Schuman Plan talks."

back into the circle of civilized nations: "Thus Caux became one of the great moral forces to which we owe our new position in the world."

Notes

1. Story told in Petersen, *Sind wir noch zu retten.*

2. Story told in Hale, *The Fight to Serve.* Also described from the German side in Gareis, *Das Beste kommt noch.*

3. Caux archives.

4. Supplement to *Das Parlament,* October 31, 1981.

5. Adenauer, *Briefe* 1949–1951.

6. *News Chronicle,* May 10, 1950.

7. Johnston and Sampson, *Religion, the Missing Dimension of Statecraft.*

3

North Africa: Dialogue of decolonization

*Each time that men by negotiation and
goodwill succeed in finding an answer to the
conflict of powerful national interests,
the whole world from East to West
should pause for a moment in silence,
meditate on the lesson and draw
from it fresh inspiration.*

HABIB BOURGUIBA
PRESIDENT OF TUNISIA,
1957–87

TUNISIA: ENDING A WAR WITHOUT MERCY

It was a host's nightmare. Important guests were coming for a
private dinner in her home; they were on opposite sides of a conflict, and the third party who had invited them had begged off at
the last moment.

It was the home of the Baroness Diane de Watteville-Berckheim
on the edge of the Bois de Boulogne in Paris. The guests were
Mohamed Masmoudi, a Tunisian nationalist, and Jean Basdevant,
a civil servant responsible for Tunisian and Moroccan affairs at the
Quai d'Orsay, the French Foreign Office. The date was July 28,
1954. The intermediary was Jacques Chevallier, secretary of state
for war in the Mendes-France government.

An hour before the dinner Chevallier had phoned to say that
he had just been summoned by the prime minister to a cabinet

37

meeting. He apologized and added that he had not told the two guests that they would be meeting each other. It was a textbook example of how not to prepare people for resolving a conflict.

According to de Watteville, it was decided to welcome each guest separately on arrival, explain the situation, and open the way for them to leave should they wish to do so. Both men decided to stay, and the dinner party, which according to the baroness was "glacial" at the outset, may have played a part in Tunisia's gaining its independence with little bloodshed.

During this period, the situation in Tunisia, then a protectorate of France, was getting more and more tense. Blood was flowing. The harvest was gathered under the protection of French armored cars. Neighboring Morocco was turning to violence. Algeria's aspirations for independence were quickening. France, still engaged in a war in Indochina, was deeply concerned about the North African scene. "It was in this political climate that an event took place which was completely unknown to the press and whose consequences were unforeseeable," wrote de Watteville.[1]

A year prior to the dinner, in 1953, the Tunisian nationalist movement, Néo-Destour, was demanding full independence. Its leader, Habib Bourguiba, and almost all his lieutenants were in prison. The most senior representative still at liberty was Masmoudi. His friends had been executed by the French, and Masmoudi had been condemned to death and was living, as he says, with "the demon of vengeance." He was committed to violence, working with French Marxist organizations, and questing "how to make the task of government impossible." For five years he had been the Néo-Destour delegate in France, sometimes hunted by the police, sometimes expelled, sometimes tolerated, always under surveillance. He was working as a political correspondent for one of his country's newspapers in Paris.

At that point a senior French journalist, Jean Rous, former political editor of *Franc Tireur*, intervened. He knew of the work of Caux, was an advocate of what he dubbed the "dialogue of decolonization," and was a man whom Masmoudi trusted. Aware that the Tunisian would meet French men and women at Caux who would understand his aspirations and with whom he could work, Rous invited the young nationalist to the Swiss center.

Masmoudi was troubled and skeptical but also curious. Having no papers, he preferred to steer clear of the police. His first hesitations were overcome when he managed to get to Caux without either the French or the Swiss authorities asking for his papers. He came secretly through Saint-Gingolph, on the opposite side of Lake Geneva from Caux. "Once the hurdle of the police was behind me, I was somewhat reassured," he said.[2] At the back of his mind was the idea that he might be able to help direct an armed struggle from Switzerland.

Masmoudi's initial reaction to what he heard from the Caux platform was dismissive. The speakers were merely well-fed men and women, he thought, who could speak in a detached manner about certain matters, while he lived in a world of violence. On the first day Masmoudi was on the point of bursting at what he thought was useless paternalism when he heard impressive words from Madame Irène Laure, the French socialist personality who had overcome her hatred of the Germans.

Masmoudi stated, "I said to myself: after all, relations between France and Tunisia have never reached the degree of tension which existed between France and Germany. There was never this rage between our two countries as there was there."[3]

On the second day he began to take time in quiet to reflect on what the Germans, French, and others had said, the wide-ranging conversations he had had at meals. He wanted to react against the tendency to be swept along by the atmosphere, which was working a change in his subconscious. "What would happen," he asked himself, "if he were to run into a fanatical French colonialist?" To mind came the image of a man he and others had once tried to kill. "If this man, or if the French could see what I have seen in Caux, how would they behave? Could they, too, change?"

The third day he asked if he might speak. He told his international audience that he would be prepared to meet with anyone—even with those French who wanted to hang onto their control, so that, in the spirit of Caux, an understanding might be reached.

Masmoudi felt his hatred slipping away.

While he was in Caux, his eighty-year-old mother had written him a letter that ended, "God bless you, my son. God curse the French." Masmoudi was ready to reply to her, "God bless me, mother—yes. I need it. But don't curse the French. I have found French with whom we can work without distrust for justice in our problems and aspirations." He told her that it was essential not to push his brothers and sisters toward revenge and that instead of going to Egypt or Libya with the aim of liberating Tunisia by force of arms, he would return to Paris, trusting that a new way would be found. Masmoudi was ready to risk going to prison.

Over the next months he met with his own people, traveling the length and breadth of Tunisia. He also traveled with French people in Paris who had gotten wind of his change of attitude, some who would previously "have avoided me like the plague." He was no less committed to the liberation struggle, but he set out to help his own people take a broader view, to reach out without prejudice on all levels. "I said to them that they needed contacts with everybody, that even if the devil presented himself, we needed to dispute with him."

Through the new friends he had made at Caux he was able to meet French leaders, including Robert Schuman and another cabinet minister, Pierre Pflimlin. Schuman was deeply touched by Masmoudi's change in attitude. It was at this stage that the dinner party, to which Masmoudi and Basdevant were invited, took place.

After the initial shock, the glacial atmosphere at the party gave way to a more relaxed spirit, helped along both by black and white South Africans who described the answers they had found to racial prejudice and hatred through Caux and by the presence of French people whom Masmoudi had met at Caux. One of the French attendees, Didier Lazard, a friend of the French minister who had failed to turn up, described what happened next:

> Then the dessert arrived. I can see it still: it was portions of lemon meringue pie, all prepared on individual plates, which were placed before each guest. It was then that the unexpected happened. Monsieur Masmoudi, without even touching his dessert, pushed his plate away to the middle of the table and, leaning on his elbows, his chest thrust forward, thickset but inspired, he started to speak.

Masmoudi explained to those around the table that he had started his studies in Tunisia but had finished them in Paris. He therefore had the advantage of having a double culture. His voice was serious and calm, his sentences brief and clear. He explained how he had lost his hatred of the French, then went on to relations between Tunisia and France. "We are responsible for the south side of the Mediterranean, as you are responsible for the north side," he said. Everyone listened with rapt attention as he spoke at length.

Lawson Wood, a Scot who was present, has noted, "During all this time Monsieur Masmoudi did not say a single hurtful word about France—remarkable for a man who later said he had been as stuffed with hatred as a bomb with explosives."[4]

When Masmoudi finished speaking, Basdevant, quite naturally, felt he should respond. He did so with the circumspection of a high-ranking civil servant; nevertheless, everything had taken on a different tone. When the dinner party moved to the salon for coffee, the two protagonists walked side by side, chatting in friendly fashion.

Soon after the dinner Masmoudi met Pierre Mendes-France, now prime minister and open to new ways of doing things. Mendes-France, incidentally, had offered earlier to defend Masmoudi when the Tunisian nationalist had sat in a condemned cell in Tunisia. At that point the prime minister was involved in resolving affairs in Indochina. "The discussions with him led to historic events," Masmoudi said. "We decided that, parallel with the peace agreement which had just been reached with Ho Chi Minh, we would prepare for internal autonomy in Tunisia."[5]

Shortly afterward official negotiations began between France and Tunisia at the French Ministry for Tunisian and Moroccan Affairs. Masmoudi, though not yet thirty, was one of the representatives his country sent to talk with the French, who included his new friend, Basdevant. Both Masmoudi and Basdevant were accompanied by their experts. But according to de Watteville, they had "to negotiate less with each other than with the members of their own delegation." One of the French delegation said later, "We were often embarrassed by Masmoudi's integrity."

The negotiations took nine months.* The discussions were suspended whenever the atmosphere became too tense, and during these times Masmoudi and Basdevant walked around the ministry gardens together, seeking the best way out of the impasse. Masmoudi said of the honesty exhibited in the negotiations, particularly those with the French minister of state, Christian Fouchet, "Our negotiators said to us from time to time, 'What do you mean in making that statement?' We would respond, 'But we are saying what we are saying.' When our associates persisted: 'What is that hiding?' We would respond: 'If that was hiding anything, we wouldn't say it.'"

Masmoudi was convinced that during negotiations it was preferable to state directly what he had to say rather than play around, cheat, and scheme. This approach saved a great deal of effort. He believed, too, that he should recognize that there was always something in the person opposite him to build on and that he should not ask for more than he wanted.

---

*Lawson Wood wrote in *New World News* (May 13, 1978), "Again and again when we met Masmoudi at the end of a day, we would find him in despair and wondering whether it was worth going on. Fortunately, he did so, a decision from which many today in similar circumstances might take heart."

After the negotiations Masmoudi met with the guerrilla fighters in the hills of Tunisia and called on them to lay down their arms. "We have never been able to trust the French," they responded. "They have always broken their word in the past. How do we know we can trust them this time?" Masmoudi replied, "I can only give you my word for it: this time it will be different." A gunrunner who was present at the meeting marveled at Masmoudi's courage.

In June 1955, a year before his country's independence, Masmoudi made a statement in Washington, D.C., in which he said that if it were not for what he had learned through his experience in Caux, his country would still be engaged in a "war without mercy" with France. A draft press release containing this statement was shown for corroboration to Basdevant, who said, "Publish it."

Some fifteen years later, when Masmoudi was his country's ambassador to France, he revisited the scene of his famous dinner with Basdevant in the house he calls "the embassy of the heart." He talked to a group of young people there, saying, "I was but one of the instruments in disentangling the events. But at a given moment I had the chance to push forward violence or stop the diabolical rhythm."[6]

During the 1956–57 session of the UN General Assembly in New York, Tunisian President Bourguiba phoned Dr. Frank Buchman in Arizona and said, "MRA created the atmosphere in which peace negotiations were successful; now we need to create that climate throughout our country."*

Subsequently, Masmoudi has laid himself open to criticism on various counts, as most politicians do. However, there is no denying the fact that at a critical moment in Tunisia's struggle for independence from France, while retaining friendship with France, he played a courageous and constructive role.

---

*Reported by the Reverend Harry Almond, who translated the message from Arabic during the phone conversation between the two men.

MOROCCO: UNEXPECTED ROUTE TO
INDEPENDENCE

Along with Masmoudi there were at Caux in the summer of 1953 other personalities whose presence was part of the process of change in another North African country: Morocco. They included the French foreign minister, Robert Schuman, and the future Moroccan prime minister, Si Bekkai.

Although Schuman had never been to Caux, its ideas were, of course, not new to him. When he first visited Mountain House in 1953, he heard a World War II German general staff officer, Colonel Eberhard Böhm, declare, "No German can just say, 'Let us forget the past.' We have done too much harm to France to have the right to speak in that way. But we can ask forgiveness and we can change. Europe will find its place in the new world only when we Germans have changed enough for our neighbors to be able to trust us."[7]

Moved by such words and by the warm welcome of more than a thousand people from all over the world, Schuman asked if he might speak. He had been impressed by the way the ideas of Caux worked out in the domain of relations between people and in international affairs: "I leave in a very different spirit from that in which I came. And with much less skepticism. Thank you for having given me this hope; we need it and now one won't give up."

As he was leaving, Schuman asked Frank Buchman if he would help him in North Africa, particularly in Morocco where civil war and a struggle for independence from France raged. There were some 360,000 French in the country and 7.5 million Moroccans. In 1912 the country's traditional rulers had been placed under French control. Resistance had grown over the years, and by 1944 the political party Istiqlal had been formed and was calling for independence. The leaders of Istiqlal were arrested, thousands demonstrated and dozens were killed or wounded, and the opposition went underground. Violence mounted steadily. In 1953 Morocco's ruler, Sultan Sidi Mohammed Ben Youssef, was deposed by the French and deported to Madagascar.

Two weeks after Schuman's visit Moroccan Si Bekkai arrived at Caux along with Masmoudi and journalist Jean Rous. Si Bekkai had been a colonel in the French army and was much respected in Morocco for his moral authority. He had resigned from his post as pasha (regional ruler) of Sefrou as a protest against the deposition of the sultan of Morocco and had gone into exile to a precarious existence in Paris. Although Si Bekkai was not a member of Istiqlal, his loyalty to the sultan was acknowledged widely. When he arrived at Caux, he was perplexed and bitter about what had happened to his country.

The biggest surprise for Si Bekkai, as it had been for Masmoudi, was to meet French men and women like Irène Laure, who were prepared to face up to their country's wrongs. He heard Count Armand de Malherbe speak at a session:

> We French have no right to wash our hands of responsibility for the government or for the French in Morocco. I would like to ask the Pasha Si Bekkai to accept my apologies for my indifference and irresponsibility about Moroccan affairs. I have no right to speak in the name of France but I believe I have the right to speak in the names of hundreds of French, bosses, trades unionists, and political men, who have participated this summer at Caux. With all our strength we have decided to fight side by side to build these African countries and to rebuild France and the world.[8]

Si Bekkai spoke to those at the conference, saying that he had been ready to give up on humanity. The drama in his country was becoming a tragedy, the victory of material over moral forces. "I have been trying to find a formula which will enable my country and France to break the present deadlock and preserve Franco-Moroccan friendship," he said. "Caux has miraculously provided the answer to the questions I have been asking, without any hatred or bitterness."

Committing himself to put into practice the principles of

Caux, which he saw as a complement to his Muslim beliefs, Si Bekkai said that he knew that in order to change his country, he had to change himself. He said, too, "If for a moment I have had doubts about France, I apologize to my French comrades here." He asked them to pray for a peaceful solution that would maintain the friendship between their two countries.

Si Bekkai was able to brief Buchman on the situation in Morocco. Over the next months he visited the de Watteville home in Paris and brought along his fellow nationalists. "How pleasant to have a meal in a dining room," said one of them, Si Omar Benabdeljalil. Pressed for an explanation, the Moroccan said he had just been released from a French prison. Some of the French guests remarked on Si Bekkai's conciliatory spirit; others, however, particularly in the administration in Morocco, were upset that he had been given an international platform in Caux. They had read what he had said at Caux in their daily newspaper, *Echo du Maroc.*[9]

In early February 1954, responding to Schuman's request, Buchman and some companions arrived in Morocco. There they got to know people with differing points of view, including the family of El Glaoui, the pasha of Marrakech who had sided with the French in the deposition of the sultan. They also befriended two French families, the Chavannes and the Lobsteins, who were to become involved in the events that followed. Pierre Chavanne was a second-generation settler, and Philippe Lobstein was an inspector of schools. Both decided to attend the Caux conference the following summer with their families.

That visit to Caux led to a decision by both families to apply the principles they had learned there to their personal lives; this, in turn, caused them to adopt a different attitude to the events in their country. Chavanne had thought it was the other French—the "ultras" who wanted to maintain the French presence—who were the problem; Lobstein, as a liberal, had never regarded himself as a colonialist. Honesty brought new perspectives.

Pierre Chavanne had always assumed that he was on the "right" side, describing himself as an agnostic tainted with Marxism. He could not escape what he felt was "the uncomfortable logic" of the thought that to change a situation, you must first look inside at where you need to change. Not knowing where he needed to change, he asked his wife, Jeanine. She was thrilled at the question: "I was very moved, not wanting to abuse the situation. I didn't know what to say. I suddenly remembered a stupid scene six months earlier which had left me with a feeling of frustration." She said to her husband, "Do you remember that day when to please you I read the newspaper and I asked some questions because I hadn't understood what I was reading? Why did you react angrily instead of explaining to me?" He replied, "It was easier to say that you were stupid than to admit that I didn't know the answer. Please forgive me."

For Jeanine it was "like the uncorking of champagne." For the first time after six years of marriage, the couple felt they could say anything to each other. They went on to work honestly through their relationships with their family, co-workers, friends, and people they didn't get on with. "It was the turning point in our lives," she said, "the beginning of an absolute trust and a transformation in our relationships which was going to lead to bringing the world into our home."

The experience also gave them a new sensitivity to the Moroccans and eliminated Pierre's fear of them. In a later Luxembourg radio interview, he drew the parallel between his attitude toward Jeanine and the French domination of Morocco:

> I realized how much of an imperialist I was, even in the family. Most of the time I didn't realize it, because there was no revolt. But I took all the decisions and imposed my choices without giving a thought to the feelings and opinions of others. And I disregarded their advice.[10]

The experience at Caux was equally overwhelming for the Lobsteins. Mila Lobstein said, "We were never colonialists, but in practice our way of living did not mark us out in any way different from them. We needed to work for *entente* and peace because

it was right—not so that we could later stay in the country."
Both couples left Caux with a commitment and a new motive to
seek their God's will for their lives and for Morocco.

On their return they began to build friendships with Moroccans. One of the first was Ahmed Guessous, head of the Provincial Agricultural Department. In his morning time of quiet
reflection, Pierre Chavanne had the thought to thank Guessous
for his effective work in combating a plague of locusts. He was
not to know until later, after having won the man's trust, that
Ahmed Guessous was working closely with Istiqlal and had spoken of French colonialists as "two-legged locusts." Chavanne
told Guessous that he had recently become aware of the selfish
way he had lived in the country, preoccupied above all with
enriching himself and profiting from his position. He described
his visit to Caux and said that the standards he had been exposed
to there were the basis on which he wanted to live, and that, in
his view, they were indispensable in solving larger problems.

Guessous was polite but guarded. He wondered whether his
visitor was an intelligence agent and suspected him of involvement in clandestine activities. Nevertheless, Guessous was
intrigued. Chavanne was, after all, the first Frenchman who had
ever taken the trouble to thank him for his work. Through his
workers and overseers he knew the Chavanne farm had a good
reputation. He invited the Chavannes for a meal at his home, an
unusual step at the time; Guessous had professional, but not
social relations with the French. A simple gesture may have
helped establish confidence. A bottle of wine remained unopened
on the table. The Chavannes had by then decided not to drink
any more alcohol because of the harm it did to society. This decision, a gesture toward the inhabitants of the country whose religion did not permit them to drink, was much appreciated.

A similar incident happened when the Lobsteins were guests of
Guessous. Guessous had contacted Lobstein when he suspected
that his daughter had been refused admission to a school for reasons of discrimination. Lobstein had been able to sort out the
matter satisfactorily.

Intrigued by his new friends' experience at Caux and puzzled by what had made such a respected figure as Si Bekkai use such conciliatory language, Guessous decided to go to Caux with the Chavannes and the Lobsteins. One of Buchman's companions from his Moroccan visit, Paul Campbell, was chairing a session when Guessous arrived. To put the new guest at ease, Campbell spoke of his time in Morocco and in particular of his meeting with the El Glaoui family. Campbell described what happened at the end of the meeting in his book, *A Dose of Your Own Medicine:*

Up came Guessous, whom I had never previously met—an extremely angry young man, with eyes flashing and voice trembling with rage. "I came here thinking this was holy ground," he said. "But all you've done is talk about the Devil. The Glaoui of Marrakech is the devil incarnate. He is a friend of the French. If I'm to remain here another hour you must promise never to mention his name again in my presence."

I invited him to sit down to lunch with me. He spent most of the meal pointing out where I had given a misleading impression of the country to the representatives of many nations. I kept thinking, "What can I say to this man that will make any difference?"

My only thought was to say to him, "In my own personal life I know I am no closer to God than I am to the person from whom I feel most divided."

"What was that?" he asked in surprise.

I repeated what I had said.

The young man put down his knife and fork and left the table. Later he told me that the idea went round and round in his head, and every time it came to the front, there was the image of El Glaoui, the feudal chief he hated.

"If I'm no closer to Allah than I am to El Glaoui, I'm a long way from home," Guessous admitted to me.

The next day Guessous spoke to the conference:

Yesterday someone said to me, "I am no closer to God than I am to the person from whom I feel most divided." I felt a long way from God. And that means I have a lot to change for I feel quite incapable of apologizing to certain people in Morocco. I would like to thank all the friends who have let me hope for the freedom of my country and the world.

During the following days many things were to move Guessous's spirit: the atmosphere of Mountain House; the international dimension of the meetings; and the raising up of the Moroccan flag, a gesture of courtesy rare before independence. He had also found an appropriate verse in the Qur'ān: "Respond to a bad action by a better action. Go towards your worst enemy and be reconciled with him. He will be transformed into an ardent protector."[11]

While Guessous was in Caux, three journalists and forty-five French people, including children, were killed in different parts of Morocco. Guessous decided to move up his departure date. He spoke again before leaving Caux:

> I came to Caux to replenish the moral strength necessary to combat hatred. I firmly intend to contribute to spreading the moral virtues which we here all honor. I thank all my friends who have given me such a warm welcome. I thank particularly all those who have been able to get through to the intimate thoughts of my heart, who suffer with me and with the Moroccan people. I particularly pay my respects to the French who understand the situation.

Lobstein was struck by the difference in Guessous on his return from Caux. "I couldn't recognize him any more," he wrote. "He wanted to reconcile everybody, including the most reactionary and incorrigible of the 'French presence.'"[12]

Violence through terrorism and counterterrorism had continued to mount in Morocco, particularly after the exile of the sultan in 1953. Tensions were evident in the big cities. By 1955 the French resident general in Morocco, Gilbert Grandval, would write, "The situation is untenable."[13] That summer the minister for Moroccan and Tunisian affairs, Pierre July, reported to the French National Assembly that the situation was at an impasse. He and Prime Minister Edgar Faure were tired, "with empty heads from too much thinking about the problem and not seeing a way out."[14]

In August talks between French and Moroccans, in which Si Bekkai participated, were held at Aix-les-Bains. Si Bekkai sent a message to Buchman from the talks, assuring him that he had not lost sight of the principles he had learned at Caux and was counting on Buchman's help in resolving the crisis. Indeed, in his memoirs Pierre July confirmed his surprise at Si Bekkai's frankness and conciliatory spirit at Aix-les-Bains.

Si Bekkai wanted to take part in the talks with the exiled sultan in Madagascar. Prime Minister Faure wrote, "I was delighted to authorize Si Bekkai to accompany the new delegation because he couldn't fail to play the role of a mediator."[15] For his part Grandval found the choice absolutely right.

At the beginning of October the prime minister feared a vast insurrectional movement in Morocco. He needed to act fast. It was hard to put together the Council of the Throne, which had been agreed on at Aix-les-Bains. It was difficult to create a balance between the members because each group wanted to be represented or did not want to see one of their opponents being part of it. He tried to find some more or less neutral people. Si Bekkai, under nationalist pressure, turned down the invitation to participate. Faure recorded in his memoirs that he felt despondent and had told his wife that they were at a dead end: "I see no way out. That happens very rarely to me. There is always, if not a solution, at least a way."[16]

After Faure had laid out the situation, his wife had the idea to speak to Si Bekkai, whom she was to meet at a friend's house that very evening. The idea pleased Faure and gave him renewed courage. He hoped that Si Bekkai would be able to save the situation by agreeing to sit on the council. Si Bekkai did accept, and the nationalists, because of his authority and integrity, had to swallow hard and go along with the decision. The situation was saved.

51

Earlier that same month the French Parliament had approved a government policy envisaging the return of the sultan to the throne. The principal obstacle was El Glaoui, a major player in Morocco and also in the designs of the French conservatives who wanted to bring down the government. But by the end of the month, a dramatic event broke the logjam.

Before leaving Caux, Guessous had told Campbell that he had to see El Glaoui and the leaders of Istiqlal. Unknown to anyone but his son, Sadeq, and others in his family, El Glaoui was by mid-October beginning to think of calling for the restoration of the sultan. Guessous was soon involved by Istiqlal in something that he would never have considered a few weeks before: preparing a meeting between adversaries who hated each other.

On October 25 three members of Istiqlal, including Guessous, met with El Glaoui in Casablanca. Guessous embraced El Glaoui. Only two months earlier Guessous had said of El Glaoui, "He is the devil. I would never be able to shake hands with him."[17] They had a moving time together, and Pasha El Glaoui then invited them for lunch. Ever since his experience in Caux, Guessous had wanted to bring the pasha and the sultan together; he felt that national reconciliation had to begin with reconciliation between the two men.

In meeting with the pasha, Guessous was putting aside not his political convictions but the hatred he had felt toward someone he had regarded as a traitor. The tension was defused, Guessous said, when he spoke of his past feeling toward the old man. He also said that they were taking this step for both the well-being of the country and for the sake of his family's future. Sadeq El Glaoui said, "Guessous was charged with informing the Istiqlal about my father's actions. He had to make a considerable effort in spite of himself to meet him." He added, "Everybody helped in creating the ambience."[18]

That same afternoon El Glaoui headed for Rabat. The French thought that he had given in to their pressure and was coming to give his blessing to the council. Guessous made a hurried phone call to the Chavannes to tell them that the ideas of Caux had worked: "You will see in the newspapers. I haven't time to explain."

In Rabat Sadeq El Glaoui read his father's message to the assembled press. It was not what was expected:

My visit to the members of the Council of the Throne should not be interpreted as my gratitude for the Council for which I have never ceased and do not cease to deny its legality. I call to the Moroccan nation for the prompt restoration of Sidi Mohammed Ben Youssef and his return to the throne, a return that can bring an orderly unification of our spirits and hearts.[19]

There was jubilation at what many newspapers called "the pasha's bombshell."

On November 5 the Council of Ministers approved the return of the sultan to the throne. On November 8 El Glaoui paid his allegiance to the sultan, now King Mohammed V, prostrating himself at his feet in ritual obeisance. The king forgave El Glaoui with the words, "We are the sons of the future."[20]

"The bloodbath predicted by General Boyer de Latour did not take place," wrote Pierre July. "The war, our permanent preoccupation, was avoided. At one blow all the obstacles were lifted to permit the return of Ben Youssef."[21] Gilbert Grandval said, "Everyone was flabbergasted, beginning with his [El Glaoui's] friends in France, of which the most starry-eyed still believed at the beginning of the summer that he would never give in."[22]

Sociologist Stephane Bernard wrote:

The simplicity, spontaneity and extent of the movement that flung the whole of traditional Morocco at Mohammed V's feet by the end of October 1955 proved that El Glaoui's about-face was not an old man's sudden whim, but an act of political realism instinctively understood by all who shared his position. The idol who for two years had been the hope and inspiration of so many French in Morocco had suddenly crumbled, leaving only a tired old man very close to death.[23]

On November 15 the king returned from exile to Morocco. On November 19 independence from France was declared, ending forty-three years as a protectorate. On December 6 the first Moroccan government was announced, with Si Bekkai the first prime minister. The king said, "Our wish is to see Moroccans and French cooperate for the prosperity of Morocco and the good of all with a view to consolidating their relations and safeguarding the friendship between the two countries."[24]

El Glaoui died a few months later, at age eighty-six. He had told his son, Sadeq, after the visit to the sultan, "Now I can die at peace. I may leave you a fortune. But don't rely on it. What I leave you above all is my reconciliation with Ben Youssef."[25]

It is difficult to discern what role others played in El Glaoui's decision and whether his act was inspired by more than political realism. What might have happened if men like Guessous and Si Bekkai had been less conciliatory in their approaches may never be known. Certainly some of the major players in Morocco felt that Caux played some part in the unfolding of events that so surprised all the experts. Just hours after Si Bekkai signed the agreement with the French, Lawson Wood and Matt Manson, two Scots who had worked with Si Bekkai after his return from Caux, visited him in Paris. Wood wrote, "We found him with a room full of tough-looking characters. Si Bekkai introduced them to us with a sweep of his arm, 'These are my militants!' Then he turned and introduced us to them, 'And these are the militants of Moral Re-Armament, without whom we would not be here today!'"[26]

In January 1956 King Mohammed V, receiving a group representing Caux, said to them:

I want to thank you for all that you have done for Morocco, the Moroccans and myself in the course of testing years. Your principles of virtue, of neighborly love and of unselfishness are noble. They are just and they are also of Islam. I wish that they be spread in Morocco as well as in the four corners of the world. You have contributed to the ushering in of a better situation in Morocco. Continue to help us in the course of the negotiations which are to follow. Help France too. You do not diminish yourself by recognizing your mistakes, rather you raise your prestige. For what is most serious about mistakes is not that you make mistakes but that you continue in them. Let us have the humility to recognize our mistakes and correct them.[27]

Frédéric Chavanne, analyzing what had happened through the efforts of some of these people in North Africa and the relevance of their experiences to other situations, drew three conclusions:

• The course of history is linked to the motivations of men and women, and these motivations can be changed.

• It is by the small (or large) acts of obedience to those thoughts or truths at the depth of a human being that the individual can be brought to the heart of those problems with which the country is confronted.

• Just as big doors swing on little hinges, ordinary citizens can have an influence on events even if they seem enveloped in a struggle for power in which they are not involved. They can always do something for specific people: Quest for ways to an answer and encourage changes in attitude that allow solutions whether in their private life or in their social and political action.[28]

A French member of parliament, Pierre Mesmin, referring to the efforts to help Tunisia and Morocco gain independence and to bring France and Germany together, put it less analytically when he said at Caux, "The method is always the same, the persevering search for the moment when heart opens to heart, when ears are no longer deaf and tongues no longer tied."[29]

Garth Lean wrote in *On the Tail of a Comet*, "To say that Buchman or Moral Re-Armament brought independence to Morocco or Tunisia would, of course, be nonsense. The tides of the times and the determination of the people would eventually have achieved that in any case. But it was Robert Schuman who wrote to Buchman, 'There can be no doubt that the history of

Tunisia and Morocco would have been different if it had not been for Moral Re-Armament.'"

ALGERIA: AN OPPORTUNITY MISSED

Later King Mohammed V was keen to enlist the help of Caux in extinguishing what he called "the fire in Algeria." "Your neighbor's house has caught fire," he said. "You have the water to put it out."*

Buchman and his French, Moroccan, and Algerian associates tried to live up to this conviction. Jean Rous, the French journalist who had arranged for Masmoudi and Si Bekkai to go to Caux, took a team to Tunisia, haven of the Algerian provisional government. Edmond Michelet, the French minister of justice, went to Caux, followed by seven generals.

Over the next few years French and Algerians met in Paris or made their way, often incognito, to Caux. They went with the support of Paul Delouvrier, the minister-resident in Algeria. The trips were dangerous, as there were many assassinations in France at the time. Algeria's great journalist, Jean Amrouche, speaking at Caux, described this "powerful assistance for all those who burn to see the end of the Algerian war."[30]

In some cases courageous initiatives stopped some of the fighting. However, when this quiet diplomacy eventually became public through news published in the French and North African press, the effort foundered, and Algeria had to go through a much more bloody baptism than Tunisia or Morocco.

---

*A message from King Mohammed V, published in *Echo du Maroc* (July 27, 1956), stated, "My desire is that your message, based on necessary moral values and the will of God, reach the masses of this country. We have full confidence in the work that you do."

Notes

1. De Watteville discusses the dinner party in *Le fil conducteur.*

2. Ibid.

3. "Plus radical que la violence," a speech by Masmoudi printed as a supplement to *Courrier d'information du réarmement moral,* December 28, 1968.

4. Letter to the author.

5. "Plus radical que la violence."

6. Ibid.

7. Caux archives. The author is particularly indebted to the thoroughness of the research on the subject by Frédéric Chavanne in his 1995 monograph, "Où aimerais-tu que je change?"

8. *Courrier d'information,* October 1, 1953.

9. Lean, *On the Tail of a Comet.*

10. *Courrier d'information,* May 17, 1957.

11. Sura 61:34.

12. Chavanne, "Où aimerais-tu que je change?"

13. Grandval, *Ma mission au Maroc.*

14. July, *Une république pour un roi.*

15. Faure, *Si tel doit être mon destin ce soir.*

16. Ibid.

17. Chavanne, "Où aimerais-tu que je change?"

18. Ibid.

19. Ibid.

20. Ibid.

21. July, *Une république pour un roi.*

22. Grandval, *Ma mission au Maroc.*

23. Bernard, *The Franco-Moroccan Conflict, 1943–1956.*

24. Chavanne, "Où aimerais-tu que je change?"

25. Ibid.

26. Letter from Lawson Wood to author, July 9, 1995.

27. *Courrier d'information*, February 17, 1956; also published in slightly abbreviated form in *La vigie marocaine* and *Echo du Maroc*, January 17, 1956.

28. Chavanne, "Où aimerais-tu que je change?"

29. Caux archives.

30. *MRA Information Service*, October 24, 1959.

4

Japan: Struggle for the soul of a nation

In the present age we face new challenges,
as Japan becomes more and more
involved in global community. We in Japan
must become more considerate of the
world in our thinking and actions.

YASUHIRO NAKASONE
Prime Minister of Japan
1982–87

AWAKENING JAPAN'S CONSCIENCE

When he speaks, Yukihisa Fujita* always has stories at his fingertips, for he feels they illustrate an element that his country—
Japan—needs. Fujita will tell you of Queen Beatrix's admission
to the Israeli Parliament in 1995 that her people had not prevented the slaughter of Dutch Jews in Nazi concentration camps,
and that in Jakarta she expressed her "profound sadness" at
Indonesia's suffering under Dutch colonial rule. He will also
refer to the French president's acknowledgment in 1995 of his
government's responsibility in the Vichy years of World War II
for the death of Jews, and to the assertion of President Roman
Herzog of the German Federal Republic during a ceremony in
Berlin marking the fiftieth anniversary of the end of World War II,

---

*Yukihisa Fujita is executive director of IMAJ, International Moral Re-Arma-
ment Association of Japan.

59

that the German people were probably more aware of their responsibility for the holocaust than they had been fifty years earlier.[1]

Fujita, a member of Japan's postwar generation, is impressed with what he feels is the frank way Germany has dealt with its past. He is also impressed with the generosity of some of the victors in World War II in exposing their own shortcomings. It may be that the world is entering an "era of collective repentance," as a July 3, 1995, *U.S. News and World Report* article suggested. Among other examples, the magazine article referred to Pope John Paul II's request for forgiveness for Catholic-Protestant wars in Europe and for the church's complicity in the African slave trade. But Fujita, although aware that the Japanese have done more to make amends than the world realizes, is conscious that there is some truth behind the August 12, 1995, headline in *The Economist*: "The Japan that cannot say sorry." He wants the examples of other countries to awaken Japan's conscience. Outlining these aims again at Caux in August 1995, Fujita said that to sustain the healing and restitution processes, his people would have to go through deep changes in their attitudes about the past, toward neighboring countries, and toward each other. This was his "agenda for reconciliation."

As director of the Association to Aid Refugees, Fujita had been involved in situations in Burma, Cambodia, India, the Philippines, Thailand, and Tibet. He was grateful when Japanese Prime Minister Tomiichi Murayama spoke in 1995 of his "feelings of deep remorse" and extended his "heartfelt apology" for the atrocities Japan had committed during World War II. "Allow me also to express my feelings of profound mourning for all victims, both at home and abroad, of that history," Murayama said. "Our task is to convey to the younger generations the horrors of war, so that we never repeat the errors in our history."[2] Responding to what the *New York Times* called this "unambiguous apology," the newspaper editorialized, "How much better to look ahead to the emerging issues of the 21st century than to continue tongue-tied about the horrors of the mid-20th."

Fujita is building on foundations that were laid soon after the end of World War II. In 1950 a plane brought some seventy Japanese to Mountain House in Caux.[3] It was said to be the largest and most representative group of political, industrial, and civic leaders to leave Japan after the war. The group included seven members of parliament and seven prefectural governors. Before the delegation left Japan's Prime Minister Shigeru Yoshida had told them how in 1870 a representative group of Japanese had traveled to the West and on their return had changed the course of Japanese life. He believed that when this delegation returned, it, too, would open "a new page in the country's history." In a message delivered at Caux by his representative, Chojiro Kuriyama, the prime minister suggested that the ideas of Caux could give moral content to Japanese democracy.

While at Caux the Japanese delegation witnessed firsthand the reconciliations between Germans and their former enemies and learned about the efforts of Germans to give the moral content Yoshida spoke of to their new democracy. They also experienced dramatic personal reconciliations. One of these occurred between Katsuji Nakajima, a leader of the All-Japan Metalworkers Union, and Eiji Suzuki, Osaka's chief of police. Nakajima, who had been in Hiroshima when the atomic bomb exploded, said at the conference that although he was trying to find the peace of Caux, he had great bitterness toward Suzuki, the man he hated most: "Labor in Japan hates this man who represents the most reactionary group in the country, and I told them to do so. Yesterday I found the answer and that was to offer my hand in apology to Mr. Suzuki." Nakajima said that getting rid of his hatred of the police chief, whom he had refused to speak to in the plane to Caux, "was to me an even greater spiritual shock than the physical shock I received at Hiroshima." Suzuki responded, "I was overcome by the tremendous spirit of Mr. Nakajima, and through that I had a chain reaction in my own heart which resulted in my losing completely my hatred of the Communists whom I blamed and fought for years."

The youngest member of parliament, Yasuhiro Nakasone, later to become prime minister, was struck by the fact that what he heard at Caux showed that confrontation and class war were not inevitable for industry. He wrote from Caux to his hometown paper:

> People who spoke at the assembly were largely representatives of labor and management from various countries. The thing that drew our greatest interest was the fact that many Communists from the Ruhr coal mines of Germany and the longshoremen's union of England have changed their way of thinking and are now becoming passionate, moving forces for this new program in these same areas . . . The ice in the Japanese hearts was melted by the international harmony that transcends race and class in this great current of world history moving through the continents of America and Europe.

JAPAN'S EMISSARIES OF RECONCILIATION TO THE UNITED STATES

Leaving Caux, the Japanese went on to other cities in Switzerland, Italy, Germany, France, and Britain before visiting the United States. In Washington, D.C., two parliamentary members of the delegation were invited to speak to the U.S. Senate and House of Representatives. U.S. Vice President Alben Barkley, who had himself been to Caux with a congressional delegation, welcomed the Japanese and led the parliamentarians to seats on the floor of the Senate. Introducing them, he spoke of the long friendship between the two countries and expressed the hope that the friendship "may not only be resumed but may be permanent in status between the two countries." Four other senators, Republican and Democrat, then spoke before Barkley invited Chojiro Kuriyama to address the Senate. The prime minister's representative expressed "our sincere regret that Japan has broken an almost century-old friendship between our two countries."

The visitors were similarly welcomed in the House of Representatives. For the first time in its history, the House received a foreign delegation on its floor. The Japanese group was led down the aisle by the majority and minority leaders and was given a standing ovation as the members were introduced to Speaker Sam Rayburn. Diet member Tokutaro Kitamura, speaking from the rostrum, apologized for "the tragic trouble that we have caused to the people of the United States." For the sake of an Australian parliamentary delegation that was in the gallery, Kitamura also added his deepest regret for what Japan had done to Australia. His speech drew a standing ovation. One of the Australian members of parliament said later:

> We saw the spokesman for the Japanese nation apologize for the wrongs, suffering and heartbreak Japan had caused. There was a hush, the most intense silence I have ever encountered. . . . It was history being made. We from Australia realized that in our global problems in the South Pacific we had only looked to our mother country, Britain, and to the United States for assistance—but now we had a third partner in terms of Pacific global strategy.

Commenting on Kuriyama's apology, the *New York Times* wrote in a July 29, 1950, editorial, "For a moment we could see out of the darkness when all men may become brothers." Noting that the mayors of Hiroshima and Nagasaki were among the visitors, the editorial commented, "If they, too, felt that they had something to forgive they had achieved that miracle." The *Saturday Evening Post* said, "The idea of a nation admitting it could be mistaken about anything has a refreshing impact. . . . Perhaps even Americans could think up a few past occasions of which it could be safely admitted, 'We certainly fouled things up that time.'"

From Caux, Shinzo Hamai, the mayor of Hiroshima, expressed gratitude for the sympathy and assistance his people had received since the bomb was dropped on August 6, 1945, and said they had to do away with all hatred in their hearts. No matter how difficult it might be, Hiroshima had to be rebuilt as a "city of true peace" for the future.

At that time there was considerable pressure on the Hiroshima authorities to have the inscription on the memorial in the heart of the city be one of blame toward the United States. Instead, anxious that the citizens' genuine feelings not be exploited to make Hiroshima a platform for divisiveness, they chose something different: "Rest in peace; we will never make the same mistake again."[4]

CHANGES AT HOME

Upon its return to Japan, that 1950 delegation, as Yoshida had predicted, had a marked effect on Japanese life. They wrote about their experiences, spoke about them at hundreds of meetings, and applied the principles they had learned to their work. Each year more Japanese went to Caux or to similar conferences in other parts of Asia or in the United States—more than six hundred in the next ten years alone. There were particularly impressive results in industry, growing out of a new teamwork between management and unions. Describing how a minority had helped change the nation's course in what he called a "decisive decade," writer Basil Entwistle said:

> Among the most insistent ideas competing for acceptance in the economic area were Marxist class war and Western-style industrial confrontation. Japan could well have followed either of these paths. She did not, largely because a third way was demonstrated by some of her citizens. It was a way which combined the best of her traditional culture with a realistic response to the problems of the times. And it proved to be a road, not only to economic recovery but to a renaissance in many areas of national life.[5]

In 1951, a year after the first delegation returned from Caux, the Japanese Peace Treaty was signed in San Francisco. Frank

Buchman had his people there to help facilitate understanding. Hisato Ichimada, governor of the Bank of Japan and one of the Japanese signatories to the peace treaty, said that Buchman's efforts had been the one means of bridging the gulf between the Japanese and other delegates. Ichimada helped secure a house in Tokyo as a base for nation-building work. This house first became a place where Americans could meet and get to know Japanese; then it became a neutral ground where Japanese men and women from the most varied backgrounds and political views could interact.

Later, on the initiative of Masahide Shibusawa, author and lecturer on Asian affairs, a conference center was built at Odawara. It was opened by Prime Minister Hayato Ikeda in the presence of three former prime ministers as well as Korean leader Kim Chong Pil. Pil's presence gave Japanese Foreign Minister Masayoshi Ohira an opportunity to have secret talks with him, which resulted in official negotiations and—within months— diplomatic recognition.

IMPROVING RELATIONS IN ASIA

This decade after the delegation's return from Caux also saw Japanese efforts to improve relations with other Asian countries. In 1955 a senior member of the Japanese Diet, Niro Hoshijima, was sent by Prime Minister Nobosuke Kishi to Manila. There, during a public occasion, he asked forgiveness of the Philippine people for Japan's wartime atrocities. His action came at a time when negotiations on reparations between the two countries, deadlocked for ten years, had finally collapsed. The bitterness was intense. Philippine Foreign Minister Carlos Garcia was the first to grasp Hoshijima's hand afterward. Negotiations were reopened the next day, and within a year the matter was settled.

In March 1957 several Japanese, including Hoshijima and opposition Senator Shidzue Kato, attended a conference sponsored by Moral Re-Armament in Baguio, the Philippines. With the permission of the prime minister, Hoshijima, who was chairman of the Japan-Korea Society, began exploratory talks with a Korean parliamentary delegation that was attending the conference. At Baguio the Japanese apologized to the Koreans for Japan's behavior over the years. Hoshijima undertook the personal step of returning three Korean treasures that were in his possession, including a massive, two-thousand-year-old stone carving of a lion once owned by the last emperor of Korea. It rightly belonged, he said, to Korea.[6] On April 8, 1957, *Yomiuri Shimbun* headlined a report describing the informal talks between the Koreans and Japanese, "Beginnings of a solution to the Japanese-Korean problem."

In a subsequent parliamentary debate Kato spoke of the Baguio conference and drew an encouraging response from the prime minister, who agreed to address the issues that most troubled the Koreans. That autumn, on the prompting of Kato and Hoshijima (who had become speaker of the House of Representatives), Prime Minister Kishi decided to make apology a cornerstone of his tour through seven Southeast Asian countries, a tour that evoked a positive response in the countries visited. In Australia, for instance, the ex-servicemen's association endorsed the visit. At the state luncheon given by Australian Prime Minister Robert Menzies, Kishi expressed his sorrow at the war and asked for forgiveness.*

The *Washington Evening Star* commented after Kishi's trip, on December 18, 1957:

> Premier Kishi is now back in Tokyo after having completed one of the most unusual missions ever undertaken by a statesman of his rank. Over the past three weeks he has visited no fewer than nine nations that Japan occupied or threatened with conquest and in each of these lands he publicly apologized for his country's actions during the war.

---

*The *Sydney Morning Herald* editorialized, "We cannot afford the luxury of living in the bitter past. Kishi handled a delicate mission with skillful tact. His ice-breaking tour . . . could hardly have been a pleasant experience. But no one could have gone further in making official amends for the sins of his country."

Kishi said the following year, "I have myself experienced the power of honest apology in healing the hurts of the past. We need the statesmanship of the humble heart to bring sanity and peace in the affairs of men."

On the last day of 1957 a preliminary declaration on the terms of a settlement between Japan and South Korea was signed. The following year a reparations accord, diplomatic recognition, and trade agreements were completed between the two countries. When President Carlos Garcia of the Philippines, who as foreign minister had shaken Hoshijima's hand three years earlier, paid a state visit to Japan in December 1958, he said on TV, "It may be truthfully said that the bitterness of former years is being washed away by compassion and forgiveness."[7] Garcia's address to the Japanese Diet, the first ever by a foreign dignitary to that body, was given a standing ovation.

INTERNAL STRIFE

In 1960 Senator Shidzue Kato played another distinctive role when the question of the renewal of the U.S.-Japan Security Treaty came up. This treaty had been the greatest single cause of friction between Japan's conservative and Socialist parties ever since it took effect in 1952. The United States had approved the renewal of the treaty, but because of rioting, U.S. President Dwight Eisenhower was prevented from visiting the country. The prospect of renewing the important treaty relationship therefore was uncertain. An all-out effort was made to avoid nationwide divisiveness at a time when the Diet building was surrounded by demonstrators and the basis of the political system was under threat. The house in Tokyo that had been set up in 1951 as a site for nation-building was one of the few places where socialist and conservative members of parliament and politicians could meet.

It was at this time that Mrs. Kato wrote an open letter to the press and the country urging changes in the policy of the Socialist Party that, if not carried through, she felt might lead to the division of the country. The response to this letter was over-whelming. Millions of citizens sensed the need to return to common sense. The Socialist Party tried to discipline Mrs. Kato, but public support for her was too great. The publicly voiced condemnation of violence and the widespread appeals for moderation put a halt to violent demonstrations that had been planned.[8]

AN ONGOING COMMITMENT TO CHANGE

In 1956 Frank Buchman was decorated by the Japanese government for his service to the country. In 1958 Prime Minister Kishi gave a reception to acknowledge the part played by Buchman and his colleagues in helping Japan regain the respect of other nations.

More than thirty years later, on the fortieth anniversary of Mountain House in 1986, Prime Minister Yasuhiro Nakasone sent a message recalling his visit to Caux in 1950 as one of a delegation representing the major sectors of Japanese life. He spoke of Caux's influence in bringing Japan back into the family of nations. He also noted that in the following decade, Caux had played "an important role in the rebuilding of Japan, in helping people accept the need for clear moral principles as a foundation for effective democracy." He said, "In the present age we face new challenges, as Japan becomes more and more involved in the global community. It is my firm conviction that we in Japan must become more considerate of the world in our thinking and actions."

Mrs. Yukika Sohma is one Japanese who strongly feels this dimension of being "more considerate." Mrs. Sohma was at the heart of these developments over the years.[9] She is vice chairperson of the Ozaki Yukio Memorial Foundation. The foundation honors her father, who is regarded as the father of Japanese parliamentary democracy. She has also served on the Japanese National Advisory Board, a prestigious body whose main concern is education.

At the end of 1978 Mrs. Sohma received a letter from a friend in Canada. He enclosed a report on Asia that called Japan a shameful nation because of its refusal to admit Asian refugees. When she approached government officials privately on this matter, she was rebuffed; consequently, she began to speak publicly about the need for Japan to change its policy. She prevailed on Senator Renzo Yanagisawa to raise the matter in a Diet committee. As a result, the cabinet decided to take in five hundred refugees.

Mrs. Sohma then set about raising money for the refugees. Asked on television what her plans were, she said, "If every Japanese gives one yen, we will have at least one hundred twenty million yen." The local post office had to hire extra staff to handle the more than twenty thousand letters she received. The donations enabled her to reach her target.

Yukika Sohma went on to found the Association to Aid Refugees and began providing clothing and housing for Cambodian refugees. Later, she broadened the association's work to other continents. Now, she is also tackling corruption in her country.

As part of an ongoing commitment to bring new thinking to Japan, Yukika Sohma, Yukihisa Fujita, and others have introduced annual initiatives for the past nineteen years. These efforts have been directed at helping Japan find honesty about the past, unity between management and labor, integrity in public life, and compassion for the suffering of its less fortunate Asian neighbors. It is part of an overall commitment to help Japan discover its appropriate role in the modern world.

Through his position with the Association to Aid Refugees, Fujita is working for something even deeper than apologies. At the time of the fiftieth anniversary of the end of World War II, he described in the leading Japanese daily *Asahi*, his wish for the country that Japanese leaders and groups of international standing visit places of symbolic significance from World War II and from other confrontations. They would be "ambassadors of reconciliation" to apologize for what Japan did in the past, pray for the deceased victims, and attempt to heal the grief of the bereaved families. "This kind of direct and continuous approach to the hearts and eyes of people in the countries involved would be essential—and far better than an inward-looking Diet resolution," Fujita wrote.

In addition, the Japanese emissaries would start projects in cooperation with host countries. Fujita listed these projects as:

• Editing history textbooks through collaboration between Japanese and local experts.

• Introducing into Japan Asian textbooks and movies dealing with Japan's actions before and during the war.

• Conducting fact-finding surveys on war victims.

• Documenting the circumstances under which the war began and the lessons it has taught.

• Describing Japan's apologies, the results of postwar recovery aid, and war reparations.

Japan, which he says owes a debt to many nations for its postwar peace and prosperity, should express its thanks for their support in such a way that the historical records can be handed down to future generations. In particular, Fujita suggested that the following statements of appreciation be issued:

• A statement in memory of Chiang Kai-shek, the Nationalist president of China before the Communists came to power, whose conviction that good should overcome the desire for vengeance compelled him to reject a plan to divide Japan at the war's end, repatriate Japanese soldiers still in mainland China, and give up claims for reparations.

• A statement thanking Mao Tse-tung, former chairman of the Chinese Communist Party, for relinquishing demands for reparations.

• A statement recognizing the key role played by former Sri Lankan President J.R. Jayawardene in winning over the nations opposed to a peace treaty with Japan at the San Francisco Conference of 1951.

• A statement expressing gratitude for U.S. postwar aid.

• A statement thanking the Allies for the return of Okinawa to Japan.

Fujita recommended further that young people bearing these messages be sent to the nations involved as part of the effort to build mutual trust. "A program of reciprocal visits by social studies teachers and former service people also merits consideration," he wrote. He feels that if Japan could gain a position of moral authority through such efforts, it would become possible to discuss objectively such contentious issues as the pros and cons of the atomic bombings and the validity of the Tokyo International War Crimes Tribunal. Coming to terms with the past can also serve Japan's national interest, he believes, by helping the country restore international trust and assume an "honored place" in international society, as stated in the Preamble to the Constitution. "That is the way," he believes, "to truly honor our war dead, a challenge to be effectively addressed by the Japanese people as a whole."

Fujita had begun to develop this new attitude to Japan after traveling for several years with a group of Asians who were working to help their continent "break the chain of hate." He had learned from them how Japan was regarded, and had left his work as an aide to a member of the House of Representatives to join them. "Being accepted by other Asians helped me to be able to apologize to them for what our country had done. . . . Since then I have taken various opportunities to apologize to the Asians for the past and in this process I was able to make many trusted friends."

The end of 1991 was seen by some as a defining moment in Japanese life. The fiftieth anniversary of the "sneak attack" (or "daring raid," depending on one's perspective) on Pearl Harbor only heightened the surfeit of soul-searching that the Gulf War sparked. Despite being one of the world's largest donors of overseas aid, and despite the fact that it had given $13 billion to the Gulf War and peace efforts, Japan had taken a psychological beating from the world for shirking its responsibilities. Indeed, in its concerted effort to rebuild from the ashes of war, Japan almost stumbled into first Asian and then world leadership, for which it was mentally unprepared.

Foreign criticism had fueled anxiety about Japan's image and the question of its role in the world. Shibusawa was quoted in the *Japan Times Weekly* in February 1991: "History has just leapt forward and left Japan without a role." Was it true, as Mortimer Zuckerman wrote in *U.S. News and World Report,* that "Japan's traditional low profile in the affairs of nations needs to give way to a role more in keeping with its stake in the international order"? The new prime minister, Kiichi Miyazawa, was recommending a greater international role so that Japan could "occupy an honored place in an international community and be a country of quiet dignity that its people can be proud of."

Should Japan play such a role? And, if so, what form should it take? How could other nations learn to trust Japan? To focus the issue, in November 1991 Fujita invited an ecumenical group of visitors to Japan, including the Dalai Lama; Jaime L. Cardinal Sin, Catholic archbishop of Manila; Dr. Inamullah Khan, secretary-general of the World Muslim Congress; and Rajmohan Gandhi, a grandson of Mahatma Gandhi and a well-known author. He felt that these men, when united, could help Japan underline the peace-building dimension of its world role. They all accepted Fujita's invitation. The Dalai Lama was prevented by ill health from participating, but his convictions were conveyed on videotape. The men spoke at twelve formal occasions for business and spiritual leaders and at a symposium that was broadcast to the nation. They addressed the subjects of reconciliation, universal ethics, and Japan's reform and contribution to peace. In a joint statement they underlined the need for a moral foundation and hearts attuned to conscience as the "only adequate basis for working together to meet the needs of our time."[10]

Toshiaki Ogasawara, publisher of the *Japan Times,* said that it was perhaps too short a visit to report a profound impact. Nonetheless, it had made people desirous for the spiritual leadership that their country was lacking. "We realized," he said, "that we have come to the stage when Japan can take initiative and responsibility for global peace. Even people at the grass roots show a strong interest in helping the world."[11]

Japan

The vision of Hiroshima as a rebuilt city of peace that had been expressed by Hiroshima Mayor Shinzo Hamai at Caux in 1950 was clearly fulfilled in 1995 at the fiftieth anniversary ceremonies marking the blast. Thirteen thousand guests gathered as a bell tolled, fifteen hundred doves of peace were released, and at 8:15 A.M.—the exact moment when the world entered the nuclear era—a minute's silence was observed. Hiroshima Mayor Takashi Hiraoka said, "With the suffering of all the war's victims indelibly etched in our hearts, we want to apologize for the unbearable suffering that Japanese colonial domination and war inflicted on so many people." Mayor Iccho Ito of Nagasaki spoke in similar terms at a ceremony in his city: "Without reflection and apology on Japan's own past," he said, "our calls for the abolition of nuclear weapons will not be heard by the people of the world."[12]

Notes

1. *Japan Times,* June 13, 1995.

2. *International Herald Tribune,* August 16, 1995.

3. The story of this group and their effect on Japanese life is told in Entwistle, *Japan's Decisive Decade.*

4. *MRA Pictorial* 22, Summer 1960.

5. Entwistle, *Japan's Decisive Decade.*

6. *MRA Information Service,* October 10, 1959.

7. *MRA Information Service,* December 29, 1958.

8. Entwistle, *Japan's Decisive Decade.*

9. Yukika Sohma is profiled in Henderson, *All Her Paths Are Peace.*

10. *Asia's Contribution to Peace and New Order,* November 1991.

11. *For a Change*, February/March 1992.

12. Reuters, August 10, 1995.

5

Prisoner 8231

The most sober—and most hopeful—
form of international remembrance is forgiveness,
that long, many-sided, seldom-completed
process of rehabilitating broken
human relationships.

DONALD SHRIVER
president emeritus and professor,
Applied Christianity at Union Theological
Seminary

CAN ONE LOVE ONE'S ENEMIES?

The interview was taking place on the tenth floor of the Hotel Belgrad in Moscow. It was early December 1990. All around the nation symbols of communism were being toppled, new countries were being born, and former citizens of the Soviet Union were having to come to terms with the previous seventy-three years.

Janna Vasilyeva, a journalist with *Literaturnaya Gazeta,* was pleased with the relaxed atmosphere as she sat on the sofa in the hotel lobby, recording the responses of some overseas guests to questions about their work of bringing people together. "As I rapidly took notes we smiled at each other. Everything was going well," she remembers. That is, until the Norwegian in the party, Leif Hovelsen, an older man of few words, entered the conversation.

"It happened during the war," Leif said. "I was a member of the Norwegian resistance." He had been caught by the Gestapo, sentenced to death by shooting, and was waiting for the order of

74

the court. For some reason the sitting of the court was postponed and the war ended . . . Ordered to guard the very Gestapo man who had been torturing me more than all the others, I was confronted with a problem: How to relate to him? I thought for a long time and at last reached the conclusion that I had to forgive him."

"Forgive!" exclaimed a rather perplexed Vasilyeva. Is that what the man really said? Had the translator gotten it right? The issue of blame was a real and current live concern for the Russian people. Can one actually forgive?

"Yes," said Leif. "According to our laws after the war, those who had suffered under the Nazis had to report this to the courts so that a court case could be made. I decided not to report my case, and my mother supported me. She asked me to tell this man that she was praying for him. I passed on my mother's words and said that I was abstaining from making a criminal case against him."

"Was he released?" asked the Russian journalist.

"No, he had distinguished himself with his brutality and was executed. But afterward, after the execution, a priest told me that before his death he asked to take communion."

Seeing that Vasilyeva did not take it all in, Leif went on: "You see, if God opened himself to this man, that means that before God, he and I are equal. And I have no right to condemn or accuse someone else."

"I was at a loss to understand," Vasilyeva wrote when her interview was published in *Literaturnaya Gazeta* on May 1, 1991. "The story that had just been told had hopelessly complicated the situation which until then had seemed clear. Because it is impossible to understand and practice literally what was said two thousand years ago: 'Love your enemy, praise those who heap abuse on you and pray for those who hurt and persecute you.'"

Yet the man she was interviewing evidently thought otherwise.

"At last I dared to ask Leif Hovelsen what he felt after what had happened," Vasilyeva wrote. He replied, "Free at heart. I stopped hating the Germans."

Such surprising words came naturally to the Norwegian. They are the fruit of having dealt with hatred at an early age and, as he says, finding the power of God to heal and direct has been effective and productive. A deafness in one ear as a result of Gestapo beatings was the only outward trace of the wartime experiences he described to the Russian journalist.

IN THE HANDS OF THE GESTAPO

In the early hours of June 9, 1943, nineteen-year-old Leif, who had just finished his final examinations, was yanked from his bed by five Gestapo officers, handcuffed, thrown into a waiting car, and taken to 19 Møller Street, the Oslo central jail. He had been distributing shortwave radio receivers and illegal newspapers, and he had been betrayed.

Leif feels that he laid some of his most important life foundations in cell B24.

One day a Gestapo officer told him he was on the list for execution. A week later another officer came to him and offered to set him free if he would inform on the resistance. It was a testing time for the nineteen-year-old. Here was a man whose word meant life or death. Everything in him wanted to live. But a clear voice told him what to answer.

"No, I can't," he said. "It's against my conscience."

The officer laughed. "You've been betrayed yourself. It's normal to inform; there's nothing wrong with that. We can guarantee that not one single person will know about it."

"No," repeated Leif. "I can't do it."

"Think about it," said the officer. "I'll come back next week, and we can find some arrangement."

"I never saw him again," says Leif. "He instinctively knew that he had lost and they could not get me under control. At the very moment I decided to say, 'No,' I experienced the inner freedom that conquered the Nazi ideology. A force within me speaking through my conscience made me resist."

Alone after a particularly brutal interrogation in which he had given more information than he wanted to, Leif knew he would not survive another session. Realizing that his life and that of two of his friends depended on their telling the same story, the thought came, "Why not pray?"

He didn't believe in prayer. He argued with himself. But finally he decided to make an experiment. "God, if you exist," he prayed, "and you are here and see everything, then you know how helpless I am and what is at stake. Will you help Albin and Erling to get through and say the right things?" Then he added, "If you can give me the answer and proof that you exist, I will give myself wholly to you."

A few days later Leif was suddenly taken out of his cell to get his hair cut. This was strange, for it was not his turn. He was placed on the stool by the exit to the courtyard. For some reason the barber turned the stool to the left. Just then two other prisoners were marched down the stairs and halted opposite him while the two sets of guards conversed. Those prisoners were Albin and Erling, and in the few seconds the three had together, they were able to establish that they had all told the same story.

Back in the cell Leif danced for joy; then he suddenly remembered his prayer. Was it chance that he'd been taken out of turn to the barber and that out of 450 prisoners, those two should, at that moment, be transferred to another camp?" Leif burst out, "God, I believe." Outside it was dark and dramatic, he recalls. There was thunder. "I was a different man."

Despite the impending threat of execution, Leif found those days in prison the richest he had ever lived through. In the cell he began to think back to his boyhood days, to communion services that he hardly understood. In the dark confines the words of an old communion text came back to him; he started to sing, "In the same night as he was betrayed he took bread. And when he had given thanks, he broke it."

As he thought about the words, he realized suddenly what Jesus had gone through. "He had been betrayed, and I had been betrayed. He had been tortured, and I had been tortured. He had been crucified, and I was going to be executed. It was as if Christ were physically walking beside me saying, 'Don't be afraid, Leif. I have been through all this for you. I am with you. I am the conqueror. Follow me.'"

At that point Leif felt that neither the Gestapo nor the fear of execution had any power over him. He was free. He knelt down and prayed, "Whatever be your will, God, let that come to pass. But if I may live and even be free again, I give you the whole of my life to use as you see best."*

From Oslo he was transported to Grini, the infamous Nazi concentration camp northwest of the city. Here, as prisoner 8231, he was to spend sixteen months awaiting execution. For Leif, Grini served as a further school for character training and for deepening the faith in which he had been brought up but from which he had been moving away.†

Leif points to several events in the Grini camp, events that served as markers along what he likes to call his "lifetime walk with God."

Through another prisoner, a professor of history named Eiliv Skard, Leif learned the discipline of listening to his inner voice. He was skeptical at first that his God could actually communicate with him. But one day, standing by an electric fence and looking out over a snowy landscape, the thought hit him, "You told a lie." A fellow prisoner, Trygve, had asked whether Leif had said anything about him when he was being interrogated, and he had replied he had not. Now, he felt he should go tell him the truth. After much hesitation and at the end of a long walk, he did so. "It's all right, Leif. I knew it," Trygve said.

---

*After the war Leif met another prisoner who, unknown to him, had been the one who had shoved his food tray in each day and had observed him through the slot. "What happened to you?" he asked Leif. "I was worried. You looked so depressed and down. Then one day you were so different. It was as if the whole cell was lit up. You had joy and peace of heart."

†Leif had been distinctly embarrassed when he was being bundled into the Gestapo car, as his mother had called out, "Leif, don't forget Jesus." That sort of thing, he thought, was only for old women and invalids.

It was also at Grini that Leif learned to stand up for his beliefs despite ridicule. He had become acquainted with a Christian prisoner named Olaf, and they had shared their hopes and longings. Then one day, Olaf was condemned to death and taken to another cell. Before the evening roll call Leif walked under the cell's window, wanting to show solidarity. Other prisoners, including some radical intellectuals he was eager to please, were milling around. Suddenly, Olaf pulled himself up by the bars, his eyes took them all in, and in a strong, clear voice he called out, "Thanks for your comradeship, Leif. Never give up in the fight for Christ."

Leif looked at his other friends and said nothing. Later, back in his room after roll call, Leif thought about the biblical account of the apostle Peter's actions when he heard the cock crow, and he wept. "It was like Christ touching me and saying, 'Don't be distressed, stand up and follow me.'" He decided never again to deny the truth of Christ and to follow his way regardless of his own shortcomings.

In the spring of 1945 Leif and several hundred other prisoners were transferred to a special SS camp at Mysen. Soon liberation came, and Leif, as he related to the Russian journalist, suddenly found himself in charge of guarding some of the SS officers. At first he began to take revenge on them, putting them through the same punishment drills he had endured. He was then startled to discover that the same root of evil he despised in the Nazis and the Germans was also within his own nature. It was this realization that led to his later decision not to press charges against the man who had tortured him.

SHARING EXPERIENCE WITH GERMANS AND RUSSIANS

Soon after the war the conviction grew in Leif that he should be ready to go with others to Germany to help with the rebuilding of the country. The decision was not an easy one, as there was criticism from fellow Norwegians that he had "gone over to the enemy" and was "betraying Norwegian interests." In 1949, however, Leif and his colleagues traveled to Germany.

In those first months in Germany, as Leif met the people, lived in their homes, walked among the ruins, and saw what the Germans had gone through, he learned a valuable lesson in compassion. He began to understand that the deeper he went, "the less it is a question of German or Norwegian, Russian or American, but that we are all part of one suffering human race." He became involved in trying to improve relations between the war-ravaged countries of Europe, particularly between Germany and her former enemies, including Norway.

One of the prisoners with Leif at Grini had been Einar Gerhardsen, the former mayor of Oslo. At the end of the war Gerhardsen had been restored to his mayoral post and then had become prime minister. Leif paid a visit to the prime minister, bringing a number of Germans with whom he was working. When one of the Germans apologized to the Norwegian leader for what had happened between their countries, Gerhardsen was touched. The encounter was markedly different from the formal ones to which he was accustomed.

During this postwar period there were difficult negotiations going on regarding reparations for former political prisoners. The negotiations dragged on for years. Thinking he might be able to do something, Leif went to see Gerhardsen, who was on vacation in the mountains. The prime minister gave Leif some ideas that he was able to pass on to the German cabinet.

As a result, Dr. Theodor Oberländer, German minister of refugees, came to Norway in 1959. He met Norwegian representatives, including the prime minister. The meeting took place in the home of another of Leif's friends, Hans Cappelen, a resistance leader whose life had been saved during the war when Count Folke Bernadotte from Sweden had recognized him half-dead in a ditch in Dachau. In a few hours the participants worked out a strategy that produced a solution at a time when no one else could see a way out. Halvard Lange, the Norwegian foreign minister, thanked Leif and his friends publicly for the part they had played.*

Leif also wrote articles that helped pave the way for the visit to Norway in 1970 of Gustav Heinemann, then head of the German Federal Republic.†

In October 1990 Leif received a letter of thanks from a group of Germans. In part, it said:

> You came to Germany in the very early years after the war. You shared with us hardships and insecurities. You helped turn desperation and resignation into faith and active responsibility. You built friendships, personally and in national dimensions. You helped lay a foundation of confidence in a democratic way of organizing society and international relations. Today, as Germans, we want to thank you most warmly for what you did for our country. The process of freedom and unification only became possible because of the broad foundations that had been laid in the decades before. We think with gratitude of the vital contribution you made.

For more than twenty years, because of a shared bond of suffering and his own dislike of totalitarian dictatorship, Leif also built friendships with dissidents from what was then the Soviet Union and other East European countries. He became a member of the Helsinki Watch Committee, which monitored human rights abuses in the Soviet Union; he was involved in the cam-

---

*On his father's seventy-fifth birthday in 1952, Leif's parents were visited in their home by Georg von Breich-Oppert, the German ambassador to Norway, who came to thank them for permitting their only son to come to his country and work tirelessly for the moral reconstruction of Berlin and Germany. His parents were deeply touched. The last Germans in their home had been the Gestapo members who had arrested Leif.

†Gustav Heinemann's trip was the first visit to Norway by a German head of state since 1905.

paign to free Vladimir Bukovsky from a KGB prison, and helped get Andrei Sakharov nominated for the Nobel peace prize.

For the sake of the future Leif wanted the dissidents to find the freedom and power he had found. The core experience he shared with them, he says, is one of total helplessness in the face of evil. At "rock-bottom reality," as he calls it, the discovery of inner freedom through moral choice comes as a revelation. "For me this was also a discovery of a spiritual dimension beyond my physical existence or my intellectual understanding and the knowledge that no earthly might or man-made hell can prevent the power of God breaking through."

He wrote to one Soviet dissident:

> Anyone can be given the gift of being a free man, free of hate, revenge and bitterness. What happened to me was a divine intervention. At the moment when I acted on the compelling thought that had come to me, I neither understood nor grasped what I did, nor did I fully realize how deep my fear and hate against the Gestapo and the Germans were. But by obeying, God took out the seed of hate in my heart and replaced it with a seed of love. And I became a free person. And because of that I was used in an amazing way to build reconciliation between our two countries.

Now, with the ending of the Cold War, Leif has been to Russia more than a dozen times. His visits led not only to the interview in *Literaturnaya Gazeta* but to further press, radio and TV interviews.* This exposure in the media has carried his experience of healing the past to millions.

"The ways of God are inscrutable," Leif says. When he was "struck like a bolt from the blue," as he puts it and prompted to forgive the Gestapo man who had tortured him, it could not

---

*In an interview for the Moscow television station RT which was broadcast all over Russia in May 11, 1996, the first question asked of Leif by Leonid Mlechlin, a deputy editor of *Izvestia*, was, "Is it possible to forgive your enemy? This is the most important question in Russia today."

have been more illogical, more unpopular, and more inconceivable. This was especially true in those days of May 1945. Many friends could not understand him; some even looked at him as a traitor. Even Leif himself could not grasp this unlikely epiphany. However, he could not resist the call that had stirred inside him.

Today, looking back over fifty years, Leif Hovelsen believes time has proved that God's way was the providential one. "It was the salvation for the Gestapo man who was executed because of his crimes but who found peace with his maker and victory over death. It has also become a door-opening experience to so many people—Germans, Poles, Russians—in their struggle to find inner freedom and deliverance from the evil of hate."

Vasilyeva made this comment to her Russian readers after listening to Leif: "You probably have to reconcile yourself to the fact that this is impossible to explain. And it is impossible to cover this stretch of road in the footsteps of someone else." She concluded:

> It seems that as long as people will not enter this other road, history will go on in a closed circuit and will demonstrate with the insistence of idiocy the bloody reality of war, hunger or enmity. A reality that at the end turns upon us.

Vasilyeva's article was published under the headline, "Is it possible to learn to love your enemy?"

Leif says simply, "It all goes back to my experience in the camp. God gave me life. It was for a purpose. I'm not bogged down with bitterness or bad feelings about people. It's a wonderful gift."

Leif's travels to Russia after the breakup of the Soviet Union to help lay the moral and spiritual foundations of the new democracy are described in section two, chapter 7.

Notes

This chapter is based largely on the author's conversations with Leif Hovelsen and on Hovelsen, *Out of the Evil Night*.

SECTION TWO

No End to History

6

Cambodia: After the killing fields

*The United Nations planted the seeds of
democracy. But someone has to be here to
fertilize and care for it. Cambodian
democracy is still a very fragile thing.*

CHEA SOKHA
*survivor of Khmer Rouge reign
of terror, Vietnamese occupation,
and refugee life*

LEGACY OF HORROR

Millions of land mines lurk unobtrusively in the killing fields of
Cambodia; they still kill. There are more amputees per thousand
people than in any other country in the world. Millions of Cambodians mourn family losses in one of the great tragedies of Asia.
Bitterness can devastate the spirit; the scale of the problems can
daunt even the most courageous. Words can hardly capture the
horror of the four years from 1975 to 1979.

In that period nearly a quarter of the population died during
Pol Pot's regime through the cruel treatment imposed by the
Khmer Rouge cadres as they deliberately set out to eliminate the
intellectuals, the middle class, and anyone who had received a
formal education or showed initiative. Ninety percent of the six
thousand-strong artists union were killed. And the country's
Buddhist roots, its connections to the past, were severed: Monasteries were closed and desecrated; statues of the Buddha

smashed, beheaded, or used for target practice; and ancient scriptures burned or used as cigarette paper.

From 1970 onward, the country was ravaged by a progression of U.S. bombing during the Vietnam War (more tons of explosives were dropped on Cambodia in the early 1970s than had fallen on Japan during the Second World War[1]), revolution, genocide, invasion by Vietnam, and thirteen years of civil war that destroyed the country's social fabric. In some parts of the country the infrastructure was nonexistent, government workers often were not paid, and corrupt officials thrived in the political vacuum. Millions of Cambodians with skills, if they had not been killed, had fled abroad. Some 370,000 displaced Cambodians were in camps in Thailand, and nearly 200,000 others were in camps in Cambodia. Then in 1993, when free elections were supervised by the United Nations and a new constitution was introduced, a fragile peace was established.

Can peace be maintained in this gentle land, a peace in which development can flourish and some of the world's poorest people can be lifted up? Can the past be healed? To expect individuals who have survived the Cambodian torture rack to put the past behind them and to forgive almost defies belief. Yet there are Cambodians who feel that only in doing so can Cambodia move forward, and that in adopting this approach they are being faithful to their Buddhist tradition and to those who died. Such selfless men and women, working to awaken the Khmer conscience, have to contend with those who enrich themselves at the expense of the poor and terrorize those who would frustrate their activities. Meanwhile fighting against the Khmer Rouge still continues in parts of the country.

A START AT HEALING

In the spring of 1972 John Graham was with the Americans helping the South Vietnamese defend the city of Hué from the Vietcong. Dith Sawaeng (a pseudonym) was a Cambodian fighting with the North Vietnamese against the Americans at the same place. It was there that he was recruited by the Khmer Rouge. In April 1994 Graham, now a retired U.S. diplomat, and Sawaeng, still with the Khmer Rouge, met at a time when U.S. diplomats were forbidden by congressional order to talk to the Khmer Rouge. Graham and others wanted to try to convince the Khmer Rouge to join the process of peaceful reconstruction in Cambodia, then starting tentatively after decades of war.

"The prospects were slim," said Graham. At first Sawaeng gave Graham a standard ideological lecture defending the Khmer Rouge role. But away from where they could be overheard, the two men began to talk about the cost of war, to share the personal experiences that revealed that twenty-two years earlier they had been fighting each other. Sawaeng said to Graham, "You are a strange man. We both learned to kill as young men." Then he asked a question: "Tell me, how did you learn to stop?"[2]

In an assessment of the situation in the country today, Graham calls the magnitude of the challenges mind-boggling. Creating a viable economic, social, and political structure is almost the "easy" part. Underneath all that is the need to help heal deep and pervasive scars in the national psyche, to, in effect, "restart" the culture and to renew traditional spiritual and religious life after the devastation of twenty years of war and genocide. There is a widespread feeling among Cambodians of all types that the country cannot be allowed to slide back into violence—no matter what the provocation; this belief lends currency to reconciliation efforts that might not otherwise be taking place, considering the political differences that exist.[3]

Two Cambodians who are in the vanguard of that reconciliation are educator Renée Pan and human rights activist Kassie Neou. Renée does not know to this day what happened to her husband, Sothi Pan, the deputy prime minister, after she fled Cambodia in 1975; Kassie's wife disappeared in the exodus when Pol Pot took over the country. Both must assume that their spouses are among the millions who died. Both are bringing something more precious than mine detectors to their country: the art of healing wounds in a society where everyone is wounded.

Renée says, "Our most urgent national need is for a new Cambodia where enemies are made into friends. National reconciliation must begin with each one of us."[4] Renée and Kassie and those working with them describe their aims as "reconciliation and active conflict resolution at all levels of Cambodian life and moral regeneration for effective participatory democracy, building on the traditional values and strengths of the Cambodian people."

With the help of the international community, Cambodia was given the opportunity for a fresh start. On October 23, 1991, a political agreement was reached in Paris, brokered by members of the UN Security Council after two years of negotiations spearheaded by France and Indonesia; it was signed by representatives of eighteen nations and agreed to by the four main Cambodian political factions. French President François Mitterrand said, "A dark page of history has been turned. Cambodia is about to resume its place in the world."

Prisons were opened up and detainees freed. The UN agreed to oversee the return of refugees, the administration of the country, the demobilization of rival armies, and the preparations for the first multiparty elections since 1972. A Supreme National Council was formed to rule the country in consultation with the United Nations. The UN mounted its largest peace-keeping operation ever, with twenty-two thousand personnel helping to oversee the transition of authority from a one-party communist state to a multiparty democracy under a constitutional monarch. It enlisted volunteers from forty-six countries, and Cambodians like Renée and Kassie, to help prepare and supervise the elections and deployed more than ten thousand UN troops with weapons and flak jackets at fifteen hundred polling sites to cope with the expected violence and intimidation.

Despite repeated predictions of failure, the election, held May 23–27, 1993, was a resounding success, with 90 percent of those registered turning out to vote. The *Christian Science Monitor* on June 2, 1993, called the vote "a testament to the resilience of the Cambodian people, who in the late 1970s and early 1980s were subjected to some of the most brutal terrors of the period." It was also a victory for the United Nations, which had spent $2 billion in Cambodia since 1991 and held to a course of multiparty elections despite Khmer Rouge attacks that killed ten soldiers and officials and the assassination of many electoral agents and party militants of the BLDP and FUNCINPEC political parties.

The Australian ambassador to Cambodia, John Holloway, said that in one village, the police upon seeing crowds moving in distant hills, feared a Khmer Rouge attack. The movement turned out to be whole families, dressed in their temple best and led by older women, coming to vote. The UN representative, Yasushi Akashi, called the result "a stinging rebuke to the men of violence." *The Economist,* giving voice to the surprise in international circles, headlined its May 29, 1993, account of the elections, "Shock in Cambodia—nobody killed."

In 1994 the United Nations withdrew, having fulfilled its eighteen-month mandate. Cambodia's path toward democracy still traverses a minefield of violence, corruption, poverty, AIDS, and illiteracy. Again there are predictions of failure. But Renée, Kassie, and many others are determined that their country will succeed with democracy. Their convictions grow out of the profound changes both have experienced in their lives that freed them from lesser preoccupations.

AN EXILE'S CONTRIBUTION

When Renée Pan escaped from Cambodia, she went to the United States. Living in exile, she never dreamed that her country would experience such a sudden and dramatic turnaround and that two decisions she made in the United States—to learn computing and to give up her hatred of the Khmer Rouge—would prove valuable to the new country.

As a refugee, she struggled first to become economically independent. It took her four years to get a master's degree in statistics and computer science. She then decided to devote her time, money, and energy to the welfare of her community and country.

She was encouraged in this goal by remembering what her parents had told her as she grew up. "Good deeds receive good deeds," they would say, and, quoting Buddha, "A good deed will follow you like your own shadow, while bad deeds are like the trace left behind by the wheel of the ox cart."

As well as helping other Southeast Asian refugees settle in the United States, she became involved in promoting unity among those of her compatriots in exile who were working for liberation but who were often divided by political feuding. Realizing that change had to start with herself, she once decided to apologize to a political leader who was refusing to meet her. Her efforts only seemed to create more distrust. She became discouraged and felt tempted to give up. "My energy did not regenerate itself," she recalls. "My brain was empty and my heart was numb and insensitive. I got angry very easily, hated bad people, was unhappy, selfish, and did things foolishly."

At this stage she saw a film about the life of Irène Laure,* *For the Love of Tomorrow.* At Caux after the end of World War II, Irène had asked the Germans present to forgive her for her hatred of them. Renée decided to visit the Frenchwoman. From Irène she learned about the importance of *le silence,* times of quiet for reflection. "I was always wanting so much to help others, I had never thought of liberating myself," she said. "Through that quiet time the Buddha teachings became real to me for the first time. I realized my mind was consumed by the 'three fires of the world'—greed, anger, and foolishness." The result of that experience was a decision—like Irène Laure's toward the Germans—to forgive those who had killed her husband and destroyed her country and to ask their forgiveness for her attitude. When she did so, she says, "the burden of revenge that I carried for a decade was lightened. It became less hard to endure the discipline that leads to enlightenment."

---

*Laure's story is told more fully in section one, chapter 2.

Later she had the chance to express her forgiveness personally to Khmer Rouge officers, when she spoke for three hours at a camp on the Thai-Cambodian border. "I delivered a powerful speech in front of forty Khmer Rouge teachers. I was quiet and calm. I knew that the hatred was over at that moment." Driving her home afterward, a Khmer Rouge officer asked, "Can the world ever forgive us?"

As a computer specialist, Renée likes to use computer images to describe what happened to her. Human memory, she maintains, is unlimited compared with computer memory. If, however, the human memory is loaded with impurities, it is unable to solve even a simple problem.

"Forgiveness freed up some megabytes in my memory," Renée says. "I dare to solve problems on a larger scale with less CPU [central processing unit] time in a more efficient way." And when freedom came for her people, she was ready to use both her computer and her bridge-building skills for the country. One of the tools she uses is a Khmer-language version of the film about Irène Laure. At the suggestion of Surya Chhuy, a Cambodian student living in France, the film was dubbed into Khmer. Surya says, "I have learned to forgive the Khmer Rouge. If I have succeeded—because I had a terrible hatred in me—it is because of Madame Laure."

REEDUCATING CAMBODIA'S PEOPLE

It was Kassie Neou[5] and his second wife, Polly, who translated the film about Irène Laure into Khmer. Before fleeing his country, Kassie had been a teacher, producing English instruction courses for Cambodian TV. He sees Irène Laure not as a Frenchwoman but as a Cambodian woman. "There is one sentence of hers that I love: 'All these things I cannot forget, but I can forgive.' Someone has got to say that to Cambodians."

Translating the film was important to Kassie because, he says, it gives people courage "to say 'sorry,' to be responsible, to admit mistakes, to have enough courage to fight within themselves, and to change themselves into the will of a society that can live in peace together." He feels that the film promotes what he describes as "moral repentance, forgiveness, reconciliation, and the unity needed to create a society that can live in peace."

In the United States Kassie was the executive director and human rights spokesman of the Cambodian Network Council, a coalition of fifty-six community associations representing two hundred thousand Cambodians living largely in the United States, working toward healing. He was one of the founders of the Cambodian Documentation Committee that, for years, compiled evidence to bring the top one hundred Khmer Rouge officers before the International Court of Justice in The Hague.

He is a survivor of Pol Pot's terror; his father was executed. When a few careless words in English revealed his social status, Kassie was sent to a "reeducation camp." During his 195 days there he was beaten unconscious five times by Khmer Rouge soldiers, who had orders to eradicate social classes identified with the old regime. Yet Kassie never revealed his identity. Each time he was beaten, he looked at his torturers and told himself that, when the time came, he would do "three times worse to them." He was saved from execution by a young guard whom he had entertained secretly with classical children's stories.

When in 1978 the Vietnamese ousted Pol Pot, Kassie was released and escaped into Thailand with his mother and two children, only to be forcibly returned to Cambodia with forty-three thousand others across a mine field. Injured by an exploding mine, he walked with his family for fifty-nine days, surviving by eating weeds. After recovering, he escaped again into Thailand and spent eighteen months there until he and his family were resettled in the United States.

At Caux Kassie described all he had been through and then said, thumping his chest, "The battle for peace has to be won from here first." While working with relief agencies in Thailand, he had suddenly recognized one of his torturers. With his army connections, Kassie could easily have gotten rid of the man. But as a boy Kassie had lived in a Buddhist monastery and had attended Christian church. Both faiths had stressed forgiveness. As one who felt the need to reach national reconciliation to achieve the reconstruction of the country, he decided to abandon the revenge that he felt had become part of his culture. He took the man to a warehouse where he got food and medicine for him and his family. "I gave him one hundred baht in cash. His hands were shaking as he took the money, and tears were in his eyes. Then I knew I had won the battle."

CAUX'S INFLUENCE

The long-term commitment of those associated with Caux to the Khmer people and their care began in 1954 when, at a conference in Paris, Daniel Dommel, a senior French civil servant, met and befriended a Cambodian personality, Son Sann, who later became chairman of the Cambodian National Bank and then prime minister of his country. Through Sann those associated with Caux were put in contact with many other Cambodians, especially those exiled and resettled in different countries. At their request training sessions were offered in Caux and similar facilities elsewhere to prepare them for an eventual return to Cambodia. In the 1970s exiles from the Indo-Chinese countries regularly met to address their grievances and seek reconciliation at the de Watteville home in Paris, which had played a role in bringing together French and North Africans. For ten years starting with 1984 at the request of Son Sann and others, workshops on democratic citizenship and moral renewal were conducted at refugee camps along the Thai-Cambodian border.

At the first Paris Peace Conference in 1989, Cambodian delegates had asked for help in holding a series of private meetings at the de Watteville home where discreet, off-the-record encounters could facilitate more intimate communication among the various rival factions. They were assisted by experienced diplomats and negotiators. The interaction continued through the stages of the peace talks, and, as the conference came to a close, a dinner was given for Prince Norodom Ranariddh—then commander-in-chief of Prince Sihanouk's army and later the first prime minister of the Kingdom of Cambodia—by his new French friends. As he was leaving, the prince encouraged them to continue to participate in the national reconciliation of all the Cambodian people.

In the early 1990s support groups developed for Cambodian youth and community leaders in Australia, France, Malaysia, and the United States. In Australia in July 1992, for example, 180 Cambodians took part in a week-long, student-led conference, "Your Part in the New Cambodia," cohosted by the Cambodian Youth Association of Victoria. Kassie Neou spoke there on "Freedom and Responsibility—the Ingredients of a Sound Democracy."

In August 1994 another conference, on "The Dynamics of Change," was held at the Center for Khmer Culture and Vipassana (the latter is a form of meditation) near Phnom Penh. This center was developed by Professor Chheng Phon, former Cambodian minister of culture. Encouraged by seeing Cambodian youth actively involved in their country's reconstruction, he made the center available at no cost. The conference was addressed by Kassie and by Son Sann's son, Son Soubert, then vice president of the Cambodian Parliament, who spoke from his own experience on the theme, "Personal Forgiveness and Reconciliation." He had apologized to his younger brother, he said, for the breakdown of their relationship: "If our families are not united, how can we unite our country?"

Financial support for the August 1994 conference came from the Australian Embassy in Cambodia, the Asia Foundation, and the American Friends Service Committee. As a result, a camp was set up for 150 people at Sihanoukville in Cambodia. Cambodians in Australia produced thousands of copies of *Which Way, Cambodia?*, a handbook on moral responsibility, in Khmer and English. It quotes the Buddha: "Hatred does not cease by hatred. Easily seen are the faults of others, but one's own faults are hard to see. . . . conquer the angry man by love, conquer the miser with generosity, conquer the liar with truth."

FINDING NEUTRAL GROUND

Throughout these years the facilities offered by the conference center in Caux proved a useful neutral meeting ground where Cambodians of different factions could find a degree of trust with one another. In 1985, for instance, two senior representatives of the Phnom Penh government attended a summer conference.* Beginning in 1990 dozens of Cambodian community leaders from Australia, France, and the United States visited Caux each year.

One encounter was particularly dramatic. Each evening the Cambodians were in the habit of meeting for hours to discuss how reconciliation could be brought about, not only among their own people but with the Vietnamese who had invaded and ruled their country. One evening two Vietnamese approached the Cambodians as they were meeting and expressed their apologies for the way Vietnam had treated the Khmer people over the years.

It so happened that the next day a Khmer Rouge official turned up unexpectedly for dinner. On the way to his table he met some other Cambodians who were at the conference. At dinner his hosts briefed him on the conference and mentioned the Vietnamese apologies. Tears started to roll down the official's eyes, which he tried to mop with his paper napkin. After a long silence he apologized and explained with a broken voice that a cousin living in the United States had visited him recently and shown him the picture of both his father's and mother's bodies. His parents had died during the Khmer Rouge killing-fields period, and he was finding it difficult to get over his grief. He went on to say that out of his eight brothers and sisters, six had also died because of the Khmer Rouge's brutal treatment of hard

---

*A leader of another faction attended a Caux conference prior to the meeting in Beijing where the impasse over the formation of the Supreme National Council was broken.

work, little food, and no medicine. And his tears kept rolling down his face.[6]

It was clear to his hosts that he could no longer keep his pain in check and that he had taken a risk in coming to Caux. They sensed that, although the official might have been a victim of circumstances, he also knew that he had been a part of the system that had destroyed his family and that his conscience was troubling him.

One of the Cambodian leaders who had greeted him when he had entered the dining room passed him a note asking whether he would be willing to meet some of his compatriots on the terrace after dinner. While others at the conference attended a concert by a Czechoslovakian orchestra, five Cambodians—two from the United States, two from France, and one from Australia—sat with the Khmer Rouge official. They were still talking in the dark when the concert ended. On the way to refreshments one of the Cambodians confided in a friend that the official had told them he regretted very much the suffering imposed on their people under Pol Pot's regime and apologized for it. The Cambodian said, "Think of it. It happened on the same terrace where Madame Irène Laure decided to make peace with a German lady after the Second World War."

Later that evening, as the Cambodians had their usual get-together, a row broke out between those who had met the official and a group that accused them of having personal contact with a "murderer." One of the former said with great conviction:

> We came here to find out how we could contribute to our national reconciliation, as well as to the reconciliation between our people and the Vietnamese people. Last night two Vietnamese asked for our forgiveness for the way their people had treated the Cambodians, and tonight a Khmer Rouge official also expressed his regrets for the suffering his political faction imposed on our people. I think that our two questions have been mysteriously answered. Yes, national and regional reconciliations

are possible provided we today accept to trust those men who apologized to us and to forgive them. If we refuse to do it in a place like Caux, we shall never be able to do it anywhere else.

That evening many in the delegation faced the challenge and decided to open their hearts to become creators of trust and peace.

Three months later, inspired by his "first experience of reconciliation with a brother enemy," one of the Cambodians resigned from a well-paid job in Paris to go to Cambodia and work full time for a political party to sustain the reconciliation process going on under the UN umbrella. He had no resource other than his deep conviction that Cambodia would be rebuilt only through the personal sacrifice and commitment of each of his compatriots. He went on to assume an important political position in his country. Meanwhile the Khmer Rouge official broke all relations with his political party, resigned from his responsibilities, and became a monk for a while. He now teaches in a European university and keeps in touch with the people he met at Caux, whom he calls his "trusted friends."

RECONCILIATION AT PHNOM PENH

After the Paris agreement made it possible for Cambodians in exile to work in the country, three visits to Phnom Penh were made in early 1992 by groups of people at the invitation of Cambodian leaders from the political groups represented in the Supreme National Council who wished to extend the nation-building work in their country and to get help in expanding national reconciliation. A cabinet minister who had served his country after the Pol Pot regime was ousted from Phnom Penh told the visitors, "All moral values are gone: national, societal, familial, individual. People are frightened and dare not tell the truth. We need spiritual help more than material." They met with Prince Norodom Sihanouk and with Yasushi Akashi, head of the UN mission, and his staff.

In March 1993 two hundred Cambodians—political leaders, members of the Buddhist hierarchy, UN volunteers, university students, and foreign diplomats attended a two-day seminar in Phnom Penh on the theme "Confidence-Building for Peace in Cambodia." A message from Prime Minister Hun Sen expressed the strong belief "that the seminar will bring some light to the darkness of the Cambodian tragedy."

The international Buddhist patriarch, the Venerable Maha Ghosananda, participated and gave the invocation. He believes that "out of great suffering comes great compassion."[7] His efforts to bring peace to the nation earned him a nomination for the 1994 Nobel peace prize. Ghosananda, whose name means "great joyful proclaimer," invited seminar participants to join in a peace march. The film, *For the Love of Tomorrow,* was shown along the route. He said, "Each step is a prayer. Each step must build a bridge." International visitors contributing their perspectives included General Joseph Lagu from the Sudan, whose spirit of forgiveness toward Northern Muslims had helped pave the way for the accords in his country that led to ten years of peace,* and Datu Paduka Hajjah Saleha from Malaysia, who attended the seminar with the support of her prime minister and spoke about what it had taken to unite the people of her country.

Rajmohan Gandhi from India cited the lessons his country had learned.

"Why did Indian fight brother Indian in the past?" he asked. "Why did prince fight brother prince? Why did trust between rulers and the ruled break down? If we study the past for answers to such questions, we make the past our servant for building a happier future. If we rake up the past, to spread bitterness, we become servants of the past, which then swallows our children. To the past let a portion of our minds be given, a cool, detached,

---

*One member of parliament said a year later that listening to Lagu had turned him away from the revenge he had planned against police officers who had harassed him during the election campaign. Lagu's story is recounted in section four, chapter 14.

searching portion. But our faces, our eyes, our emotions, our dreams should be turned towards the future. This is one lesson that Indian events have produced." He quoted his grandfather, the Mahatma: "If we do not condemn our own violence, we will have tyranny after India wins independence."

In March 1994 another conference was held, this time on the theme "Change in the Heart: The Key to Change in Society." It was attended by 350 political leaders, students, monks, diplomats, and workers from nongovernmental organizations. It was cosponsored by the Cambodian Institute of Human Rights. Opening and closing addresses were given by two deputy prime ministers from previously opposing parties. The foreign minister, Prince Norodom Sirivuddh, called for "a process of permanent consultation" to end the nation's ongoing conflict with the Khmer Rouge. In closing Interior Minister Sar Kheng called for "a nonviolent formula to solve our problems." He laid aside a prepared text and spoke from his heart. Using his own experience of making peace with five former colleagues who had tried to kill him when he defected from the Khmer Rouge, he related that later, as a government official, he went back to assure them that he desired peace.

Finance Minister Sam Rainsy, Education Minister Ung Huot, Information Minister Ieng Mouly, and Second Vice President of the National Assembly Son Soubert, who all had previous contacts with Caux personalities in France and Australia, also participated.

CORRUPTION OF THE EDUCATION SYSTEM

In August 1994 and 1995 Cambodian delegations to Caux included members of the royal government. One of them, Ung Huot, then education minister and later foreign minister, told a Caux conference that his priority had been to eliminate corruption in school examinations in order to restore credibility to the education system after its complete destruction by the Khmer Rouge. When he was appointed, it was clear to him that exam results did not correspond to ability. Degrees and diplomas had lost their credibility. On one hand, high-level officials would intervene with the Education Ministry to make sure that their children passed. On the other, students would pay bribes to teachers and supervisors to pass them.

Beholden to no one in Cambodia—he had earned degrees in commerce and business administration from Melbourne University—he decided to tackle the situation. First, he secured the backing of the country's two prime ministers in halting the practice of intervention by high officials. Then he made a three-month tour of the country to explain what he was doing. He knew he would have to "market" the answer to the corruption if he were to carry with him teachers, students, parents, and politicians. He told the people that they had to want change in their hearts, that Cambodia was getting a bad reputation all over the world because of the corruption in their education system. The going rate to pass an exam then was $200, and corruption had become a six-million-dollar industry. "I told the people to forget the past," he said. "I was not going to put blame on anyone, but instead to look to a positive future."

Huot instructed supervisors to remove all the special markings that were left on papers by students to signify that they had paid a bribe. He sent supervisors away from their teaching areas when students were taking exams so that there could be no collusion. He also ensured that teachers would not correct papers at the same center where they had monitored an exam. He punished dishonest teachers, not by stripping them of their qualifications or ranking in the profession but by sending them to jail, where they could "continue their teaching inside."

The dramatic drop in test results showed that progress had been made. "Because only 4 percent passed the eleventh grade exam, if there was any attempted corruption, it obviously did not work," he said. "The people who accepted bribes will have to give the money back." He said he believed that such poor results could only encourage students to work harder. His aim is that by the year 2000, Cambodia's educational standards will be among the best in the world.

THE WORK OF REBUILDING CONTINUES

Through all the efforts to help Cambodia stand on its feet—along with the emphasis on awakening the individual conscience, particularly among the nation's elite—there has been a bid to strengthen the cultural and traditional values in the country, which for centuries have been found in Buddhism. English film-maker David Channer, who made *For the Love of Tomorrow,* has also made *The Serene Smile.* Ghosananda says of *The Serene Smile,* "We will show it from temple to temple in the countryside and the cities."*

The film is an exposition in contemporary images of the qualities in Khmer culture that can inspire social and spiritual renewal in Cambodia. Channer's son, Alan, who directed the film, hopes that it will raise awareness among Cambodians, who have known little but insecurity, hardship, and isolation, that the Khmer people have a great spiritual legacy. He also hopes it will foster a sense that a peaceful, just, and harmonious Cambodia is a vision that can be realized. At the same time, he wants the film to sensitize the rest of the world to the dignity and forbearance of the Khmer people.

The Konrad Adenauer Foundation bought four hundred copies of the video and presented them to the king, senior Buddhist monks, the cabinet, members of the National Assembly, and government officials. The film has been broadcast repeatedly on national television.

Renée Pan and Kassie Neou continue their work. Renee is focused on education. Once she was freed from her bitterness, she was inspired to found the Cambodian Children's Education Fund, with the aim of developing "education for all." It is designed to upgrade the quality of teaching skills and education, emphasizing the moral and traditional values of the Khmer peo-

---

* The Serene Smile was shown at the second national seminar on Buddhism and the development of Khmer society in Battambang. The response to the film by Buddhist leaders is recorded in an article in *Cambodia Today* (December 8, 1995), "Buddhist medicine for Cambodia's ills."

ple and education for democracy, and to introduce strategies of dialogue, critical thinking, and problem solving. Renée wants, she says, to complete the unfinished work of her husband, who was minister of education, to heal the wounds and work with all factions. Her organization first developed courses in the refugee camps and now works within Cambodia. Many of the first participants in her courses hold leadership positions in the country.

Kassie Neou, as director of the Institute of Human Rights, today is charged with writing the human rights curriculum for the national education system and implementing it by training all seventy thousand school teachers at primary and secondary levels. One of his priorities is the building of a Mohajeti Jati, a national memorial near Phnom Penh where the names of all the dead of the last two decades will be recorded. He hopes this memorial will replace the grotesque display of skulls that now exists and is in contradiction to Buddhist tradition. The Mohajeti Jati was conceived by a nonpolitical coalition of Cambodians around the world. They aim to give the remains of all victims proper Buddhist rites and house the ashes in a traditional Buddhist stupa (shrine). They see the memorial as a symbol of the first steps toward the moral and spiritual healing of the Cambodian people.

"We Buddhists believe that unless we give our loved ones proper service, their spirits cannot rest in peace," says Kassie. "It is impossible to bring peace to Cambodia unless there is a proper place to put the ashes and for people to come together and pray. It is healing at the grass roots."

In the summer of 1995 an American Catholic monk, Bob Maat, found himself in the midst of artillery fire in northwest Cambodia. He saw some villagers running toward a ditch and, assuming that they would know where there were no land mines, threw himself down in the ditch, too. As the firefight blazed overhead, he handed each villager a text on peace written by Maha Ghosananda. It read: "We must remove the land mines in our hearts which keep us from making peace—hatred, greed, delusion. We can oppose hatred with loving kindness, greed with generosity, and delusion with wisdom. Peacemaking begins with us." One villager exclaimed as he read it, "This is completely right."[8]

Notes

1. *Far Eastern Economic Review,* April 27, 1995.

2. Unpublished memoir by Graham, "Sit Down, Young Stranger."

3. Letter from Graham to Dick Ruffin, executive director, Moral Re-Armament in the United States, March 31, 1994.

4. Renée Pan is profiled in Henderson, *All Her Paths Are Peace.*

5. Kassie Neou is profiled in *For a Change,* January 1992.

6. This story is told in a memo by Alain Tate, a Frenchman who was present.

7. Maha Ghosananda is profiled in *For a Change,* October 1994.

8. A Christmas letter to friends from Alan Channer, December 8, 1995.

7

From Russia
with hope

*The vigorous debates over the size and
structure of Western economic assistance
to the Soviet Union should not overshadow the
need for another, more subtle, but no
less important, aid, aimed at reweaving
the spiritual fabric of Soviet society.*

DR. ALEXEI IZYUMOV
*political analyst and economist,
Soviet Academy of Sciences*

BREAKING THE CIRCLE OF HATE

For Russia there was no line drawn after the Soviet system collapsed, as there had been in Germany after the defeat of Nazism. It was a disillusioned, but not a defeated, country. There were no trials: The perpetrators of many human rights abuses were alive and free; collaborators, including those in the church, went unpunished. The Communist Party was still strong. The Nazis' reign lasted only twelve years, compared with the Communists' seventy-four years.

Frank Buchman, the initiator of Moral Re-Armament whose work is described in the appendix, used to say to his younger colleagues, "One day you will be working in Moscow," a remark regarded by some as visionary but unrealistic. He also spoke about Marxists finding new thinking in a time of crisis: "Why not? They have always been open to new things. They will go to prison for their beliefs. They will die for their beliefs. Why should they not be the ones to live for this superior thinking?"

His successor, Peter Howard, liked to make it clear that, whether or not communism existed, the work of Moral Re-Armament remained the same. Both predictions have been borne out by the events since the collapse of the Cold War.

During the Cold War, Moral Re-Armament was at work in many areas that Communists outside the Soviet Union were also making their priority. It was promoting the idea, particularly in the trade union and industrial sectors, that the class struggle was not the basic struggle. Rather, the eternal struggle between good and evil was more fundamental than the battle between right and left. Marxists who responded to its ideas soon found themselves under attack from those who wanted to maintain the ideological purity of communism. This inner-party strife was increasing as members of the Communist Party in different countries, including some founding members like Hans Bjerkholt in Norway, Eudocio Ravines in Peru, and R.S. Nimbkar in India, began working with Moral Re-Armament.

The language used in attacks on Moral Re-Armament was often extreme. The Moscow English-language *New Times,* for instance, on July 21, 1948, spoke of "Buchmanism" as "a tool of world reaction" that "is to supply Marshallized Europe with spiritual pablum which is to prevent minds from being swayed by the progressive ideas of our day." It described Caux:

> Imagine a gathering of politicians, industrial bigwigs, shady dealers of various kinds, retired generals, wealthy widows and tipsy landlords, publicly, for all to hear, repenting of their sins. In a fine religious frenzy, they proclaim to the world the frauds and swindles they have committed, their political intrigues and downright criminal offenses. Then they all join voices in a hymn and betake themselves to their homes or drinking houses.

On February 9, 1950, the *Manchester Guardian,* reporting on recent changes in the leadership of the Communist Party in West

Germany, stated that the new Communist Party chairman for the Ruhr was drawing special attention to the influence of Moral Re-Armament on members of the party:

> He thought one of the most dangerous symptoms was the growing connection between party members and the Moral Re-Armament movement. One reason for this may be the recent successful introduction of Moral Re-Armament as a working principle in a large factory in the communist stronghold of Wuppertal.

In a review of a book about Moral Re-Armament[1] aired by the USSR Radio Home Service on November 21, 1952, Georgi Arbatov, who was later to be top adviser to five Soviet leaders, said:

> The ideological arsenal of the imperialists must look rather pitiful that they present a whole lot of church psalms, hypocritical truths and middle-class vulgarities as a progressive ideology. . . . The attempts of the imperialists to distract by means of Buchmanism the working people from the struggle against war and fascism are suffering a disgraceful defeat.

Responding to an initiative by Moral Re-Armament to speak directly to Communists, the Moscow Communist Party organ, *Kommunist,* wrote in the early 1960s:

> Not long ago they issued a call to Communists through full pages in the press. In this the Communists are challenged to take part in "the greatest revolution of all time." These people say the problem is neither Communism nor capitalism, but the necessity to change human nature to the roots. They puff themselves up with pride and even suggest to Marxists they should change and take up an ideology that is for everybody. This is really the most bold stroke that has come from these propagandists of reconciliation and forgiveness."[2]

This call, appearing as a full-page advertisement in several countries, piqued the interest of a Russian journalist, Eduard

Rozental, who was shown it by a French settler in Africa. It challenged Communists to accept "a superior ideology" above divisions of class. He wrote about the encounter in a pamphlet, "Man—His Ideals and Reality," and decided to visit Caux in 1968. There he was given the chance to meet many people, including a Swiss employer who had found new attitudes toward his workers and become honest with them. On leaving Caux and "coming down from above the clouds," as he put it, Rozental wrote an article belittling those he had met there that appeared in January 1969 in *Izvestia*. "The superior morality must not rock one to sleep," he wrote, "but call to the struggle."

Another Russian journalist, Victor Rodionov, who represented the *Economic Gazette* in London, also had contact with Moral Re-Armament in the mid-sixties. He responded to Moral Re-Armament's work to reconcile peoples, nations, and races. He would have liked to have written about Moral Re-Armament, "but for the Soviet leadership of that time such an organization was unacceptable and consequently a story about it could not appear in our press."

Rodionov says it would be a mistake to think that all those who were harnessed to the chariot of propaganda thought in unison and that none had any doubts about what they were doing:

> Western analysts long ago noted our technique of introducing long quotations from our "enemies," ostensibly to refute them. But clever readers understood us. I think a lot of our editors understood us too and sympathized with us. Though there were many exceptions.

On January 23, 1991, forty-three years after the first attack on Moral Re-Armament, the first positive assessment of its work was sent out to the Soviet press by *Novosti* in an article by Rozental. Returning to Caux after thirty years, he was touched by the warm welcome and the willingness of his hosts "to turn the other cheek." He apologized publicly for what he had written in *Izves-*

tia in the late sixties. He had been following the party line, as he said, "under orders."

This time he wrote in a different vein. His article was headed, "We found a common language." He also omitted the negative references to Moral Re-Armament from a new edition of an earlier book.

"I was wrong," he says today. "I was under the pressure of the communist ideology. We had the attitude that anyone who was not for us was against us. MRA was preaching peace between capital and labor, and so we were against it. But now I believe we must have peace. Caux has given me a lot."

His father, Mark Rozental, was a well-known Russian philosopher. Stalin had summoned him and fifty other Jewish intellectuals to the Kremlin in January 1953, instructing them to write a letter condemning many of their fellow Jews as unpatriotic. Eduard remembers his father returning home in deep distress with a draft of the letter. When Eduard asked what he would do, his father replied, "I will condemn myself." The letter was to be made public on March 15; Stalin died on March 5. The letter was never published. Eduard remembers his mother saying, "Now I believe in God."

In 1995 Rodionov, too, came to Caux. He had fought against the Germans in World War II and now wanted to help build bridges with them. He could now write what he wanted and had already done so. He had ended a long article that was published a year earlier, on February 18, 1994, in *Vechernaya Moskva* by saying that each person is capable of freeing himself from hate and the desire for revenge:

> Such a way is suggested by Moral Re-Armament's more than half a century of experience, by its actions which are inconspicuous day by day but visible over a half-century of human life. It teaches us what is simple and great. Forgetting strife and holding out our hands to each other, we can break the vicious circle of hate and by that means discover a new world. We have the

duty, we must rearm morally. In this lies the chance of salvation and of entry into the family of civilised nations.

In November 1994 Russian philosopher Grigory Pomerants wrote a substantive article in *New Times*, which had been the first to attack Moral Re-Armament in 1948. It was headed, "Action out of silence—not only the guerrillas in Sarajevo need to be morally rearmed but also the citizens of the affluent world." Pomerants described the experiences of Leif Hovelsen, who had invited him to Caux. He wrote:

> It is not a matter of victory over Communism but of changing the whole character of civilization, which has lost the balance between contemplation and action, of the spirit of Mary sitting at the feet of Christ, and the spirit of Martha taking care of many things.

Pomerants quoted his wife, Zinaida Mirkina, a poet, who said that Mountain House was the exact opposite of the Tower of Babel: "Then a single language broke up into many languages, whereas here people are taught to speak a common divine parent language and we, like children, are learning to understand this silent language which opens the soul."

At the height of the Cold War, MRA literature had often put forward a stark choice between its ideas and those of communism. It was particularly so in a pamphlet, *Ideology and Coexistence,* which went to millions of households around the world. As these new opportunities opened up in Russia, many of those working with MRA felt they should acknowledge that at times they had adopted a too simplistic and self-righteous world view. In 1990 Dr. Bryan Hamlin of Cambridge, Massachusetts, who had gone with Hovelsen on many of his Russian visits, was asked to write a major article on Moral Re-Armament and the role of forgiveness in international affairs. In the article, published in September 1991 in the Moscow-based magazine, *Druzhba Narodov,* he apologized on behalf of Moral Re-Armament to the Russian people. He quoted the earlier attack in *Kommunist* and wrote:

> In the spirit of this article, a few words are in order about the relationship of MRA to the Soviet Union. As the article in *Kommunist* cited earlier recognized, MRA challenges the materialism of both the Communist and capitalist worlds. We felt compelled to take a stand against policies in the Soviet Union that were against democratic values and human rights. However, in the fifties and early sixties some statements in our literature did not differentiate adequately between a people and its government policies, thereby encouraging negative sterotypes of Soviet citizens and erecting barriers between peoples. We regret this and are grateful for this opportunity to give an account of this work of Moral Re-Armament to Soviet readers.

A DIALOGUE BETWEEN EAST AND WEST

One of the first impulses toward a new approach to the people of the Soviet Union came from Franz Cardinal König, the archbishop of Vienna.

Cardinal König is no stranger to Eastern Europe; Russian is one of the ten languages he speaks. In 1956, at the prompting of Pope John XXIII, the cardinal began his visits through the Iron Curtain. It was at one of his first audiences that Pope John asked him to see Cardinal Jozsef Mindszenty, in exile at the U.S. embassy in Budapest.

König thought it would be difficult to get through to him. "What's so difficult about it?" the Pope asked in his direct way. "Walk to the station in Vienna, buy yourself a ticket to Budapest and simply go there."

For fifteen years Cardinal König was president of the Secretariat for Non-Believers, an organization set up after the second Vatican Council to further relationships with non-Christians. In that capacity he helped formulate, at the philosophical level, relations with the communist countries.

König returned to this theme at Caux in 1986, on the fortieth anniversary of the Caux conference center. He suggested that it was now a further task for Caux to initiate a common thought process that would start a dialogue between East and West, despite all their differences. Among the people in the East, too, there was a longing to be able to make things happen themselves, not just to follow the bureaucracy or the mass media. He said:

> We must have the faith that these people have the strength in themselves to find an appropriate way of changing their own way of thinking and living. At the same time we must also rediscover in ourselves that truth of our Gospel that will help us to alter our own life in an appropriate and lasting way.

This humble approach, and the readiness of those at Caux to respond to the cardinal's words, led to a steady interaction between the Swiss center and the peoples of the countries that then made up the Soviet Union. The dialogue began, and more than four hundred Russians and seven hundred from other countries of Central and Eastern Europe have since attended Caux sessions. The Russians have come from a dozen cities. Most are neither Communists nor dissidents. They reflect the general population that wants to see changes and more freedom. They have included concert pianists and other cultural figures, respected intellectuals and fighters for human rights, as well as Orthodox priests and pioneers of university religious education.

In part because of his own imprisonment by the Nazis and in part because of his close friendship with many dissidents who had spent years in the *gulag,* Leif Hovelsen made his first visit to Russia in 1989 with some trepidation. It was the time of *glasnost* and *perestroika,* but nobody had dreamed that the changes would lead to the breakup of the Soviet Union and the end of the Cold War. As Leif's plane landed at the Moscow airport, gun-toting Soviet soldiers surrounded him. Fearing that his hotel room might be bugged, he went outdoors to discuss his program of visits each day. One dissident friend had KGB officers outside his apartment building. For Leif it was all too reminiscent of his Gestapo experiences as a member of the Norwegian resistance.*

Leif was accompanied on his first visit by an English lecturer in Russian, Philip Boobbyer, whose links were with academics; on his second visit he traveled with a Norwegian foreign editor, Frank Bjerkholt; and on many subsequent visits he traveled with Bryan Hamlin, whose first contacts were with people from the Philosophy Institute who were closer to the Soviet establishment. Leif had believed at the height of the Cold War that the Soviet Union would be changed by the dissidents pulling her out of the ashes and ruins of communism. But with the collapse of communism he began to realize slowly that a new Russia would not be built without including the former and present Communists.

With some hesitation Leif agreed to meet Communists who had been part of the system.

"What a pain and change it was for me to join Bryan Hamlin in the first meetings with those people who had been part of the USSR *nomenklatura* [communist party élite]," says Leif. "But God put it in our hearts and then gave me what I needed to rise to the challenge."

Leif soon found that his wartime experiences gave him credibility with all sides. He began to broaden his concepts of who would help Russia come out of the past. "We cannot exterminate people," he would say, "or jump over a generation." There was no alternative but to offer the people of the *nomenklatura* the experience of moral and spiritual change.

Responding to criticisms of what he was doing, Leif wrote:

The jungle of falsehood, of corruption, of rottenness, of immorality and still worse, the devastating destruction of the

---

*On another visit, at the end of November 1990 when tension was growing in the Lithuanian Republic and there were rumors of a crackdown in Moscow, Leif woke in the middle of the night shouting, "The tanks are coming." There were tanks outside, he said, but the noise proved to be only the early morning garbage trucks.

human soul and mind which is now being revealed is far worse than I had imagined. Yet from the rubble and ruins and thorny minefields of the communist period there are people whom God is preparing. Not only because a catharsis of forgiveness, repentance and the will to restore for the past is essential but also because if this does not happen the former Soviet Union will be the breeding ground for tragic events as in former Yugoslavia.

He pays honor to Andrei Sakharov, Alexander Solzhenitsyn, Vladimir Bukovsky, Andrei Amalrik, Mstislav Rostropovich, Ernst Neizvestny, Sergei Kovaliov, as well as countless other dissidents who disappeared because they paved the way for ending communism. But could it be, he asks, that the mending job—the task of conquering the grip of the past that still lingers over Russia—can only be done through those who committed, executed, and condoned the evil that has now been revealed?*

Leif and his colleagues are concerned with helping Russia find the best way to evolve from a state-controlled economy to a free-market system and from a one-party totalitarian state to a multi-party democracy. They are grateful for the many experts who are also trying to help on that front. They feel that their own contribution is to help create the moral and spiritual foundation from which the structured, Soviet-made person can be transformed into an independent and responsible human.

If it was difficult for Leif to make the transition to giving care to those who had gone along with the regime, it was doubly hard for some of the Russians who had courageously resisted to

---

*Bryan Hamlin describes visiting Yuri Zamoschkin, a senior researcher in the Soviet Academy of Sciences, in November 1991. Zamoschkin was dying of cancer and told Hamlin he had quit the Communist Party recently after being a member for forty years. In earlier years he had thought Sakharov was an extremist and had wasted his career. Zamoschkin had even signed an Academy document attacking Sakharov. "Now I realize I was wrong and Sakharov was right," Zamoschkin said. "I need to repent," and, as tears came to his eyes, he said, "I do. I do repent."

stretch out a hand of friendship to those who, if they had not personally tortured them, had been a part of the regime that had done so. He and others found themselves helping dissidents reduce their self-righteousness and rid themselves and those in the system of their bitterness and guilt by arranging seminars on issues like opposing destructiveness, the problems of guilt and personal responsibility, and the role of forgiveness in overcoming hate—the very areas of Leif's early experience.*

SEMINARS AT CAUX

In August 1992 Leif helped initiate a five-day seminar at Caux on the theme "The Moral Lessons of Soviet History." It drew Russian historians, philosophers, and journalists. Both academic knowledge and what Yuri Senokosov, chairman of the seminar, one of the first people whom Leif had met in Moscow, called "an element of personal life-experience" were shared during the seminar. Speakers included Len Karpinski, a former national leader of the Soviet youth organization and editorial board member of *Pravda* heading the department of Marxism-Leninism, and Yeltsin adviser Yuri Karyakin, a Dostoevsky scholar who was a leading radical deputy in the Congress of Peoples Deputies. Vyacheslav Igrunov, a former dissident and cofounder of Memorial, the nationwide human rights organization, said that although he had fought the communist system through much of his life, he questioned whether he had done all he could to oppose communism. He suggested that "we all lack courage to find evil in ourselves" and that the Communist Party could never be blamed for wrongs for which the whole nation was guilty.

Among the Russians in Caux two years later, in 1994, were Sergei Kovaliov, chair of the Russian Parliament's Human Rights Commission, and constitutional court Judge Ernest Ametistov, a

---

*Section one, chapter 5 discusses Leif's work in the Norwegian resistance, his imprisonment, and his spiritual reawakening.

member of the Caux fiftieth anniversary committee. Judge Ametistov warned that freedom could be transformed into its opposite if its enemies are suppressed. "What are the guarantees against such transformation?" he asked. "Russian democracy faces this dilemma—the dilemma between justice and tolerance, civil war and civil peace."

Kovaliov spoke of "the miracle in Russia": "The superpower that tried to teach the world for years is now sitting in school learning about democracy," he said. "This revolution has changed the map of the world. Those under the evil will of this state have become free." He thanked the Western intellectuals who had seen through the lie and supported the forces for change. The truth was, he said, that for seventy years "some simplistic, naive people in Russia believed that freedom was every human being's birthright; they naively believed that they could think and speak freely—and they were sent to prison for that. But they were the real creators of the Russian 'miracle.'"

During one Caux seminar Kovaliov said:

When we Russians discuss our tragic history, we have no sense of guilt. We blame everyone else except ourselves. But we are guilty of the fact that we permitted this regime to exist for 70 years and all that went with it. So the responsibility applies not only to the Communists, but to everybody including those of us who were politically repressed. Without looking into the past properly, I do not believe we can look into the future with clarity.

Kovaliov told the hundreds there from all over the world that he had been helped by two things: being in prison and being a scientist.

When you are out in a punishment cell and you are given nothing to read and not even the possibility of writing a letter, and you are cold and hungry, what can you do but think about your soul? Science is that region of activity which dispassionately, disinterestedly and unselfishly aspires to truth. And the

117

scientist is the man who can assess things in that way. If you start with that, I don't think it is an impossible sequence to start to understand our own national guilt, and my own personal guilt as well.

Some months later he headed a group of parliamentarians and human rights experts who went to Grozny to monitor the Chechen people's fight for independence from Russia. He was described on Russian TV as "the keeper of Russia's conscience," and *Izvestia* hailed him as "man of the year." In the United States the ABC television network's evening news program profiled him as the "person of the week."

In the first years after the Cold War, just as there was occasional tension in Caux between Russians who had been proponents and dissidents, and between those in the *nomenklatura* and those from the *gulag,* there was also tension between the Russian people and those whose countries had been suppressed by them. But in the atmosphere of Caux, the chance to work together and share past experiences helped build understanding. Sometimes there were unexpected chain reactions of change. For instance, a young Austrian medical student told the five hundred-member assembly that she had never been willing to identify with her country's history—particularly with the fact that Hitler was Austrian. But unless she identified with her nation's history, she said, she could not be responsible for its future.

Touched by her words, Vladimir Zelinski, a Russian philosopher and journalist who once had been expelled from the Academy of Sciences for deviating from the official ideology, asked to address the conference. He realized that he also needed to take responsibility for his nation's history and asked humbly for the forgiveness of the nations surrounding the former Soviet Union.[3]

The need to heal relationships between the Baltic countries and Russia is crucial, Zelinski said. Tens of thousands of Russians from the Baltic states were deported to Siberia, and the settling of Russians in those states is part of the background to the present ethnic conflict; nearly 40 percent of the Latvian population

today is Russian, Byelorussian, or Ukrainian, as is 35 percent of
the Estonian population. Zelinski became aware of the urgency
of doing something about this legacy when he sensed the strong
anti-Russian sentiment of the people from the Baltic countries
whom he met at Caux. On his initiative a group of Swedes
hosted the first "Baltic seminar" in Stockholm in 1993.*

TALK ABOUT MISTAKES AND HONEST ADMISSIONS

Many from the Nordic countries have committed their energies
to help their neighbors meet the challenge of democracy. One is
a Finnish businessman, Paul Gundersen. As a young man Gundersen volunteered for the army when the Russians bombed
Helsinki in 1939. He had been on his way to a university lecture.
After serving three years as an artillery forward observation officer, in 1944 he was wounded on the Karelian Isthmus in the
biggest battle in Nordic history. Gundersen now is classified as
35 percent war-disabled.

Gundersen's work with NOKIA, an electronics giant, has
taken him all over the world. Between 1970 and the early 1990s
he made forty business trips to the Soviet Union, East Germany,
Bulgaria, Czechoslovakia, and Poland. "I began to build links to
people," he says, "and discovered a reality of a remarkable people
ready to pay a price for their personal integrity and operating in
very difficult circumstances."

After the end of the Cold War, Gundersen was able to operate
more openly. His business friends particularly wanted him to
arrange seminars on the moral basis for a market economy, which

---

*Norwegians also arranged two-week courses for Polish parliamentarians and
municipal leaders on the structural, moral, and spiritual foundations of democracy. And in Britain a program, Foundations for Freedom, has been launched
for eighteen- to thirty-year-olds in Central and Eastern Europe. As part of this
program eight young politicians and senior administrators from the Ukrainian
Parliament attended a two-week seminar in Britain in November 1994.

he did. The first was in 1991 in Tallin, Estonia, in the former headquarters of the Communist Party, put on at the request of a cabinet minister. Gundersen was asked to bring with him half a dozen executives from other Western countries. "What would you like us to deal with?" he asked. "Tell us about your mistakes," the minister said. Gundersen did not think it sounded very sophisticated. But the man repeated, "Yes, tell us about your mistakes."

Gundersen's hosts had heard exemplary economic theories from the West but felt these theories did not apply to the problems of Estonia. His hosts wanted to hear not just what went well but also what went wrong and why. Gundersen assembled a team from Sweden, Denmark, Finland, and Britain. They did not go as people who knew and gave wise advice. He says, "We came as co-discoverers."

Some twenty business men and women attended the first seminar, most of them heads of their own companies in Estonia. After a full day Gundersen asked what they would especially like to discuss the next day. One executive shouted eagerly, "Don't you have any more mistakes?"

Gundersen says that, as a result of this first seminar, they were asked to conduct further seminars in Tallin and other Estonian cities; for instance, one for forty managers of the National Co-Operative movement from all over the country. "For some of the Estonians," Gundersen says, "it was a different way of conducting business and to find the motivation and initiative which had been stifled under Communism." This group had been afraid of expressing their own views.[4]

In the spring of 1995 Gundersen participated in a similar industrial seminar in Novosibirsk. Many of the participants in these seminars have since visited Caux.

After World War II apologies by the French for their hatred had disarmed Germans to the point that they were ready to admit where they had gone wrong as individuals and as a nation. In the 1990s German admissions of these wrongs led Russians to greater honesty as well. Sometimes this happened at Caux, sometimes at some of the regional conferences arranged in Russia. For instance, retired coal miner Hubert Eggeman spoke at a conference in Gatchina, near St. Petersburg. He had last been in the area fifty-four years earlier as a soldier at the German siege of Stalingrad, where some 800,000 soldiers and civilians had died. It was moving for all present to see how former antagonists, some of them members of the Society of Survivors of the Leningrad Siege, took in his words and, as a sign of reconciliation, embraced him. His apology to the Russians was reported on April 18, 1995, in one of Russia's largest dailies, *Vechernaya Moskva.*

Dr. Sieger Ernst, a German who had served in the medical corps on the eastern front, in 1990 was finally able to revisit the village near Minsk in Belarus where he had been stationed. He was welcomed as a hero because he had saved the lives of local inhabitants during the war. A group from Belarus then came to Caux and later established courses in the values that underline freedom for the young people.

THE ROLE OF THE MEDIA

An International Communications Forum was held in Russia in Nizhny Novgorod in September 1993. Highlighting the importance of a free press, it drew fifty-six Russians as well as representatives from other countries. Its theme was "The Media—A Decisive Force in Building a Free and Just Society." Olga Noskova, a director of the regional television system, said, "We are suffering from a rare clinical case—the freedom of the madhouse. We live in a society without any values. We have destroyed the old values but not created the new."

This forum arose out of the conviction of a professor of English at the University of Nizhny Novgorod, Dr. Bella Gribkova, who had been introduced to the ideas of Moral Re-Armament at the Moscow International Book Fair. She felt that through the media she could help to build the foundations for democracy.

Assessing the forum, Philip Boobbyer, then a lecturer at the London School of Economics, wrote in the October 15, 1993, issue of *The Times Higher Educational Supplement:*

The Russian media faces a long-term challenge. Its representatives will need to acquire the courage and culture not to be intimidated by authority, coupled with a sense of responsibility for the freedoms they do achieve. If, as is increasingly happening across the world, the media have the power to shape social values, then they will need to develop their own discretion about what to print or show.

HABITS OF THE HEART

For the first time in seventy years there is a chance that a free and democratic Russia may take its place alongside the other free democracies of Europe. However, the changes inherent in moving from the kinds of habits of the heart ingrained through communism are painful. It will take time, even generations some say, to establish an open, stable, and normal functioning democratic society. As Tocqueville wrote about the birth of freedom, "Liberty is generally born in stormy weather, growing with difficulty among civil discords, and only when it is already old does one see the blessings it has brought."

Leif Hovelsen says that seventy years of indoctrination have had a far deeper effect on the personality of the people than he ever envisaged. He believes that those in the West must respond with care and sensitivity and see it as a priority "to inspire the Russian people to conquer the 'homo sovieticus' syndrome and to free themselves from the grip of the past."

The men and women he and his friends are working with are, he says, finding a platform inside themselves from which they can spot and embrace the truth about themselves and their historic path, "learning to discern between good and evil, detecting what is true and genuine and what is false and mendacious." His priority is to help create the moral and spiritual foundation of the new Russia. To do so, he says, is equally a challenge to the Western nations, which may be compelled to find a more mature conception of what freedom with responsibility and care could mean in the modern world.

His friend, Professor Grigory Pomerants, put it to Leif this way in Caux:

We Russians seem mostly to pick up the worst excesses of freedom which you in the West have brought forth. But you can put up with it because through centuries you have been able to counteract the excesses, obtaining a tradition of qualities like inner discipline, respect for the law and being responsible. This heritage has given the West a certain stability even if destructive ideas and passions are tolerated. But in Russia we have no such tradition, and I fear that with no antidote to the destructive excesses we have picked up, it could be fatal for us. We need a moral and spiritual renaissance that can give our freedom a deeper content and the democratic process a stable framework through which it can evolve.

Notes

1. Howard, *The World Rebuilt*.
2. Quoted in the international edition of the *New York Times,* April 30, 1963.
3. Described by Jens Wilhelmsen in *NIRA Review,* Summer 1994.
4. The author spoke with Gundersen in August 1995.

8

Southern Africa:
Forgiveness as policy

*We enter into a covenant that we shall
build a society in which all South Africans,
both black and white, will be able to walk
tall, without any fear in their hearts,
assured of their inalienable right
to human dignity—a rainbow nation at
peace with itself and the world.*

PRESIDENT NELSON MANDELA

APARTHEID ENDS IN SOUTH AFRICA

The behind-the-scenes story of how South Africa ended apartheid is a fascinating one. As Allister Sparks writes in *Tomorrow Is Another Country,* "For four years before the rest of the world knew anything of it, the future of South Africa was being explored in secret conversations in hospitals, prisons, and a cabinet minister's home between government officials and their principal political prisoner." Talks were also going on between senior men from the Broederbond organization, an influential secret Afrikaner society, and leaders of the African National Congress (ANC), the first and longest-lived African organization.

The late Archbishop of Canterbury William Temple once said, "When I pray, coincidences happen." Much prayer enveloped South Africa's 1994 elections. A number of coincidences also

124

played their part. For instance, when Winnie Mandela found herself in November 1985 on the same plane as South African Minister of Justice Kobie Coetzee, she seized the chance to sit next to him and talk. Subsequently the minister decided to visit her husband in the hospital.

Broederbond member Professor Willie Esterhuyse, the author of *Apartheid Must Die,* who was involved in secret negotiations with Thabo Mbeki and other ANC leaders in London, described his meeting with African nationalists as "one of the most liberating experiences of my life." He said, "The one lesson we learned during these delicate days was that trust and confidence does not come from public statements. It is built through personal contact, a spirit of openness and honesty. As early as September 1988 I went back to South Africa and told my wife as well as the senior government official I had to liaise with, 'I am prepared to entrust my life to Thabo Mbeki.' "

In a meeting at Caux, Esterhuyse said, "The majority of South Africa's political, business and other leaders displayed incredibly high levels of boldness, courage, perseverance and vision in pulling South Africa away from the abyss." Esterhuyse paid tribute to the leaders of all races who had helped the thrust for reconciliation and nation building to get off the ground, singling out Nelson Mandela:

> If leadership and moral force are determined by a person's ability to overcome and neutralize good reasons for being bitter and revengeful, President Mandela is one of the greatest leaders of the world. He did not allow himself to become a prisoner of bitterness after his release from jail.

In a speech Professor Esterhuyse delivered at Caux on August 14, 1995, Esterhuyse said that before the election of April 1994 and while constitutional negotiations were still taking place, South Africans of all cultures and colors had joined at the local and regional levels in forums and other organizations to address common problems and to get involved in projects on the ground. "These initiatives, in my opinion, contributed substantially to the process of healing."

In the period preceding the first multiracial elections in 1994, a snag threatened to derail the process. Chief Mangosuthu Buthelezi, leader of South Africa's Inkatha Freedom Party, was refusing to participate. James Baker, former U.S. secretary of state, predicted the loss of a million lives if no way out was found. On March 1, only eight weeks before the scheduled elections, Mandela, the ANC leaders, and Buthelezi were still at loggerheads. They agreed, however, with the encouragement of UN representative Lakdar Brahimi of Algeria, to pursue international mediation. Various distinguished foreigners, including Henry Kissinger, a former U.S. secretary of state, and Lord Carrington, a former British foreign secretary, were invited to form a mediation team. A week later, at a seemingly coincidental meeting with a key figure, Michael Cassidy, head of the missionary organization African Enterprise, discovered that, not only was the list of mediators not finalized but that he would be welcome to submit names. It seemed vital to him to secure the participation of a Kenyan friend, Washington Okumu.

Okumu, a Harvard- and Cambridge-trained economist and international civil servant, had worked with Kenyan leaders for his country's independence. Later, he was imprisoned for two years for exposing corruption in Kenya. While imprisoned, he became a Christian and, after being released, got to know Buthelezi at a prayer breakfast in Washington, D.C. In the 1970s and 1980s he undertook secret diplomatic missions in South Africa on behalf of the Front-Line* States to try to persuade then-South African Prime Minister John Vorster to release Mandela and others from Robben Island Prison. Okumu was also involved in secret shuttle diplomacy and negotiations with Rhodesia's Prime Minister Ian Smith for the convening of the Lancaster House Constitutional Conference, the return of exiled political leaders, and the eventual independence of Zimbabwe.

*Angola, Botswana, Mozambique, Tanzania, Zambia, Zimbabwe

Speaking of Okumu, Smith predicted then, "There is a black man who will play a major role in the politics of this region."

Okumu's service with the United Nations had ended unhappily in the mid-eighties as the result of a clash he attributes to Arab-African incompatibility and intrigue. In August 1989 he attended a Caux conference, where he faced his hatred toward the man under whom he had worked. The Kenyan, known for his height and girth, told the conference that an Arab neighbor had said that Okumu's hatred was so great that it was directly in proportion to his size. Referring to the reconciliation that had taken place at Caux between France and Germany, and the spirit at Mountain House, Okumu said:

> One cannot come to this place without undergoing some kind of radical transformation in one's thinking. And so to the burden of hatred that I was carrying against my brothers, particularly the Arab. My own leader, Jomo Kenyatta, when he came out of jail said, 'I forgive you,' and I think I feel the same way. So I think I will leave the hatred now to those who want to continue to hate. Within the context of Caux, one would say that one has undergone a transformation, and I would like to shed this burden—I don't know if it will reduce my weight, but if it will, I will be very happy!

Okumu was ready for the call from Cassidy, with whom he had worked in the Newick Park Initiative.* In his book, *A Witness For Ever,* Cassidy described his conversation with Okumu:

> "But what about the security problem in South Africa and Natal right now?" Okumu asked one night on the telephone.
> "Brother," I teased him, "Sadat went to Jerusalem, so you can come to Natal!"

---

*A group of Christians who sought policy options for South Africa based on biblical principles. The Newick Park Initiative had conducted secret informal negotiations between the South African government and the ANC and had prepared nearly a hundred research papers on related subjects.

"Come now," he replied with a twinkle, "I'm not sure I like that analogy when you consider what eventually happened to Sadat!"

He said he'd pray about it, but sounded rather reluctant about the idea.

Three weeks later Okumu had not been accepted officially as a member of the mediation team. To Cassidy's consternation there was still no African presence on the international panel. At his urging Okumu flew out on a personal basis. Okumu arrived in Durban on March 27, immersed himself in the concerns of the Inkatha Freedom Party, and three days later had his first meeting with his old friend Buthelezi. That night he was also able to meet with the South African Minister of Home Affairs, Danie Schutte, and before heading back to Kenya, with all the senior ANC leaders. This brief foray was enough to raise the question of whether Okumu should be the official African adviser to the international mediation process.

On April 5 Okumu had a "very urgent" sense that he should return to South Africa. Suggestions that he be included in the summit meeting between the disputing parties were ruled impossible. But out of the summit came the decision that Okumu could come as official adviser to the international mediation exercise set for April 12, two weeks before the election. On the initiative of an Afrikaner policeman April 6 was the start of new prayer chains and a chain of prayer rallies throughout the country.

On April 12 Okumu arrived at the airport but, because his baggage was the last off the plane, he arrived late at a hotel reception for the international mediators. He decided not to stop to change his clothes. The press conference was winding up as he arrived, and Okumu was ushered to the front of the room and welcomed with a hug by Henry Kissinger. He was invited to speak, and for the first time took center stage.

Following his speech Buthelezi took him by the arm and said, "Since I first met you in 1972 I never knew that a time would come at a critical moment in my country's history when you would come to help us." Cassidy pointed out in his book that if Okumu had gotten there on time, he might not have spoken or, if he had, his speech would have had less prominence. "But in this situation he was the climax to the evening, the cherry on the top, as it were! Yes, perhaps it was indeed God playing his own card in a completely different and unorthodox way and showing sovereignty, even over delayed suitcases as he lifted his servant into the key position."

On April 14 the international negotiations broke down, and the negotiators, including Lord Carrington and Henry Kissinger, were set to head home. After further talks with some of those involved, Okumu needed to see Buthelezi again. A message was sent to the chief, asking for a meeting at the Lanseria airport. The chief, who did not want to be late for a scheduled meeting with the Zulu king, could not wait. His plane took off.

Both Buthelezi and Okumu describe what happened subsequently as an intervention by God. The compass in Buthelezi's new plane started acting up, and the pilot had to return to Lanseria, where Okumu was waiting. Buthelezi greeted him with the words, "You know, my brother, God has brought me back like Jonah. It is obvious he wants us to meet." The conversations at Lanseria were, in Okumu's mind, a turning point. He also points out that when the plane landed, the technical trouble had disappeared.

During the next two days Okumu, assisted by South Africans Colin Coleman of the Consultative Business Movement and Michael Spicer of Anglo-American, worked with all sides on the peace agreement. On April 17 Okumu handed the agreement to Buthelezi as the Zulu chief was heading for a Jesus Peace Rally attended by 30,000 people who gathered in the King's Park stadium. Buthelezi showed the document to Mandela's representative, Jacob Zuma, who thought it would work. It did. BBC reporter John Simpson said, "It was the Jesus Peace Rally which tipped the scales."

On April 19, after a flurry of talks, the agreement was signed, and Buthelezi was back in the electoral process a week before the elections were scheduled to take place. With a prodigious logistical effort eighty million stickers reflecting the participation of the Inkatha Freedom Party were printed and attached to the ballot papers. The Natal *Sunday Tribune* wrote, "It's still the age of real life miracles, even if they take their time."[1]

Speaking in Nairobi six months after the elections, Okumu said that like Frank Buchman, he had been moved by the holy spirit in the South African scene.* In the foreword to Michael Cassidy's *A Witness For Ever,* Okumu wrote that this confidentiality and trust are the preconditions for successful peaceful negotiations.

When a settlement comes about like that in South Africa, Okumu says, people find it very difficult to mention the name of God. They will say that the international political situation has changed or that certain economic forces at work enabled statesmen to succeed. They will rarely mention spiritual factors or faith. "If you believe in witchcraft," he says, "you might think a witch doctor did it. I don't. I bring in the angle of God and divine intervention because I believe in it." He also describes it as "the African option."

Asked what he does to prepare himself for such responsibilities, he says that, though he is not always faithful to the process, he finds it useful to take time to look at the word of God and to have the discipline to structure the time with humility. You don't always get what you want, he says, but "with quiet you get some very useful inner feeling that girds you up for the day." Okumu continues to work on conflict resolution, where he likes best to be, out of the limelight. He says about negotiations, "To be trusted, you don't beat drums before it happens."

When Queen Elizabeth II visited South Africa in 1995 for the first time in forty-eight years, she said, "I have come back to see for myself what is little short of a miracle."[2] As we peer into the

---

*Like Buchman, he said, he had recognized that a precondition for success in mediation efforts is an ability to keep confidences.

twenty-first century, she explained, the view might be a little obscure, "but the events in South Africa of the last few years have helped to bring rays of sunshine to pierce the mist."

Her words mirror comments made soon after the 1994 elections that made Nelson Mandela the first nonwhite president of South Africa. "Miraculous" was the view of South African playwright Athol Fugard. "By the standards of today's world, the election in South Africa is a political miracle," wrote Anthony Lewis in the *New York Times.* "A 'miracle' for all humanity," proclaimed a headline in the *Christian Science Monitor.*

In his inaugural address South African President Nelson Mandela said, "The time for healing of the wounds has come."

HEALING IN ZIMBABWE

Fifteen years earlier, in 1980, Zimbabwe (Rhodesia) had found an unexpectedly swift end to its civil war and a peaceful transition from constitutional talks to independence against a background of expected violence, a predicted coup by whites, and a bloody civil war. As the peaceful election unfolded, *The Times* of London quoted Lord Carrington, then Britain's foreign secretary: "I think we are seeing something of a miracle."

Lord Soames, the son-in-law of Winston Churchill, who was the transitional governor, told the press on his return to England on April 19, "Every time we thought the thing would explode in our faces, some miracle came about. When we went out there I was not one who believed in miracles. I think I am reversing my position now." In a lecture at Oxford on May 19 Soames talked about a process that accompanied the constitutional changes:

Concealed within the forms and even the aridities of constitutional behavior, there is a subtle healing art—an art which closes wounds, which unites what has been divided, which subdues antagonisms, and which brings people together. We have only to look at the most recent months in the history of Zimbabwe to see into the heart of this great truth.

For South Africa and Zimbabwe the handing-over of power was only the first hurdle in a long race. In both countries the "miracle" that intrigued the media and baffled the experts was but one outward manifestation of a struggle that goes back decades and has to be carried forward into the future so that the hopes of millions for a better way of doing things are not dashed. The work of reconciliation is perhaps even more important for these countries because they continue to face the challenges of high expectations and limited resources to do the job.

STEVEN SIBARE

Steven Sibare is responsible for a leadership training program in Zimbabwe that is becoming increasingly recognized for its contribution to nation building. This program is an extension of the efforts that began in the period preceding independence.

Sibare's courses at the Coolmoreen farm in Gweru, Zimbabwe, focus on turning competition into cooperation, criticism into caring, opposition into opportunity, and enemies into friends. The courses, wrote Sibare, stress the need for each person to mirror in his or her own life the qualities the country needs:

> Changing oneself is an essential, inescapable first step in changing anything or anyone else. When we learn under the leading of the inner voice to share from our experience of dealing with wrongs within us, then time and again it leads to a similar quality of change in others. With this key experience so many social and international issues have been untangled—not overnight, but as men and women remain undeterred and faithful to the inner direction, the speed is often surprising.

For Steven these principles are not theory. They stem from his own experiences as his country approached independence. As a cashier in a supermarket, he was familiar with insults and prejudice by whites. He lived in a hostel with five others and shared a bathroom and a toilet with a hundred. After being sacked from one job after being falsely accused of stealing, he began spreading lies about the white woman he felt was responsible. Deciding that his country needed more than a recurring cycle of blame, Steven decided to ask forgiveness of this white woman. As a result, he says, the blinders of bitterness were lifted, and he began to see people differently. He found himself firmly able to tell white customers without anger that he and his fellow black staff should be called "men," not "boys." He wrote to all the staff, black and white, about his change and new convictions. He confronted racial issues in company policy and fought for higher-quality food in the staff canteen.

At that time he shared a room with a young white church minister. The minister voiced some theological objections to what Steven was doing. "We try to follow Christ," responded Steven, and he told the minister how he had met friends who had treated him as an equal and helped him to take time to search for God's plan for his life. "Even some ministers rarely invite black people for a meal," he commented.

Before going to bed, they knelt together and Steven prayed aloud. Then they knelt in silence for ten minutes. The minister said, "I am not able to accept what I have to face." But after another five minutes, he prayed for God's love to enter his heart.

Steven gave the minister a book about the work of reconciliation around the world, which he read until 2:30 A.M. In his sermon the next day the minister thanked God for the "new experience of Christ" that had come into his life. In the afternoon he conducted a service in the Shona language, with Steven interpreting for him. But when it came time for the sermon, he felt unable to preach. He and Steven went into the vestry, leaving the congregation singing. Steven asked him to take time in quiet for what God might say to him, which they did. When they went back into the church, the minister told the congregation that he was not going to preach. Instead, he spoke of his experience and apologized for "living under a system that was wrong and doing nothing about it." The black congregation, in tears, got on their knees and prayed. The service ended with Communion.

Word of the new note in the minister's sermons was soon attracting young people from many miles. An English visitor commented at the time, "Perhaps this story is an indication of what African people and Zimbabwe itself will give to the Western world, the faith black will give to white."[3]

After his own experience of change Steven Sibare began to take his convictions to the leadership of the country, white and black. As a member of the Shona tribe, he decided to learn the language of the Ndebele tribe to help bridge tribal differences. He wrote a play, *Turning Enemies Into Friends,* depicting the war situation from the perspective of a young black. It was shown at the opening of the Coolmoreen conference center in Gweru, for which Steven is now responsible as a member of the Council of Management of Moral Re-Armament in Zimbabwe. He was part of the Zimbabwe "miracle."

ALEC SMITH

In 1965 Rhodesian Prime Minister Ian Smith made a unilateral declaration of independence (UDI) and said that "never in a thousand years" would there be black majority rule in his country.[4] The United Nations declared Smith's action a "threat to world peace." In the next dozen years some twenty efforts were made to resolve the problem of UDI and white rule. In 1972 a guerrilla war for independence started. During the seven years that followed nearly thirty-five thousand lives were lost. Atrocities on both sides led to the disruption of all areas of life, including serious food shortages. More and more white Rhodesians began emigrating, and more and more black Rhodesians began turning to violence to achieve justice. By its end the war was costing nearly a million dollars a day.

Ivor Richard, chairman of the 1977 Geneva conference that attempted a settlement, spoke of "the mountains of mistrust to overcome." British Foreign Secretary David Owen predicted in 1978 that unless a settlement could be negotiated, "the war will soon become unstoppable." The U.S. ambassador to Somalia,

Donald Petterson, wrote to a friend saying, "It is not too late for a miracle in Rhodesia today. But it is probably too late for anything else."

In 1972 something had happened in the life of Smith's son, Alec, that had helpful repercussions in the country. Alec Smith had been a dropout and a drug addict, rebelling against his father and going off to study in South Africa. There he was expelled from the university and convicted of drug smuggling. In 1972, at his lowest point, he had, while on a "vague religious search," what might be described as a "born again" experience.[5] "It was as if a thousand knots in my stomach had suddenly become untied," he said. He began to get a sense of "God's guiding hand." Then he gained some further insight. He discovered, as he puts it, "that there is a difference between giving my life to God so that my problems can be sorted out and giving my life to God to work toward establishing his authority in the power structures of your country." He decided to do both.

Until then Alec had given no thought to the position of blacks in his country, taking his own privileged position for granted. He told BBC Television, "I didn't really care about academic freedom, black rights or anything else, just about satisfying the ego of a young man who wanted to be himself, not someone else's son."[6] Alec was suddenly aware that his country was being torn apart by a terrible war of hatred. He also realized that sooner or later the war would be over and people would be needed to rebuild. He describes the experience as "scales falling from his eyes." Alec saw for the first time "the link between my faith and the society in which I lived and the change that needed to take place in it."

In 1975 Alec began to work with a group of people of different races:

> They came from all sorts of different churches and from every walk of life; some were students, some were civil servants, some were university lecturers, some were housewives. The one thing which they obviously had in common was the conviction that

God, through the power of the Holy Spirit, could not only change the lives of men but change the lives of nations—that a political solution alone could not solve Rhodesia's problems. Somehow there had to be a real healing between black and white, between tribe and tribe, if there was to be any lasting peace and we, under God's direction, had to help that healing come about.

Alec and his new teammates decided to hold an international conference in 1975 in Salisbury to take their ideas to the nation. In the invitation they stated:

> Those who have called this conference, both black and white, are united in a common aim: to bring the change in people which alone will make political changes work. This starts when everyone admits his own faults instead of spotlighting the other fellow's. Our goal is to create the new society where all are free to do what is right—in a continent that is hate-free, fear-free, greed-free and famine-free. God has a plan. We have a part. The choice is God's way or man's way—for Africa and for the world. God will show his will and way to those who listen and are willing to obey.

It was a chance for Alec to put his newfound convictions before the public. He told the audience of nearly a thousand people, including many white leaders, that had gathered at the University of Rhodesia that it was fashionable to blame the communists for everything. Though the abused, humiliated, frustrated black Rhodesians might be influenced by Cubans or Russians or Chinese, "It's people like me who have sent them there. I am deeply sorry for the thoughtlessness of my past life and I have now committed myself to finding a solution for our country."

ARTHUR KANODEREKA

One man who was struck by the unexpected words of Alec and other white speakers was a black Methodist minister, Arthur Kanodereka. Arthur had been arrested three times and tortured by the authorities; his only sympathy toward a white man was to a dead one. After the conference he said, "I have met white men who really care about my country and have a vision for it and for my part in finding God's plan for it. I have decided to try the experiment of listening for His guidance every morning."

He decided also to measure his past life against the standards he had heard proclaimed at the meeting: absolute honesty, purity, unselfishness, and love. As a minister of the gospel, he had gone into politics to help his people. Now he realized he had let politics come before God. He also acknowledged that his calling was to whites as well as blacks. "I used to give the sacraments to blacks knowing I hated whites," he said. "When I saw the change in Alec Smith I had to change my philosophy. Now I can say I belong to no man's camp. For me Christ comes first."

For the next two years Arthur held church services every Sunday evening. They were perhaps the only genuine multiracial gatherings in Harare. He invited Alec to speak there, and the two began to work together. "Through Arthur I learnt of the very deep experiences of hurt the blacks had suffered at the hands of whites," says Alec. "He exposed and revealed the depths of my own prejudices; above all it was Arthur who taught me to be truly colorblind." The two men went round the country speaking together, and eventually also traveled to South Africa and throughout Europe.

THE CABINET OF CONSCIENCE

Quite naturally, at the same time, there developed a group of citizens of different races who wanted to help Rhodesia in its hour of need. They soon became known as the Cabinet of Conscience. "Not all of those who came shared the same faith and certainly not the same politics," Alec wrote in his autobiography, "but we all cared for our country and were distressed at our people's suffering."

They were a small, informal group of twelve or so who spent Saturday mornings together, discussing the current crisis; although rarely praying formally, they always took time for quiet, during which ideas would come.

It took work to build trust among the disparate elements, but one idea that helped them to get along was that "the blame game" was left outside the door. They stuck to it, seeking to remove the roadblocks of bitterness and the desire for revenge, of arrogance and insensitivity and plain misunderstanding. They tried to come to grips with specific issues ranging from unhelpful attitudes within the white-controlled media to divisions between the Matabeleland and Mashonaland tribes. They were also aware that, when the war ended, people would be needed to rebuild the country.

In *Religion, the Missing Dimension of Statecraft,* Ron Kraybill,* who wrote the chapter on Zimbabwe, said that the Cabinet of Conscience served "partly as a central strategy-planning group, partly as a place of encounter and dialogue for people of diverse backgrounds, and partly as a forum for confronting individuals with the call to change their own lives according to the four absolute standards [honesty, purity, unselfishness, love]." They carried a message of reconciliation both challenging and hopeful at a time when the nation was weary of war. "Perhaps most important, on a continent where personal relationships often transcend politics and ideology, they were tireless in cultivating friendships across the political spectrum."

"It took courage," wrote Alec, "to befriend a politician we felt violently opposed to, also conscious that many of us were very ordinary people with no claim to fame, yet we were approaching some of the most influential and sometimes the most dangerous men in our country."

Ideas would come that only a white or a black member could carry through. They would support each other. They would

---

*Kraybill was then director of training at the Centre for Conflict Resolution at the University of Cape Town.

reach out only to the most difficult in the belief that they were meant to be bridge builders. They enlisted people from other countries who had expertise in areas that could be helpful to Rhodesia, ranging from land resettlement in Kenya to ending guerrilla warfare in the Sudan, from answering corruption in government service to working out compromise solutions in politics and diplomacy. These men and women on their return home could also help their governments to become better informed.

Through their interaction at the Cabinet meetings and the actions they took together, those participating saw their views and attitudes slowly change. Whites faced their own shortcomings and began to consider how they could become people with whom blacks would want to work. A senior white university professor, Desmond Reader, recognized through his participation that he had seriously underestimated the academic abilities of a black lecturer and apologized to him. The colleague, Gordon Chavanduka, was the Secretary-General of the African National Congress; later, he became the first black professor and a vice-chancellor of the University of Rhodesia. Together they initiated a series of lunches and dinners for the senior whites and blacks at the university to meet.

Reader was also invited to speak in Arthur Kanodereka's church, where he asked the blacks present for their forgiveness and help in building a new society. There was an unexpected response. A young black Rhodesian rose from the congregation and proposed that the church be opened the following Friday, the day the president had proclaimed as a National Day of Prayer and Repentance. In spite of the fact that most blacks regarded the president's move as an action for whites only, this proposal was supported unanimously.

A white former cabinet minister, Sir Cyril Hatty, realized through his participation in the group that he must share responsibility for the voluntary exile of Herbert Chitepo. Chitepo, Rhodesia's first black attorney, had met such opposition that he left the country and went into voluntary exile in Zambia, where he became head of ZANU, the Zimbabwe African National Union headed by Robert Mugabe. Hatty wrote a letter of apology to Chitepo, asking for forgiveness. Chitepo replied:

> What has inspired me to sacrifice so much of an otherwise promising future, and to live as I do, is not hatred but love— love of a new order of society in Zimbabwe, free from racial oppression or degradation, in which all have an equal voice in deciding the policies, laws and measures under which they are to live. The best apology, if there was need for any, is the realization of these goals—the creation of a new society.

Chitepo's generous response led to the *Rhodesia Herald* headline, "Apology to Chitepo—'a great man.'" Looking out over the fertile fields he and his wife had cultivated from the bush, Hatty said, "Doris and I are going to give whatever experience we have to whoever rules this country tomorrow."[7]

A former secretary of foreign affairs, Stan O'Donnell, whose life had been turned upside down by the near death of his son in the Rhodesian armed forces, was able to inject fresh ideas into the governing circles and help give practical experience to black Rhodesians in running the economy and the government. O'Donnell said he had learned the difference between "asking God to rubber stamp my plans and asking God to make me fit to play a part in His plan."

A white accountant, Don Barnett, who was a member of the Cabinet, believed that any society that blindly accepted the lot of the have-nots when there was plenty was sowing the seeds of its own destruction. The work of the "Cabinet" was not to deal on the political level, he said, but to encourage political figures to submit themselves to their God's will. Champion Chigwida, a black supervisor in a chemical plant, warned the group that people were telling the country's leaders what they wanted to hear but that "not enough truth is being spoken." A student leader, Jos te Braake, took steps to reduce polarization on campus. And

Steven Sibare, when he was in Harare, was able to participate with the others in their work.

The Cabinet felt they needed to speak to the country. They initiated showings of the African film *Freedom,* which dramatizes the personal moral choices facing freedom fighters and how those choices affect not only how freedom is won but also how it is kept. The film was dubbed into the Shona and Ndebele languages. The group also distributed thousands of copies of a pamphlet, *The Zimbabwe We Want,* outlining the qualities the new country would need. In it one of the members, John Muzekiwa, is quoted as saying, "When I saw bodies of young black and white men dead, I began to see that violence was not the only way to win our country. A clear voice came to me, saying, 'Is this the way you want to liberate your country?' "

Steven Sibare is quoted on the importance of tackling tribalism:

> I don't think our freedom will stick unless we find the answer to tribalism. I am a Shona. Coming from a major tribe I have always felt superior and secure. I have always thought low of anyone who belonged to any other tribe. When I apologized to them, I started to make friends. And now I am learning Ndebele.

As the guerrilla war spread into the cities, the Cabinet of Conscience saw the need to reach the "crunch-points" with its message. One such point was Que Que in the Midlands. If trouble broke out, it would be there that the major tribes and parties would meet. An audience representing all the different factions packed the big hall of the Globe and Phoenix Mine to hear Alec Smith and Arthur Kanodereka speak. They said that whether this country was called Rhodesia or Zimbabwe in ten years, new men and women were needed now to make a new country.

Meanwhile—thanks to new approaches by the British government that led to changes at the commonwealth heads of government meeting in July 1979 in Lusaka, to determined efforts on all sides, and to a prevailing war-weariness—the disputing parties came back to the negotiating table at Lancaster House, London, in September 1979. Two weeks before this crucial conference where agreement was finally worked out, a group of seventeen Zimbabweans, including white and black cabinet ministers and exiles traveled to Caux. One black member of parliament who had been trained in Moscow as a paratrooper was so struck by the spirit there that he said, "If Marx and Lenin were resurrected and landed at Caux, they would find here the classless society established on a Christian basis."

The Lancaster House talks lasted twelve and a half weeks. Some who had been at Caux took part officially, others were active behind the scenes. Members of the Cabinet of Conscience who sought to build bridges between the parties were included. Both the BBC and the *Manchester Guardian* referred to the part played by "intermediaries" in helping leaders find a settlement. One member of the Cabinet of Conscience who was at the London talks was Gary Magadzire, president of the African Farmer's Union. He was able to give black leader Robert Mugabe, who would later become prime minister, details on the suffering of the villagers caught in the crossfire as the bush war continued. "Our people have suffered enough," Magadzire told Mugabe. "It's time to settle."

According to Lord Soames, "The structure of the Lancaster House Agreement was built on a basis of trust. That moral force—plus a remarkable degree of confidence on every side that they would win the elections—proved sufficient."

The election process was a dangerous one. Lord Soames, governor of a colony that had been self-governing since 1923, flew to Rhodesia with no independent armed forces at his disposal and before a cease-fire had been accepted. He managed to build bridges with Mugabe, who said at the airport as the governor was leaving, "Now we are both changed men."

It was an extremely volatile situation, particularly when it was not clear whether the guerrillas would report to the appointed assembly points.* Plans for a coup had been drawn up by senior white officers of the Rhodesian army in the event that Robert Mugabe came to power. During the election, campaign members of the Cabinet of Conscience published a manifesto calling for a commitment by citizens

> to forgive what others have done to us, and ask forgiveness for what we have done to others—which is the price of the reconciliation we seek: to live every day the way we want others to live with standards of absolute honesty, unselfishness, clean morals, and care for one another; and to help our leaders to do the same. Such a decision cannot be made for us by others—the British, the Russians, the OAU [Organization of African Unity], the Commonwealth, the United Nations or anyone else. We must make it ourselves.

A SIGNIFICANT INTERMEDIARY

One of the most significant initiatives by an intermediary occurred during the election process. A black nationalist, Joram Kucherera, who was part of the Cabinet of Conscience, had taken steps in restitution that had brought new life to his family. Armored cars were at street corners, bombs had gone off in shops and suburbs as he and a group of young businessmen met in Salisbury to consider "how to deal with fear." Someone at the meeting suggested that one way was "to think what you would do if you were not afraid and then go and do it." After the meeting Joram came forward quietly and said, "I believe God means us to get Ian Smith and Robert Mugabe to meet each other."

Henry Macnicol, a Scot who helped facilitate the meetings of the Cabinet of Conscience, was present. He remembers:

> It sounded like crazy over-reach. Mugabe's headquarters had just issued a "death list" with Smith's name at the top. Smith

---

*As part of the agreement the guerrilla forces were to stand down, move to assembly lines, and accept disarmament.

had issued a statement calling Mugabe an "instrument of the devil." But we all felt that we should trust Joram's thought.

To help bring about a meeting between the two men, Alec Smith was in touch with his father, Joram Kucherera with Mugabe's people.

The *New York Times* described what happened next:

The whites' acceptance of the Mugabe government was far from assured . . . and a military coup seemed possible. The encounter was improbable: a white leader whose government detained Mr. Mugabe and other nationalists for eleven years, then fought a war for minority rule that cost at least twenty-five thousand lives, driving across town to a suburban house that Mr. Mugabe as a black could not have owned under the segregation laws enforced by Mr. Smith. The two men knew each other from negotiations in London and elsewhere but had never shaken hands. The meeting was a success.[8]

Emmerson Munangagwa, minister for state security, commented later, "I don't know much about Moral Re-Armament but had it not been for that young man, Joram, the streets of Harare would have been running with blood."

On March 4, 1980, after the elections had been recognized as free and fair, Prime Minister Mugabe spoke to the nation:

This is now time to beat our swords into ploughshares. I urge you whether you are black or white to join me in a new place to forget our grave past. Forgive others and forget. Join hands in a new amity and together, Zimbabweans, trample upon racialism, tribalism and regionalism and work hard to reconstruct and rehabilitate our society as we reinvigorate our economic machinery. Let us constitute a oneness derived from our common objectives and total commitment to build a great Zimbabwe that will be the pride of all Africa.

In a broadcast the next day Ian Smith called on whites not to leave the country. He told his caucus of members of parliament later that, to his surprise, he had ended his talk with Mugabe convinced that Mugabe could be trusted by the whites, that he was sincere in wanting most whites to stay, and in his desire for a mixed economy and reconciliation between races and tribes.

SOME RESERVATIONS ABOUT THE OUTCOME

The Cabinet of Conscience met the day after Mugabe's overwhelming victory. During the meeting a prominent white businessman burst into the room. "God has let us down," he said. "Now there will be a flood of whites leaving the country."

The businessman had hoped that Bishop Abel Muzorewa would be the first prime minister of Zimbabwe; Mugabe had been portrayed to white Rhodesians as a Marxist ideologue. He spoke with alarm until two senior black men said quietly but firmly, "It's not like that at all." Alec Smith said,

> We have been praying for God to intervene. We must believe that he has answered our prayers—and perhaps not in our way. But it is no use praying, "Thy will be done—but in my way, not thine." We asked for peace, and God has given it. We prayed for the right man to win the election, and we thought that meant the bishop. But God may have another way.

The next morning the white businessman returned and said, "I have prayed about this matter. I realize that, in fact, I share many of the goals Mr. Mugabe has for the country. My job is to help him achieve them in the best way." For five years he served independent Zimbabwe as a managing director in two government marketing agencies. The man, in partnership with his son, is still in business in the country.

Summing up the approach of the members of the Cabinet of Conscience and those working with them, Ron Kraybill wrote in *Religion, the Missing Dimension of Statecraft* that they "maintained a clear, if often unspoken agenda. The task was to enable individuals to listen to God. This would lead to a change of heart and to clarity about the 'right' thing to do, and if leaders would get themselves oriented in the right direction, society must follow." Conflict resolution, Henry Macnicol points out, was not the primary aim but the by-product of people changing to implement God's plan.

After independence the Cabinet of Conscience met occasionally, helping to facilitate unity in the country. Younger men and women, like Steven Sibare, stepped forward to help. Steven resigned from his job to work full time on the task of nation building and reconciliation.

THE FORGIVENESS FACTOR

At a press conference with President Bill Clinton in 1994, at a time when Haitian President Jean-Bertrand Aristide was in Washington, D.C., President Nelson Mandela was asked, "What are you going to say to Aristide?" He responded, "Without in any way prescribing to the leadership of Haiti, we sincerely hope that they will realize the crucial importance of national reconciliation and to heal the wounds of the past by involving all the parties which may have been at cross-purposes with one another."

This exchange was symbolic of a phenomenon observed by Allan Griffith, an Australian foreign policy expert. He noted the encouragement that the end of the war in Zimbabwe had given to Namibia, where SWAPO leader Sam Nujoma, like Prime Minister Robert Mugabe, had adopted a policy of national reconciliation. Similarly, Namibia had given encouragement to South Africans. Sir Robin Renwick, British ambassador to South Africa, said that Namibia's peaceful transition to democracy "showed that this kind of change would not necessarily have catastrophic results." And Mandela was now giving inspiration to nations around the world. In a speech at Oriel College, in Oxford, England, on May 1, 1994, Griffith described the process as "the forgiveness factor set loose to work its power in international affairs."

Notes

1. The story of Okumu's involvement was also told in the Johannesburg *Sunday Times,* April 24, 1994.

2. *Guardian Weekly,* March 26, 1995.

3. Round-robin letter to friends in England from Jim Trehane, an Englishman visiting Salisbury, August 1980.

4. See Johnston and Sampson, *Religion, the Missing Dimension of Statecraft,* which covers much of the background and many of the experiences described in this chapter. See also Elliott, *Darkness and Dawn in Zimbabwe* and *Dawn in Zimbabwe.* Hugh Elliott is an English administrator with wide experience in Africa. Additional information was supplied by Henry Macnicol.

5. Smith tells this story in *Now I Call Him Brother.*

6. *New World News,* November 15, 1980.

7. Reported in Hannon, *Southern Africa: What Kind of Change?*

8. Also recorded in Smith, *Stitches in Time.*

9

Europe:
The ethnic crisis
that disappeared

*What is interesting is not the exposé of
a technical solution but the evidence that no
solution is acceptable if there is not
at the same time an internal change
of heart in specific people.*

GABRIEL MARCEL
French Catholic philosopher

THE BEGINNINGS OF THE
SOUTH TYROL PROBLEM

If you referred to South Tyrol today in conversation, most people would not know what you were talking about. It is a measure
of accomplishment and maturity in the German- and Italian-
speaking populations of that Italian province and a tribute to
those who labored for many years to end the conflict there, that
South Tyrol did not become, like Northern Ireland or the
Balkans, a synonym for intractable division. It might easily have
done so.

Nearly 90 percent of the countries that have gained independence since 1945 are multicultural, multilingual states. Canadian
diplomat Arnold Smith, remarking on this phenomenon, wrote,

"Learning how to build and maintain a free political society out of several cultures and national groups with two or more official languages forms one of the most important political challenges of our age."

The experience of South Tyrol should give hope to other regions with unresolved ethnic conflict. South Tyrol is a strategic point due to the linking of northern and southern Europe at the Brenner Pass. South Tyrol is on the southern side of the pass. Like Bosnia and the other countries of the former Yugoslavia, it owes its existence to the breakup of the Austro-Hungarian Empire at the end of World War I. In 1919 the treaty of Saint Germain-en-Laye joined 200,000 German-speaking Austrians from the *Bundesland* Tyrol to a nation of fifty million Italians. This major change, undertaken without any consultation with the peoples involved, had been promised to Italy as a sweetener for joining the Allied side in the war. Thus the seeds of the South Tyrol problem were sown.

Over the years a Mussolini-led Italy adopted a policy of moving Italians in from outside the region—mainly workers for the three large industrial plants that were built to "Italianize" the area—trying to drive German speakers out. German culture and language were banned, including German newspapers. Names were also changed: Bozen became Bolzano; Meran, Merano; and South Tyrol, Alto Adige. Even German names on gravestones were altered. Despite a less nationalistic leadership in Rome after World War II, provocation of German-speaking residents continued and promises of minority rights did not go far enough to satisfy the South Tyroleans or Austria. Prime Minister Alcide de Gasperi had created a new region, named Trentino-Alto Adige, with an Italian majority. It had a certain autonomy with its own parliament and government. But the South Tyroleans resented the fact that decisions were made in Trentino and always favored the Italians.

The best legal and political minds of various nations worked for years on these issues but failed to come up with a satisfactory solution. In 1959 Austria, in its role as protector of the interests of the province, asked the United Nations to tackle the conflict. The following year the UN General Assembly called on Italy and Austria to start negotiations. These made little progress, however. The violence that had started in the 1950s had become particularly bloody during the second half of the 1960s. A bomb attack by "separatists" at the Pozescharte, an Italian military training camp, killed four military men and wounded many others. There was no real communication between the two sides. Some new factor was needed that could recapture the momentum for a solution.

INTRODUCING A NEW FACTOR

Strewn with picturesque lakes and villages and set in the mountains of northern Italy to the south of Austria and Switzerland, the province is a paradise for tourists in the heart of Europe. But for those who lived there in the late 1960s it was something else. Fred Ladenius, a Dutch TV journalist, was sent on assignment there in 1967. He remembers well the scene that greeted him. As the train carrying him from Rome passed Trentino on its way to Bolzano, he began to notice armed men, mountain troops, and paratroopers watching the line. "Attacks on convoys was the order of the day. I had the impression at the station of going back in time, a jump back to the years of the last war." Even his press pass, authorized by the president and that in other parts of Italy he had waved like a magic wand, came under close scrutiny here. At street crossings in Bolzano the police carried machine guns. One politician the journalist interviewed compared the situation with Vietnam.

After completing his journalistic work, Ladenius returned to Rome and considered South Tyrol a closed chapter. But as he thought of what he had heard, of the sincerity and the concerns of those on all sides and of the legacy of World War I, he remembered a phrase he had heard from Frank Buchman some years before in Caux: "It is not a question of determining who is right but what is right." In an article he wrote about South

Tyrol in *L'Osservatore Romano,* he mentioned this phrase and the possibility that Caux might have something to offer in the situation.

Ladenius's article caught the eye of the secretary general of the chamber of commerce, Alberto Modolo, and other personalities in South Tyrol. Josef Anton Mayr, deputy head of the Tyrol government in Innsbruck, encouraged Heini Karrer, one of the Swiss responsible for the conferences at Caux, to visit Modolo and other South Tyrol leaders and invite them to Caux. (Mayr, chief editor of the *Tiroler Tageszeitung,* himself decided to travel to Bolzano to inform his friends there.) In January 1968 the first of the South Tyrol leaders, Italian- and German-speaking, made their way to Caux. Ladenius had introduced a new factor into the equation.

The group that came to Caux at the beginning of 1968— including local politicians from Bolzano as well as Mayr and political figures from Innsbruck—met for the first time. Pepi Posch, director of the Catholic Workers' Movement from South Tyrol, wrote such a convincing report for the South Tyrol People's Party that a delegation—including Armando Bertorelle, president of the regional parliament; Giorgio Pasquali, mayor of Bolzano; and Karl Mitterdorfer, a member of the Italian Parliament representing the German-speaking population—came to Caux that summer.

One of the most important experiences the South Tyroleans encountered was that of envisioning a larger perspective. At the Caux conference they heard representatives from other countries discuss how they had brought about concrete transformations in seemingly inextricable situations. Mitterdorfer said,

We came to Caux in the hope of finding an inspiration which could open the door to a solution that satisfied everybody. Finding myself here in the presence of other situations even more difficult than ours, I have had the impression that our problems have suddenly diminished a little in their importance. I have understood that in solving our problems effectively, we could become an example for all those in the world who have to come to grips with problems infinitely more complex than ours.

Bertorelle said, "We are grateful to learn here how more serious problems between races and peoples than ours have been overcome." For him the foundations had been laid and "now the new house of South Tyrol can be built."

The group returned to Italy determined to bring other colleagues to Caux. In early September another delegation arrived. This time it included Governor Silvius Magnago, leader of the South Tyrol People's Party, and Guido Bernardi, a Christian Democratic member of parliament representing Rome. In Caux at the same time was a delegation of senior figures in the Confindustria, the Italian employers association.

While they were at a meal, the representatives of the two language groups were joined by Rajmohan Gandhi from India. After he had heard their outline of the issues, he told them there were two reasons for them to resolve their problems. One was the amount of goodwill on both sides. The other was that his country had been facing similar problems for years. If these representatives could resolve their problems, they could show India the way. After all, he said, South Tyrol had only two languages and one religion, whereas India had hundreds of languages and several religions. Gandhi even suggested that they set a deadline.

That evening the South Tyroleans talked late, continuing the next morning over breakfast. An industrialist who had come from Rome with Bernardi suggested that they all observe a time of quiet to see if God could give them ideas about what steps to take. Reflecting on the issues, Bernardi wrote, "Mitterdorfer must meet Piccoli." He even wrote a date: September 20 [1968]. Flaminio Piccoli, deputy secretary general of the Christian Democratic Party, was from Trentino.

At the final meeting in Caux the South Tyrol delegation— representatives of politics, business, and youth of the region— took the platform together. Governor Magnago said he hoped for a settlement that would guarantee the opportunity to live free from fear to the German minority and a secure way of life to the Italians. "I hope the efforts of the years will be crowned with success in the near future," he stated. Magnago said that the settlement of minority problems, whether in South Tyrol, Cyprus, or in other parts, was vital because the issues affected relationships between nations and therefore international peace. He said to the Italians, "The next time we meet we shall not glare at each other but meet in friendship because of our experiences here."

The Italian speakers responded. Armando Bertorelle, vice president of the regional parliament of Trentino-Alto Adige, said, "I welcome what Governor Magnago has said and the spirit with which he has spoken. Each of us has defended the position of his own group without thinking always of the common good. There has been no lack of goodwill but in Caux goodwill immediately becomes concrete." Guido Bernardi said, "Through coming to Caux we Italians realized we had to respect the uniquely German character of the majority in South Tyrol."

A handshake on the platform between the Italian- and German-speaking delegates sealed their determination to bring an early settlement to the outstanding disagreements between their two communities. They had seen a way, they said, to break out of "the vicious circle of wrongs" that had frustrated their efforts. Mitterdorfer said, "We came for help. We got help. I leave with the conviction that we must bring a solution speedily to the South Tyrol question so that we can be in a position to help others who need it."

At Caux "our horizons have been widened," Mitterdorfer told the international audience. Referring to the grievances between the parties, he said that there would be no solution without sacrifice, that they had to help each other over the obstacles: "It is not a question of sacrificing justice but of accepting personal sacrifice to find a just solution."

Catholic Bishop Josef Gargitter commented later to a visiting journalist, "I noticed a change in the South Tyroleans and the Italian politicians after their return from Caux. They said things I had never heard them say before." He decided to go to Caux himself. He said,

> It was a question of carrying over private faith into the social sector and the life of the community and demonstrating the validity of principles of faith for life in community. We found people who had the power to draw concrete conclusions from their faith and to say: "we must cultivate dialogue, get to know each other, listen to each other and help one another."

FULFILLING HOPES

On September 20, 1968, the meeting that Bernardi had envisaged came about. Rajmohan Gandhi was invited by the delegation to join them in Rome. The encounter did not, according to Ladenius, get lost in platitudes or the usual political compliments: "It was a meeting of men conscious of their responsibility with regard to history and determined to surmount in a new spirit obstacles which up until then had appeared insurmountable."

The atmosphere was completely relaxed. Mitterdorfer gave his impressions of Caux and said that his two visits had made a deep impression on him. At that point Piccoli interrupted and said to the others, "You have already converted Mitterdorfer" and referred to the fact that he was known in Rome as *Il duro,* the tough one. Then Mitterdorfer said that he was sorry that he was not able to report the progress in the South Tyrol situation that Gandhi had asked for in September. He would like to be able to contribute to the solution of similar problems in Asia, for example, through the application of the example of South Tyrol.

"My conviction," Mitterdorfer said, "is that we must now swiftly find a solution." He asked the leaders of the Christian Democratic Party and the current Italian government to recognize the hereditary rights of the German minority and said that he would work personally for a just treaty with the Italian government. He asked Piccoli to arrange a meeting between Governor Magnago and Foreign Minister Giuseppe Medici. Piccoli replied that he would do this as soon as possible. The moment had come to end the South Tyrol problem once and for all. "It is not a chance but *the* chance," Piccoli said. He had already spoken to the prime minister about it.

Piccoli admitted that the mistrust by the German majority toward Rome was justified. The Italians had made many mistakes, both under fascism and afterward. Now, he said, it was up to the politicians to introduce a new age of mutual trust. Bernardi added that this spirit had to be spread publicly throughout Italy. "We must make peace after 50 years of conflict," Piccoli concluded.

Piccoli reported to Prime Minister Mariana Rumor the substance of the discussions and in parliament a few weeks later referred to the problem in Alto Adige, recognizing the mistakes committed on the Italian side. When Mitterdorfer shook his hand afterward, Piccoli told him to tell his friends in Caux that he had spoken in the spirit of their ideas.

In October the new mayor of Bozen, Giancarlo Bolognini, told Heini Karrer and Ladenius that there had been an astonishing change of climate compared with previous years. Politicians from both language groups were behaving as if the South Tyrol problem were already solved: "They were speaking of the common tasks which are before us instead of raising the matters which divide them."

The November 20–21, 1968, issue of the *Frankfurter Allgemeine Zeitung* bore the headline, "A new situation in South Tyrol." Its correspondent wrote:

One gets the impression that a new situation, a new climate, has come about in South Tyrol. That is a big surprise for those who set foot in South Tyrol on the occasion of last Sunday's *Landtag* [state parliament] and regional elections. No more bombs, no more assassination attempts, since the summer no more blood has been shed. Not even polemics of an ethnic character characterized the election campaign. It appears as if a turbulent period of ten years has come to an end.

Another positive factor in the political scene was a reconciliation between Mitterdorfer and Peter Brugger, a vice president of the South Tyrol People's Party. There was a danger that the clashes between them over whether to accept proposals by the Italian government could do permanent damage to the German-speaking minority. Mitterdorfer had the "necessary but very difficult" task of speaking to Brugger: "I realized that I was jealous of people who I thought were more able or more successful than I was. After long consideration and some prevarication I apologized to Senator Brugger for the things which divided us."

Brugger was surprised by Mitterdorfer's apology: "His courageous conversation began something new between us. It was a huge sacrifice on his part and I was so impressed that we became real friends."

RESOLVING THE SOUTH TYROL PROBLEM

At the congress of the South Tyrol People's Party that autumn no one knew what the outcome of the deliberations would be. At a previous congress the Italian government's proposals had been voted down. Magnago, supported by Mitterdorfer, campaigned for acceptance of Rome's proposals. Brugger opposed them. Before the vote in the Landesversammlung (provincial party congress) Magnago said, "No one who votes 'yes' will be called a traitor, no one who votes 'no' will have betrayed us. For all will have voted in good faith."

On November 22 at two o'clock in the morning, 583 voted yes and 492 no, with 39 abstentions. A few minutes after the vote Brugger approached Magnago and shook his hand, a gesture that drew prolonged applause from the thousand people present. Brugger told him, "We want to work again together." This was a surprise to everyone since the party was split from top to bottom. A further step along the way to a solution had been taken.

Two years later, in early 1970, Mitterdorfer and Brugger traveled together to Northern Ireland to describe the process of unity they had found and the new approaches and outcomes that were evolving in the South Tyrol situation. Mitterdorfer said in Belfast that although he did not want to exaggerate the significance of his reconciliation with Brugger it had bridged their political differences and might have led to a freer debate and even to the maintenance of unity within the party, which was essential for relationships with the Italian government. Brugger added, "It is the duty of each of us to develop the good in the heart of the other. I have decided no longer to construct artificial barriers to my advantage or to remain silent about the good deeds of others—a silence that can lead to violence."

The friendships developed at Caux continued as they worked together in Rome. And those who had been to Caux worked along with many others to move the process forward. Looking back, Giorgio Pasquali, Bolzano's longtime mayor who had become a member of the provincial government, says, "We were only very few then who believed that any cohabitation of the two populations would be possible. Often we were in disagreement and in spite of it we constantly met again and looked for possible solutions."

By 1972, after long negotiations, a package involving major concessions on both sides was agreed on. The German side was to give up its demand for independence or reunification with Austria. The Italian speakers were to accept that both languages would have equal status in education, the judiciary, and the civil service, and even that Italian speakers in some public offices would have to learn German. Full cultural autonomy for South Tyrol had to be guaranteed. A majority within both groups had to be convinced that sufficient trust existed for a multicultural and multilingual society to be built.

Within weeks the agreement was approved by the governments of Austria and Italy, whose foreign ministers issued a joint communiqué saying that a new era of constructive teamwork was beginning.

There were still details to be worked out. For instance, under the agreement German speakers in South Tyrol were not allowed to present evidence in court in German. And Austria was not prepared at that point to give a declaration of the formal end of conflict until every last point had been settled.

So much progress had been made, however, that British Prime Minister Ted Heath, interviewed on the BBC program, "Panorama," in January 1972 cited this success as a source of hope that the Irish situation might also be solved. The prime minister noted, "The Irish situation causes grief. . . . But other countries have had their problems, for example Italy in its relations with Austria in South Tyrol, and that has been solved."

The Italian newspaper, *Il Giorno,* wrote of the effect of the talks in Caux: "From these meetings has come the new spirit which made possible an effective solution to the problems of Alto Adige."

At the time the agreement was signed it was estimated that its 137 legislative measures would take two years to implement. In fact, it took twenty years of painstaking work (with occasional setbacks and renewed violence) for the Italian Parliament to ratify all the measures. In May 1992 Italian Prime Minister Giulio Andreotti declared in Austria that every last point of *il paquetto* (the package) had been settled. In June 1992 the South Tyrol People's Party voted overwhelmingly to accept the package. Then in 1993 the Austrian Parliament added its agreement, enabling Austria to give the United Nations the formal declaration of the end of the conflict. Austrian Foreign Minister Alois Mock told the Austrian Parliament that what had happened in South Tyrol could be a model for other minority questions and for the settlement of similar conflicts elsewhere.

Reporting on that event on June 6, 1992, the *Washington Post* wrote:

Austria's Parliament cleared the way today for peaceful resolution of one of Central Europe's longest disputes about the rights of minorities. After more than 45 years of negotiations between Austria and Italy the National Assembly voted 125–30 to declare that Italy was in compliance with a package of measures that guarantee the rights of the 300,000 German-speaking residents of South Tyrol.

Silvio Magnago, by then honorary president of the South Tyrol People's Party and a main architect of the agreement,* told the press, "The settlement of the conflict is an historic occasion." It provided, among other things, for schools to teach in German and German to be used in judicial and administrative procedures. It also guaranteed that public service jobs, housing, and other benefits would be apportioned according to the population mix.

Summing up Caux's contribution to the solution, Austrian Franz Johann Vock (now secretary general of the Catholic Men's Movement in Vienna) wrote in his doctoral dissertation that it had helped create "an infrastructure of trust":

> Through the meetings of the representatives of both national groups they came closer, first of all, as human beings—not as a political representative of this or that group. . . . The solution of conflicts in other, far bigger crisis regions and the requests for help with other conflict areas brought the problems of South Tyrol into clearer perspective. The honest reports about solutions also stimulated honest conversations on their part and corrections to their course. A sign of the readiness to come to meet the other side is seen, for example, in the fact that the Italians spoke German. On both sides mistakes were addressed and admitted, and a common basis of understanding was laid, followed by an encouragement and strengthening of responsibility. The relationships that developed between both national groups persisted over the years and set the course for the political actions that followed.

Speaking in Caux in 1994, Karl Mitterdorfer, who had become president of the Federation of European Nationalities, said:

---

*A bipartisan committee of the Austrian Parliament nominated him for the Nobel peace prize.

The negotiations took thirty years. It doesn't mean that all the problems are solved. But South Tyrolers can continue, in mutual community with others, to lead the life that they have led there for a thousand years. Both sides had to accept compromises. In the perspective of the wars that have broken out in Europe it is very important that at least in one area through negotiation and agreement such a problem has been taken in hand.

Notes

The sources for this chapter are as follows: Franz Johann Vock, Ph.D. dissertation, "Zur Bedeutung der Moral für die Politik: Eine Untersuchung der Arbeit der Moralischen Aufrüstung an drei Fallbeispielen," Salzburg University, 1989; Fred Ladenius, "Printemps à Bolzano" in Marcel, *Plus décisif que la violence;* and Pierre Spoerri writing in *For a Change,* April 1993.

Other sources are author interviews with Heini Karrer, who was involved in the process; issues of *Caux Reports* for 1968 and 1969; and the author's articles in the *Christian Science Monitor* (July 1, 1992) and *The Oregonian* (July 3, 1992).

SECTION THREE

Unselfish Capitalism?

10

New aims for
management and labor

When people change, the structure of
society changes, and when the structure
of society changes, people change.
Both go together and both
are necessary.

HANS BÖCKLER
postwar president of the
German Trades Union Federation

A DRAMATIC CHANGE IN THE DOCKS

For twenty-five years Jim Beggs was state president of the Water-side Workers' Federation (longshoremen's union) in Australia, and for four years until 1992, he was national president.[1] For a young man who joked that before he had become active in his union, the largest crowd he had ever spoken to was in a phone box, and who preferred golf and duck shooting to union meetings, he had come a long way. The chain reaction of change in him and in his family—and through him to his industry—started with a caring neighbor who challenged him to create a new spirit in the port of Melbourne.

The livelihood of four out of five people in Australia is affected by what comes in and out of the country's ports. The toughness of the "wharfies" and their tendency to go out on strike led one prime minister to joke that another recession would not hit Australia because the wharfies wouldn't unload it.

163

Beggs has lived through and contributed to decades of significant change, with a dramatic improvement in working conditions and an equally dramatic decline in industrial friction. It all began in 1951. One midnight Beggs walked up the gangway of a ship to start his first job as a longshoreman. The work was hard, dirty, and unsafe, and because of the irregular hours, antisocial. During Beggs's first four years on the waterfront, he was an apathetic union member, critical of the union leadership whether from left or right and, of course, of his employer. When he started on the docks there were twenty-eight thousand wharfies in Australia. Today there are fewer than six thousand because in thirty hours a handful of men on a container ship can do the work of one hundred men in two weeks on a general cargo ship. When Beggs joined his union it represented about 2 percent of the national workforce but accounted for 27 percent of the country's national work stoppages. When he retired, his union, which by then had absorbed members of twenty-six other unions in waterfront work, was responsible for only half a percent of the national stoppages.

One day new neighbors, Tom and Florence Uren, moved next door to the Beggs household. To Beggs's consternation Tom turned out to be a port employer. Jim said to his wife, Tui, "I've got a bloke I attack all day on the job and I have to come home and live next to him." The neighbors nonetheless began to talk over the fence. The Urens even left the night light on so that the Beggs could do some night construction work on their home. Tom Uren, who like his French counterpart, Robert Carmichael discussed later in this chapter, had faced up to the wider responsibilities of management, said to Beggs one day, "It's fellows in management like me who have made profit our main aim who have created bitterness in the workers."

Soon after a three-week strike in the port, which had set the Beggs finances back considerably, Tom asked Jim if he wanted to see changes on the waterfront and whether he knew the place to start. Jim thought immediately of the union officials, who were too political, and the employers, who were very uncaring. But

Tom had something else in mind. "No," he said, "the place to start is with yourself."

"That was when Tui and I as a young couple began for the first time to look at our extended family, the people I worked with on the docks, that I'd never cared for but drawn a living from," Beggs said.

The neighbors had put another thought in the Beggs' minds: that God had a plan for everyone and that each person who took time to listen to his or her "inner voice," or whatever name was given to it, could find a part in that plan. "We tried this experiment and our first thoughts were very simple ones. First building our own relationships and being honest with each other about the things we did not know about each other and were ashamed of. And as that unity grew I thought this is what my union needs most."

Jim's employer-neighbor told him that he had decided to live by the standard of absolute honesty and that he had lost business as an accountant because he would only prepare honest tax returns. This knowledge helped Jim focus on the fact that he himself had been dishonest: He had stolen a clock from some cargo.

"I'd always accused my employer of being dishonest," he says, "but it didn't stop me from thieving his cargo." His resulting restitution set Jim on a new course. By returning the clock he had stolen, Jim earned a nickname that followed him throughout union life.* Jim became known as "Daylight Saving" because "he put the clock back." Jim told an industrial conference in Caux in 1994, "Let me tell you it is very, very difficult to thieve something off the waterfront on my port, but, believe me, it's twice as hard to take it back."

The thoughts Jim was having in his times of quiet and these new experiences helped him see that he had been part of the

---

*Wharfies have a distinct sense of humor about nicknames. One was known as "London Fog" because he never lifted. Another was known as "Bungalow" because he had nothing upstairs.

problem. Now he wanted the chance to be part of the answer. As his interests and responsibilities broadened, he began to take an interest in the front pages of the newspaper as well as the sports pages. He began to get involved in union activities and decided to run for office. It took him thirteen years, but he finally was elected as a union official in 1965. The union's leadership was a committee called "the executive." The executive had five different political points of view, no unity in its viewpoints, and no sense of community with the employer. Jim worked to build unity on the executive and to encourage nonpolitical representatives to step forward.

Journalist Chris Mayor wrote in the international magazine, *For a Change:*

> In what is still known as "Beggsie's God, King and Country speech," he apologized to Les, a Catholic ex-boxer [and a union leader], "five foot three and a hundred pounds in a wet overcoat," for his intense anti-Catholic prejudice. The two men began to work together—and others joined them. This played a part in a political shift in the union's national leadership and in the industry becoming, says Beggs, "the most progressive in Australia."

Jim and Tui came up with two principles for the union work: one was not to take sides, the other was to treat the executive as a family. At the end of a year one of his principal opponents, a Beijing-line communist, said to him, "I've been on the executive for nine years. For eight years I've hated the job because of the backstabbing that went on. But for the last twelve months the atmosphere has been different. I've never enjoyed my job so much." At the next election this former opponent canvassed for Jim.

In 1989 the prime minister devised an economic reform package and called the employers and union leaders together on the waterfront, challenging them to build a more efficient waterfront within three years. Otherwise, he told them, he would do it in a way neither group would like. He was not interested in seeing dock workers improve their wages and conditions or employers make more profit at the expense of the community.

After hundreds of meetings over the next three years, Jim and the others produced what he calls "most historic trade union agreements." The dock labor force was reduced by 60 percent. Two-thirds of his members left voluntarily, and no one was fired. According to Jim,

> Productivity went up by a hundred percent in most of the thirty ports around the coast of Australia and in some ports, my own included, higher. Twenty-seven unions became one. And shortly the other remaining union will join it, too. The captains of ships and the able seamen, the shore-based supervisors and the dockworkers will all be in the same union.

Jim reported in 1994:

> For the first time, my workers are being properly trained and multi-skilled. When I started on the docks 43 years ago I went in as a dockworker and I left as a dockworker. Now they come into the industry as dockworkers and with this multi-skilling . . . they can finish up as the manager of the port. And all this happened without one hour of work being lost.

Jim, who in 1991 was awarded the Order of Australia in recognition of his work in industry, says that because of the reform process, costs have been reduced dramatically, exports have increased, and jobs elsewhere—particularly in agriculture— have been protected. "The trade union movement should be an instrument of change," he says, "not a means of resisting change."

Jim gives an illustration of his direct and honest approach. In the early 1980s he had read an article by a retiring president of the National Farmer's Federation, who stated that the dockers were "the garbage on Australia's doorstep." This animosity had arisen from a long history of work stoppages that had disrupted agricultural exports. Jim feared the incoming president would have the same attitudes.

"There is one way to find out," said his wife. "Ring him up. You're the national chairman for your union, he's the national president of his." Jim did so, and they met. As a result Jim took a delegation of dockworkers to meet the critical farmers.

Jim describes the scene:

> We walked into their executive meeting of twenty men. Only one shook hands with us, very few of them smiled, here was the enemy. My opening remarks were, "I understand that you people believe that we are your problem on the docks. If that is so, we want you to identify those problems so we can solve them. We want to see your goods efficiently cross the wharves, creating more opportunities for you to export, more work for my members, better for the economy. We've come to repair some fences and to build some bridges."

It turned out that nine out of ten of the farmers' problems had nothing to do with Jim's union. The group had lunch together and inspected a fruit-picking operation. At the end of the day the employer who had been the most obstinate came up to the union group and said, "I never thought I would see the day that I would shake the hand of a dockworker. This has been a remarkable experience." Jim invited the farmers to come to the port to have lunch with the dockworkers.

In 1993 $600 million of fresh fruit and vegetables passed through Jim's port, a vast increase over earlier years. He attributes much of the increase to what he learned about putting his feet in the other person's shoes and not seeing things only "from the narrow point of view of the trade union movement."

Over the years Jim has taken his ideas to some forty ports around the world. "My union and my country," he says, "have played a very significant role in trying to uplift conditions and wages of people around the world who are unable to do it themselves."

In 1987 Jim was interviewed by Caroline Jones on her popular

Australian radio program, "The Search for Meaning." At the end of the program Caroline stated, "Many people today feel rather powerless. Your way of life suggests that as an individual I do have some power to make a difference."

Jim replied:

> I am absolutely convinced of that. I am an ordinary person; no education; used to be part of the apathetic majority of the trade union movement. But history is made up of individuals who have turned the tide and most of them have been ordinary people. You may not be meant to be a leader of your profession. But if you try that experiment of listening to a still, small voice that my wife and I made thirty-eight years ago, you will have that peace of heart which is more important than wealth and power. You will never know the effect you have.

A COMPLETE REVOLUTION IN INDUSTRY

Robert Carmichael, a French *patron,* was an authoritarian employer who decided what was best for others without consulting them.[2] But he was a boss who later found a new way of doing things and a caring that spanned the globe: an attitude toward Germans that helped bridge the Rhine after World War II (described in section one, chapter 2), an attitude toward labor leaders that made them put class war aside, and an attitude toward the Third World that still has to be adopted more widely. And it came about not through a neighbor as with Beggs, but through a visiting soldier.

Shortly after World War II, Carmichael, who was president of the French jute industry and a leading Protestant layman, had an English officer as a guest for lunch. After lunch the Englishman suggested that the family might like to take time in quiet to listen for divine inspiration. Carmichael's daughter and niece liked the idea, so Carmichael and his wife, despite any reservations they may have had, consented.

DEVELOPING EMPATHY FOR WORKERS

One of the first thoughts Carmichael had when he decided to adopt a regular practice of listening was to streamline his life, cutting out unnecessary activities, and to begin to regard people as more important than profitability and success. He attended a conference at Caux and met a group of Welsh miners, who described to him the suffering and unemployment they had undergone in 1929 and how they had broken out of the circle of resentment and the desire for revenge. Their experiences, their commitment, and their sense of responsibility for industry were a challenge to the Frenchman. He decided that his business life too had to undergo a change.

Carmichael took the bold step of inviting a Communist workers' leader from one of his factories to go to Caux with a colleague to see what he had experienced there. To Carmichael's surprise the man accepted, bringing with him the secretary of the local Communist cell. The workers' leader returned home, having made a number of decisions: He gave up drinking, found a new unity with his wife, and initiated new work modes in the factory.

In their book, *The World at the Turning*, Piguet and Sentis describe what happened:

> In the following months, the spectacular change in the life of this communist worker had its effect on his comrades in the factory. The bistro over the road lost its customers, and the workers persuaded the owner to convert it into a grocery store. A new atmosphere was born in the small firm, and in this atmosphere manager and workers decided to tackle various problems together. Productivity went up, wages went up by nearly fifty percent, homes were built for the most badly housed, there was a measure of job security. Carmichael watched a loss-making firm, which he had been on the point of closing down, become a prosperous business.

In the ensuing years Carmichael's experience played a part at Caux with Germans, who saw in him a Frenchman who did not point the finger of blame; with North African nationalists, who met a Frenchman who understood their aspirations; and with French workers, who realized that employers too could find new motives.

Carmichael told his colleagues in industry:

We need a complete revolution in industry, and this implies a fundamental change in our aims. It is no longer enough for us in management to work only for our profits, nor for the workers to aim only at earning their wages. We must combine our strengths to meet the needs of all men and to rebuild the world.

A new spirit began to spread in the French textile industry as a whole, particularly after Carmichael's opposite in labor, Maurice Mercier, secretary general of the French Textile Workers, also had a fundamental experience of change in Caux. This was due in part to Mercier's observation of Carmichael's new approach. On the initiative of the two men, who had met at Caux, textile managers and workers in 1951 signed a national agreement, the first in France after the war. It guaranteed to employees that they would get a share in the benefits of higher productivity, and some 600,000 workers were given large pay raises.

That summer eighty delegations from the French textile industry went to Caux. What happened there between management and labor led to an industrywide agreement in June 1953 that covered the seven thousand factories and 648,000 workers then in the industry. The preamble to the agreement stated, "The textile industry intends to make an economic and social experiment in the interest of the nation, in the spirit of service, with a social objective." Mercier characterized this new approach: "Not one cry of hatred, not one hour of work lost, not one drop of blood shed."

Practically, this agreement meant that the textile workers were the first in France to benefit from a policy of permanent consultation, compensation for partial unemployment, bonuses for

171

greater productivity, and mutually agreed-upon restraint. As a result of the agreement the real wages of textile workers rose 3.3 percent to 5 percent each year over the next two decades.

When France was faced with galloping inflation in 1953, Prime Minister Antoine Pinay turned to the textile industry and asked the workers, whose industry had the best management-labor relationship, to take the lead. At that time, workers in most industries had forced a 20 percent rise in wages; with the consequent rise in prices, they were coming back for another wage hike. The textile workers responded by accepting an 8 percent raise, and employers agreed not to increase their prices.

Prime Minister Pinay wrote in *Le Figaro* that this agreement was "one of the first solid achievements on the road of the change which is indispensable to the economic survival of the country." This spirit held through the next decades and led to the revival of French industry. Following the student and labor demonstrations of May 1968 that swept the country, the textile industry was the only one practically untouched.

TOWARD FAIR JUTE PRICES AROUND THE WORLD

The year 1951 was also a landmark for Robert Carmichael. After seeing the poverty of the population firsthand while on an economic mission to India and Pakistan, he had a surprising thought in his early morning quiet time: "You are responsible for the millions of jute growers in India and Pakistan who die of hunger." On his return to France Carmichael decided, as a first step, to set about uniting the European jute manufacturing industries. Jute is a vital ingredient in producing twine and heavy-duty cloth. In 1954, after a series of meetings with the fourteen interested European countries, the European Association of Jute Industries was formed, and Carmichael was named president. He had explained at the early meetings that the mission was to help bring about a sound world jute economy: to give a fair return to the jute growers of India and Pakistan, the middlemen (including packers and carriers), and the Asian and European manufacturers and to provide a good product at a reasonable price.

What Carmichael had learned at Caux was a help in winning certain Europeans to these ideas. In 1959, after a stormy association meeting in Stockholm during which he threatened to resign his post, he was at last commissioned to start talks with India and Pakistan. Carmichael told his colleagues:

> If the European jute industry makes an effort to create a sane economy in this sector with India and Pakistan, it can find its true mission, its real reason for existence. To do this, the basic motives of European industrialists must undergo a fundamental change.

Carmichael made a series of journeys to India and Pakistan to convince not only the two governments but also the exporters and the jute industrialists of the need to stabilize the price of jute. Determined to strengthen the links between developing and industrialized countries, he undertook these trips on top of his other responsibilities, such as representing the French textile industry at Common Market meetings. He had to fight the speculative tendencies of certain traders and even help Asian partners find a consensus while they were at war with each other.

"As in Europe," he wrote, "I encountered fierce opposition from some industrialists and from people who wanted to play the market. But during the next five years I was able to get a number of those I had met to see the need for an agreement with the West and with India on a stable price for raw jute."

In February 1965 the UN Food and Agriculture Organization (FAO) succeeded in getting a world agreement on stabilizing jute prices. Unlike earlier agreements that had been broken, this one aimed only at fixing general objectives, leaving a committee to decide each year the terms to be implemented. A meeting was to be held in Rome six months later to fix the prices and conditions of the agreement.

As the Rome meeting approached, Carmichael knew that several countries had signed the agreement only because they were convinced that it could never work. The conditions were not favorable. Carmichael arrived a day early to see Eric Ojala, the FAO official, who was organizing the meeting. During their conversation they hit on a strategy that brought together the Pakistani representative and the Europeans—despite instructions from their governments to sabotage any such agreement.

Carmichael described what happened that afternoon, when the delegates met to work out a suggested price to submit to the full committee.

During this session I said that our aim was to fix a fair price and that there were two ways of going about this. Either we could do it the old way, where those who wanted a low price asked for half the price they expected and those wanting a high price responded by asking twice as much as they expected; the resultant bargaining invariably produced a wrong price. Or we could lay aside our official positions for a moment, and seek together, man to man, for the right price. If we agreed to try the second way, I said, I had a proposition to make.

This was accepted. I suggested that we might ask the man who, because of the importance to his country of their jute production, seemed the best person to tell us honestly what he thought was the fair price. There was no doubt, I said, that this man was the Pakistani representative. There was a long silence. Then the Pakistani delegate said that if everyone agreed that there would be no official record of what was about to be discussed, and that he would not be held to the price he would indicate at the plenary session, then he was ready, as an individual and as an expert, simply to give this price.

Everyone agreed. He then stated a price which corresponded so nearly to that which all those present recognized as fair, that the German delegate said he did not understand what was happening. The price mentioned seemed to him so reasonable that, as representative of the German government, he could not do otherwise but accept it. Within a few minutes the twenty delegates had all agreed.

At the plenary session the next day this proposal was approved by all countries except Pakistan, whose delegate explained that as he had not received instructions from his government to give his agreement, he had to oppose it. He indicated, however, that in view of the remarkable unanimity expressed, he would do everything possible to get his government to accept the proposition. It did so five days later.

The settlement came as a surprise to those who did not know what had made it possible. It was put into effect and brought substantial advantages to the workers of Pakistan and India. Two years later, in 1968, the director general of the FAO was able to say that jute had shown the way to a new type of international agreement with much wider repercussions, as the jute agreement was beginning to influence other industries such as hard fiber and rubber.

Subsequent difficulties in negotiating the price of jute do not detract from the pioneer work done by Carmichael in the area of commodity prices, which remains a source of divisiveness in the world. For the first time the price of a basic raw material, the subject of litigation between industrialized and developing nations, had been freely negotiated between equal partners. As the director general of the FAO acknowledged, the jute industry had shown nations that were divided on other raw materials that there was a way to cooperate in complete openness.

Notes

1. This discussion is drawn from speeches by Jim Beggs, including a speech to a Caux industrial conference on July 24, 1994, and from correspondence with him. He was profiled by Chris Mayor in "King of the Wharfies," *For a Change,* February 1988.

2. Carmichael tells his own story in *Robert Carmichael par lui-même.* His story is also told in Mottu, *The Story of Caux;* Lean, *Rebirth of a Nation?;* Piguet and Sentis, *The World at the Turning;* and Mowat, *Decline and Renewal.*

11

Initiatives from below: Saving an industry

*We went to the brink, we looked into
the abyss, we did not like what we saw, so we've
come back. And we don't want charity
because we've shown we can produce
goods of the right quality
and at the right price.*

DAVID JAMES
*Secretary, Supervisors' Group,
Steelworkers' Union, Llanwern Steelworks, Wales*

Paul Theroux, in his 1983 book, *The Kingdom by the Sea*, refers to the "doomed Llanwern steelworks." In 1983 this description of the steelworks was already outdated. In 1978 British Steel Corporation was losing £2 million a day, and Llanwern had the worst reputation of all British Steel plants—for poor labor relations, low productivity, low quality, high price, and failure to meet delivery dates. Even in the good years of the steel industry, it had never been profitable. In the space of eighteen months during 1978–79, twelve major steelworks were closed down or partly shut, with the loss of more than 100,000 jobs. Llanwern was the thirteenth loss-making plant due for closure, and this Welsh plant had been all but written off.

Suddenly, without a penny of new investment, Llanwern began to turn around. A 1983 article in the *South Wales Argus,* when the steelworks was still in jeopardy, said:

You cannot lay your hands on the reason and pull it out of the hat like a magician to place before the British Steel Corporation board or the government. But you can feel it. Put simply, it's the overwhelming determination of the ordinary workers at the plant to make sure Llanwern survives. It has already worked what has become known as the Llanwern miracle—turning what was not so long ago a stumbling giant into a sleek greyhound which has outpaced many of its rivals in the efficiency race. The figures speak for themselves. In the past few weeks the plant has been shattering its own output records and achieving productivity figures that can equal or better its top European rivals.[1]

The chairman of British Steel not only reprieved the plant but decided to make it the standard for the restructuring of the whole corporation. To become competitive British Steel's workforce had to be cut by half, a survival package called Slimline. Sir Charles Villiers, a former head of British Steel, took on the job as chairman of BSC Industry to help provide employment for those who lost their jobs. His company gave support to 2,700 new businesses around the nation, which in turn generated some 70,000 new jobs.

On August 10, 1987, *Insight* magazine reported, "British Steel's annual report reveals the transformation of a once decrepit company into what may be Europe's most financially sound steel enterprise." Indeed, in 1985 British Steel made its first profit in ten years—£38 million. In 1987 it made a profit of £226 million on sales of £3.46 billion.

What happened at Llanwern seems to have been the product of all sides—management, labor, and government—moving beyond recrimination. "We in management had to change our attitudes and working practices," admits the Llanwern plant director at the time, Bill Harrison. Worker-Director David Williams adds that the trade unions at Llanwern were prepared to accept their share of the blame for what had gone wrong in the past.

The turnaround was the product too of individuals who went way beyond their usual responsibilities in their thinking and planning. "People are putting in a tremendous personal commitment," comments a section manager. John Foley, then divisional officer for the main steelworkers' union, summed it up by saying, "Llanwern was saved by a team effort."

A key factor, according to Works Council member David James, was that a union branch secretary, Gwilym Jenkins, had helped set up an effective dialogue with the government, the owner of this nationalized industry. Two fellow trade unionists had suggested to Gwilym that he should meet someone in the Conservative government informally to discuss the problems of the South Wales steel industry. Gwilym's first reaction was negative: As a "dyed-in-the-wool socialist," he had no desire to sit next to a Conservative member of parliament, let alone talk to him. However, he agreed to the suggestion and met the man in the central lobby of the House of Commons.

"It was a shaft of light at the end of a tunnel that was pitch black," according to Llanwern's press officer, Howell Morgan. A spirit of trust beyond politics was born. The first visit was followed by a second and a third visit in which members of the Llanwern Works Council participated. As a result, says Gwilym, "the government became acquainted for the first time with the real hopes, fears and aspirations of the South Wales steelworkers, and in due course with what we ourselves were doing to save Llanwern."

Gwilym's decision to set aside his hatred of the establishment was to lead to his playing a significant role with the team that helped save the steelworks. His involvement was a departure from his earlier attitude, when he had said of British Steel, "They exist to pay my wages."

Later, at Caux, meeting Japanese delegations, memories of World War II in Burma returned and with them his bitter hatred of all things Japanese. His hatred was burnished by the contraction of the industry in the face of Japanese competition. Gwilym found the courage to admit his hatred and apologized for it. He was invited to Japan and soon found himself in Tokyo distributing "Buy Llanwern" stickers to his bemused hosts.

A significant part of the Llanwern turnaround is that someone like Gwilym could step forward to responsibility as he did. He now sees it in terms of God's having a plan for every person and situation. A key to the change, he says, was a "provocative suggestion" made to him by the two trade unionists who had first approached him: Although human wisdom on its own had failed and would continue to fail to resolve the problems, God had a plan for every situation, including the steel industry. "Perhaps because I was desperate and looking for solutions," he says, "I had begun to explore the implications of this concept during the ten weeks since the campaign to save Llanwern had started, and also to apply it to my own attitudes and behavior."

As he reflected, he had "two simple and compelling thoughts." First, even if the men went back to work, there would be none to do because there were no orders. Second, Llanwern somehow had to win back all the customers who had been lost.

"The next day a remarkable thing happened," Gwilyn relates. He was watching a TV program about the steel industry. One of those talking was a customer, Harold Williams, chairman of the Confederation of British Industry in Wales. "I had a clear thought to phone him, even though my union was picketing his works at the time," Gwilym explains. As a result, Williams, who says he had reached the point where he could not have cared less whether the steel industry lived or died, brought seven customers to a dinner with union and management representatives.

As employees began to feel responsible and included in decisions, production times dropped from ten man-hours per metric ton of steel to 3.27. The government, with new confidence, was able to invest £7 billion in the industry in the 1980s.

The Times of London could write in 1981:

Management-union relationships have never been better, craft and process worker demarcation lines have been dissolved and such a commitment and determination to succeed is evident everywhere. The vigor and vitality which is almost tangible seems paradoxical at a time when the steel industry is experiencing its deepest crisis since the thirties.[2]

In 1995 the Llanwern workforce was one-third of what it had been at the start of Slimline—3,500 instead of 9,600—and the capacity had been upgraded from 2.2 million metric tons to 3.0 million metric tons. This expansion is, according to a 1996 article in the *Industrial Pioneer,* "a massive vindication of the leadership provided by unions and management at the plant, not to mention the efforts of the 3,500-strong work force during the last sixteen years in particular." Today Llanwern has some of the lowest costs and highest productivity of any fully integrated steelworks in the world—a far cry from the decline of the 1970s.[3]

Notes

1. John, Peter, "Why Llanwern's Fighters Deserve to Win the Battle," *South Wales Argus,* March 3, 1983.

2. "Steel Success Story," *The Times* of London, October 14, 1981.

3. Cosens, Dick, "World Best for Productivity," *Industrial Pioneer,* February–March 1996.

12

Initiatives from the top: Leveling the corporate playing field

Although much of the impact of the Caux Round Table comes from responsible actions by its participants in their own spheres of influence, we also seek to be proactive as a group on issues where we have expertise, conviction and a high degree of consensus. We seek to affect the policies and conduct not only of internationally involved businesses but also of governments. It isn't beyond our hope that we can make changes in the world as a result of what we are doing.

WINSTON R. WALLIN
Chairman, Medtronic Inc.

THE BIRTH OF THE CAUX ROUND TABLE

As a nineteen-year-old conscripted Japanese shipyard worker, Ryuzaburo Kaku heard the blast of the atomic bomb at Nagasaki. For three days he took shelter in the mountains. Those traumatic hours confirmed in him the deep-rooted conviction that Japan was wrong to put so much reliance on military might. Fifty years later, as chairman of Canon, the camera and copier manufacturing giant, Kaku feels equally strongly that Japan is on

181

a dangerous path if it relies only on economic strength. This time the world, not just Japan, would be the loser. Kaku is promoting a philosophy, *kyosei*—living and working together for the common good—which he hopes will become as familiar a Japanese word to the outside world as *kamikaze* was in World War II.

At the time that Kaku was emerging from his mountain hiding place, forty-year-old Frederik (Frits) Philips, a Dutchman freed from a German prison camp, was helping to rebuild the fortunes of Philips Electrical Industries, the parent of Norelco and Magnavox which he would head as its chairman. His philosophy is expressed in the only words found on the back jacket of his autobiography: "Figures are important; people are more important."[1]

When these two men got together with some other captains of industry in 1986, the result was the creation of a unique grouping. There are those who say that "capitalism for the sake of others" and "business ethics" are oxymorons. Philips and Kaku and their friends are out to prove them wrong. They believe that the business leaders of Europe, Japan, and the United States can help business and industry to be a vital force for innovative change.

The story begins in 1985, but some background is first needed. In the 1970s and early 1980s Western Europe had been shaken by the quantity and quality of Japan's exports. As Japan made inroads into traditional areas of American strength, Americans began to engage in Japan bashing. The Japanese public will long remember the image of U.S. congressmen on the steps of the U.S. Capitol in Washington, D.C., taking sledge hammers to Toshiba tape recorders. The reaction in Japan, with its less demonstrative culture, may have been outwardly restrained, but underneath many Japanese seethed. The Western media and politicians fed the furor using military metaphors like "invasion" to describe the flood of Japanese imports.*

---

*Confronted by Japan's effective market techniques and unfailing quality, many Western businesses were driven out of the market, sometimes into bankruptcy, and hundreds of thousands of workers lost their jobs. An article in the *Japan Times* that describes the situation in 1986 said:

In May 1985 Philips read a company report that concluded that protectionism, dumping, theft, and blackmail were all part of a strategy by which Japan was aiming to destroy the electronics industry in Europe and the United States and that free trade and free market development were at stake. The author, R. Hamersma, had said that the Philips company took the view that free trade in the world had to be restored, which meant doing away with protectionism and trade barriers. The report appeared on May 8 in a prominent Dutch paper, *NRC Handelsblad,* headed "The false smile of Japan."

Philips was shocked by the report and its confrontational tone. "Smaller things have led to bloody conflict," he thought. Philips believed that the Japanese needed to know what image they had abroad. He knew that image can sometimes be more important than reality and that some wars had begun not because of facts but because of distortion.

Philips had close links with Japanese business leaders. In 1950 he had begun a lifelong friendship and business partnership with Konosuke Matsushita, who ten years earlier, along with his wife, had started a small bicycle lamp shop. Matsushita now was seeking help from the Philips company to manufacture lamps and radios. (Today Matsushita is one of the world's largest electronics firms.) In June of 1985 Philips sent the article to a number of friends in Japan. His accompanying letter said that the article illustrated the danger that threatened world trade and world progress in the years to come. "I know that hardly anyone in Japan is informed of what is going on," Philips wrote. "I even think that the big companies are more interested in their turnover and their profits than they are aware of this interna-

---

Japan's overwhelming strength in steel, shipbuilding, and cameras had been grumblingly accepted. But when the car industry, so important to the economies of the major European countries, began to suffer seriously from Japanese competition, an angry clamor started. As soon as consumer electronics were affected, indignation began to reign—for electronics were considered particularly essential to the future of the industrial society.

tional danger which will affect the future of Japanese industry." He added that his friendship for Japan was his main motive for sending the article.

Following correspondence back and forth, Philips invited business leaders from Japan, the United States, and Europe to meet with him in Europe in August 1986 to seek an answer to this threat to world trade. He suggested a meeting at Mountain House, the Swiss conference center that he had visited frequently. Philips chose Caux because he had seen firsthand its effect in helping to reconcile nations that had fought each other during World War II. It was there too, he said, that he had first begun as a member of management to grasp what was in the minds of workers. He believed that the setting and the spirit of Caux would help to overcome the distrust between Japanese industrialists and their U.S. and European competitors. Philips enlisted a friend, Olivier Giscard d'Estaing, vice chairman of the European Institute of Business Administration, to help host the visitors.

Nine senior Japanese executives accepted the invitation to Caux, where they met with seven American and twelve European business leaders. The Japanese leaders included Toshihiko Yamashita, former CEO of Matsushita; Masaki Nakajima, director and former chairman of the Mitsubishi Research Institute; and Toshiaki Ogasawara, chairman of *The Japan Times*. The Japanese responded with alacrity to the invitation, although some may have wondered, as did Canon head Kaku, "How can we be sure that this is not just another Japan-bashing session?" Any hesitation was overcome, however, by the sincerity of Philips's desire to bridge the differences, the urgency of the hour, and the reputation of Caux as a neutral place that had already played a part in helping Japan to regain acceptance into the family of nations after World War II.

In the first twenty-four hours at Caux it seemed to the Japanese that they might have put too much trust in the venue and to Philips that his expectations would be dashed. Some Europeans just could not resist the temptation to air their grievances against

Japan. Yamashita describes what happened: "We felt in coming to Caux that we would be coming to a heavenly place. But as we started the Round Table we felt like we were being pushed into hell." Overnight, however, what he describes as "frank and honest talk" began, and as a result "we felt we had come back to heaven again." The bashing stopped, says Francis X. Stankard of Chase Manhattan Bank, "as the spirit of Caux surrounded us."

Together, the leaders worked through to the truth about the issues dividing them. They recognized the cultural differences among the continents.* All agreed on a communiqué that stated, "Nations should set their own houses in order and maintain their world competitiveness."

The participants voiced a sense of urgency growing out of their shared concern over the danger of the rising imbalance of trade and threatened increase in protectionism. They expressed a common concern that demands for protection and trade restrictions should be resisted and that a freer and more balanced trade should be the prime objective. Agreed aims would be pursued "as a shared responsibility of Europeans, Japanese, and Americans with a clear moral and spiritual dimension." They agreed that those from each national group would take part in clarifying the actions to be taken to improve the situation within their own area, rather than prescribing actions for the others to take. This approach, which is at the heart of the spirit of Caux, was to become a distinguishing mark of this new grouping of business leaders, which became known as the Caux Round Table.

The Round Table participants went beyond their immediate preoccupations and brought a wider perspective to their deliberations, stating that "the developed nations have a common responsibility to support the economic and social progress of the third world." This consensus particularly pleased Giscard d'Estaing, who was involved in Africa and whose participation in the

---

*To use a sporting example, in sumo wrestling colossal differences of weight are not considered unfair by the Japanese, while hostile takeovers, common in the West, are.

Round Table stemmed in large part from his belief that its work might lead to a fairer deal for the Third World.*

Gerrit Wagner, chairman of the Supervisory Board of Royal Dutch Petroleum Company, wrote afterwards, "I was struck by the frankness with which views were expressed on a number of delicate matters."

Ryuzaburo Kaku was later to recommend Caux to Chinese leaders as a venue that "shows that this conference is no place for falsification or cheating. It is in fact conducive to the elimination of misunderstanding and malice, resulting in common interests." He continued:

> This is also what distinguishes the Caux Round Table from other international conferences. It is where people from different races, religions, nations, and systems gather in order to understand and communicate with each other for the sake of the happiness of all mankind by changing their own attitudes first.

THE ROUND TABLE IS INSTITUTIONALIZED

Indicative of the newfound trust and friendship was an invitation issued by the Japanese for the group to meet in Japan the following May "to continue the dialogue and get to know the Japanese situation at firsthand." The invitation was accepted by Philips, d'Estaing, and the other business leaders. They met in Tokyo with executives of Canon, Toshiba, Nissan, and Matsushita; with members of the Confederation of Economic Organizations (Keidanren) and the Committee for Economic Development (Keizai Doyukai); and with a vice minister at the Ministry of International Trade and Industry (MITI).

---

*At a Round Table session in Delhi following the Caux meeting, Giscard d'Estaing told Indian business leaders, "I believe in economic miracles. I also believe in the ability of men to change, to learn, to behave in such a way that instead of being a heavy burden they become a creative force contributing to the corporations and to their country."

The May 1987 visit took place against a background of mounting trade and monetary problems and a growing negative attitude toward Japan in the United States. Following their frank exchanges *Nihon Keizai Shimbun,* Japan's principal financial paper, summed up the visit:

> Data and information are different. Data can be misinterpreted. Real information is produced from a network of people. A new and valuable network has just been created in Japan at a time when she tends to be the target of pressure from the rest of the world.

The group agreed to meet again the following summer in Caux, and the Japanese undertook to have prepared by then concrete suggestions for action. On the initiative of Brad Butler, former chairman of Procter and Gamble, interim meetings followed in San Francisco, Cincinnati, and New York. A pattern for the Round Table was by then emerging: twenty-five to thirty business leaders from Japan, the United States, and Europe meet twice yearly, with a plenary meeting in Caux and a midyear meeting alternating among Europe, Asia, and North America. Local meetings are held periodically in each region. By the end of 1995 this pattern had meant ten sessions in Caux and meetings in Japan, Taiwan, China, India, Germany, the United States, and at the time of the 1995 UN World Social Summit, in Copenhagen. In the first ten years of the Round Table more than two hundred fifty business leaders met to discuss trade frictions, as well as related issues like unemployment and job creation and strengthening emerging democracies.

Frenchman Jean-Loup Dherse, former vice president of the World Bank and the 1994–95 chair of the steering committee for the Caux Round Table, likens the debates to a chemical reaction "in which the experience of being honest over real conflicting situations has allowed trust to develop to such an extent that there now is a common philosophy." Round Table members like to point to the value of the friendships established over the years and to the presence of spouses at all the conferences, which has contributed to warm personal relationships.

On occasions the Caux Round Table has invited nonmembers to attend its sessions. Authorities are sometimes invited to help shed light on major issues, as when the Dutch Underminister for Foreign Trade Dr. Yvonne van Rooy, helped underline the dangers of creating a "Fortress Europe."

Where appropriate, Caux Round Table members have reported to their governments. For example, after the first meeting in 1986 the Japanese group wrote an unusual letter to Prime Minister Yasuhiro Nakasone with suggestions about how to expand the domestic market, reduce the state debt, open up the Japanese market to foreign goods, and reduce trade friction. In 1990 the Japanese group made further "proposals to remake Japan": "Japan must shift its priority towards playing its part to create wealth and prosperity for all. This means accepting common moral values as the principles of the state. For business corporations it means contributing positively to resolving existing discrepancies and social ills."

At Kaku's urging the Caux Round Table has focused attention on the importance of global corporate responsibility in reducing social and economic threats to world peace and stability. It calls for shared leadership and emphasizes the development of continuing friendship, understanding, and cooperation based on a common respect for the highest moral values and responsible action by individuals in their own sphere of influence.

In 1994 after three years of work and study, the group published the Caux Round Table Principles for Business expressing "a world standard against which business behavior can be measured." It is perhaps the first time such principles for corporate behavior have been jointly drawn up by business leaders from three continents. The introduction to the Principles states, "Members of the Caux Round Table place their first emphasis on putting one's own house in order, and on seeking to establish what is right rather than who is right." In releasing the Principles, Round Table members were attempting to focus widespread attention on the consequences and cost of unprincipled business activities.[2]*

In a jointly written article that appeared in the February 18, 1995 issue of the *Japan Times,* Alfredo Ambrosetti, chair of the European Ambrosetti Group; Winston Wallin, chairman of Medtronic Inc., an internationally known U.S. medical technology firm; and Ryuzaburo Kaku wrote:

> Even the least humanistic, most bottom-line-focused executives know that global standards are the necessary base for a level playing field. They understand that corruption and other irresponsible behaviors are ultimately inefficient and wasteful because they add to the cost of each transaction in which they play a part. And enlightened executives know that these corrupt practices undermine public confidence in capitalist economic institutions. We affirm that moral values are necessary in decision-making and that without them, stable business relationships and a sustainable world community are impossible.

The Principles for Business draw on distinctive values and responsible business practices. From Japan comes the concept of *kyosei*—living and working together for the common good—and the belief that corporations evolve through stages toward full responsibility to all stakeholders. From Europe comes the conviction that there is a great potential for community among nations, as exemplified by both the founding of the European Community and the spirit of Caux. From the United States come the Minnesota Principles, a statement of aspirations intended to start

---

*At the 1995 UN World Summit for Social Development, at a forum arranged by Olivier Giscard d'Estaing, the Principles were presented on behalf of the Caux Round Table by Stephen R. Braswell, senior vice president and chief ethics officer of The Prudential Insurance Company of America. Giscard warned of a dark future if the business world did not broaden its perspective: "If the capitalist system is limited to those who can afford it and leaves out the rest, we have a problem. If we don't cope with it, there will be political instability. The unemployed and those left out will come to the point of revolution."

a process to develop a world standard of responsible business behavior.

Kyosei has been Kaku's passion since he became president of Canon in 1977 and realized that Japan needed a new way of doing things.[3] He says, "For Canon alone to be prosperous or Japan alone to be prosperous is not enough. We must share prosperity with all the world."

Companies can reach *kyosei,* Kaku maintains, through four stages of evolution. The first stage is purely capitalistic, with owners and managers reserving to themselves all profits from the enterprise. The second stage occurs when a company recognizes the contribution of all its workers and shares with them some of the profits. The third stage takes place when the company enlarges its definition of stakeholders to include not only shareholders and employees but also customers, suppliers, and the local community in which it works. In the fourth stage the company thinks and acts globally, not only in the geographical sense but in its concern for the good of all humanity. According to Kaku:

> It recognizes that the single most important factor in its long-term success is the economic, social, and political health of the communities in which it works and lives. It further understands that because national borders cannot curtail the spread of disease or pollution, nor stem the mass migration of the world's poor, the world is or shortly will become an indivisible community.

The Minnesota Principles owe their origin to pioneering work by business leaders from seventeen industrial concerns in the Twin Cities of Minneapolis and St. Paul, together with the Minnesota Center for Corporate Responsibility. They wanted to foster "the fairness and integrity of business relationships in the emerging global marketplace." Charles M. Denny, chairman of ADC Telecommunications and one of the architects of the principles, says that to be truly ethical it is necessary to "go well beyond the requirements of the law." Human nature is "so diverse and perverse that if we rely solely on the legal system we have failed. There has to be a moral basis for a business community to survive."

In its March/April 1995 issue the magazine *Business Ethics* described the launching of the Principles for Business as "a new kind of capitalist revolution" and cited the example of a German Round Table member:

> Friedrich Schock, president of Schock and Co., of Schorndorf, Germany, knows what it is like to face difficult ethical decision. "Recently we sold a license to an Italian company," said Schock, "and they gave me a check from a Swiss bank to void the 60 percent German tax. I told their boss it was wrong and I would follow the German law."

Since 1924 the three Schock brothers, the $165 million private manufacturers of "home living" goods, employing one thousand people, have always tried to live up to high standards. "Just the other day, a company from Nigeria wanted me to send a phony invoice and take a kickback. And there is a permanent temptation to avoid the European Union's TVA tax. Almost every day there are decisions like this that require absolute honesty. Business is like marriage because it requires daily practice," said Schock.

Jean-Loup Dherse believes that one of the next steps should be sharing applications of the Principles for Business in everyday business life. "This would include true stories where the lack of such principles has caused risks or even damage to a company," he says.

Although other trilateral bodies of business executives exist, the Caux Round Table is different. Its cornerstone is that everybody first look at his or her own part when in a clash of purposes and interests. The participants are committed to a joint search for what is right, rather than who is right. They believe that corporate business people—because they do not have the disadvantage of government, which cannot go beyond national interests, and the disadvantages of politicians, who are constantly concerned with their reelection—can together build a more equi-table and just world. Dherse believes that the Round Table's expressed principles, genuinely international composition, and "spirit of good communication and mutual respect" set the group apart from other international roundtables.

In a 1995 mission statement the Caux Round Table identified four major socioeconomic conditions that threaten world harmony:

• Excessive poverty within countries and regions.

• Growing economic friction arising from enduring trade imbalances, which if unaddressed, can lead to political strife.

• The gap between the increasing affluence of the developed world and the continuing poverty, concentration of population growth, and despair in less-developed countries.

• Generational burdens, such as a polluted world and over-whelming national debts, which are passed on to children.

Dherse wants to help focus for international business leader-ship the need to address these issues and "to take full account of the rights and expectations of current and future generations."

Unlike most enterprises in which businesspeople are involved, the Caux Round Table has no clear road map for the future. It prefers to remain a semi-informal network of executives whose strength is the focus it can give to the human and moral issues underlying world dilemmas and the feedback it can give through position papers and direct access to responsible leaders.

Kaku and Philips are still at grips with the issues that threaten world stability. Younger businesspeople are taking up their man-tle, but they are still thinking in big terms. Kaku dares to envis-age a great change in Japan. He says, "We need an overarching concept for the 21st century that will work for the common good of all peoples."

Frits Philips told the *Asahi Shimbun* in 1987:

It is up to us whether the next century is a golden era for the whole of humanity or not. I believe in God and I stuck to this belief while I was a prisoner of war. . . . If we fail to manage this earth which is our residence, it's the responsibility of us all, as human beings. I am convinced that the way we live—whether it is as a state, an enterprise or an individual—will be severely questioned in the 21st century. People will pay more attention to what sort of values and philosophy national leadership, top businessmen, and individuals have.

The 90-year-old Philips added, "As I don't think I'll be still alive in the 21st century, when the time comes I'll put in a call from the next world to ask what sort of society it has become."

Notes

1. Philips, *45 Years with Philips*.

2. The Caux Round Table Principles for Business were widely circulated among Fortune 1000 companies and reported on *Financial Times, Nihon Keizai Shimbun,* and the *Japan Times*.

3. Glosserman, the *Japan Times*.

This chapter also draws on the files of the Caux Round Table, reports supplied to the author by James Montgomery, former chairman and chief executive officer of Pan Am World Services, and an unpublished paper by Peter Hintzen, son-in-law of Frits Philips.

SECTION FOUR

People Power

13

America's unfinished business

Let all of us who want to stand up against racism do our part to roll back the divide. Begin by seeking out people in the workplace, the classroom, the community, the neighborhood across town, the place of worship to actually sit down and have those honest conversations I talked about—conversations where we speak openly and listen and understand how others view this world of ours.

PRESIDENT BILL CLINTON

CIVIL WAR LEGACIES

It took Dick Ruffin* some time to work through what he felt about his great, great grandfather. Edmund Ruffin is noted in American schoolbooks because he fired the shot on Fort Sumter that marked the start of the Civil War. He was a prominent agriculturalist who served in the Virginia legislature. He might be said to have also fired the last shot of the Civil War: At the end of the war this owner of slave plantations and strong protagonist for states' rights, not wanting to owe allegiance to the United States, wrapped himself in the Confederate flag and shot himself. It was

---

*Ruffin is Executive Director of Moral Re-Armament in the United States.

a war in which more than 600,000 Southerners and Northerners died, more American lives lost than in the two world wars and the Vietnam War combined.

Dick had been brought up on stories of his ancestor's passion to save the South's rural economy through slavery and secession. Despite misgivings about his relative's purposes, Dick had absorbed a certain pride in his agricultural innovations and radical politics. It was only recently that he had begun to realize that his ancestor's life had indirectly touched his own life and that Edmund's legacy had shaped his own relationships with African Americans in subtle ways.

Dick was aware that for his family, as for many Southerners, the defeat of the South was felt as a deep humiliation, leaving a residue of resentment, insecurity, and anger. One general effect was that white Southerners interpreted their experience and their history almost exclusively in relation to the North, rather than in relation to those who had suffered under slavery. This view probably accounts for the strong tendencies to romanticize the Southern way of life, in particular the antebellum period, and to villainize the North, which persisted among white Southerners for more than a century after the Civil War and are still evident to some degree in the South's modern political culture.

Less obvious, according to Dick, is how the preoccupation with North-South relations reinforced the blindness of white Southerners to the impact of slavery on black Americans. To judge from Edmund Ruffin's diaries, for example, and from Ruffin family lore, Dick's great, great grandfather was oblivious to the evil of slavery and to the havoc wreaked in the lives of millions of African Americans. Not surprisingly, in stories passed down in families like Dick's, black Americans hardly ever figured. Their reality was ignored, their true feelings denied. "Such blindness was in some measure bequeathed to subsequent generations," says Dick, "so that many in my generation still have little capacity to feel the reality of life for the bonded Americans or for their descendants today."

In a *Richmond Times-Dispatch* article on July 25, 1993, Dick

wrote an article about another, perhaps more persistent legacy—
a minimalist view of the potential of African Americans: "Those
who saw blacks as property did little to pass on to their children
a positive idea of what blacks could contribute to American
thought, politics, business and culture." People like himself, he
said, need to recognize and appreciate the extraordinary contri-
butions made by African Americans and to find a fresh vision of
their future role. Black Americans need to see whites ending the
denial that had blinded them.

In working through issues of race in his own life and taking an
honest look at the past, Dick was doing what the city of Richmond, founded by his ancestors, has been doing in recent years
to exorcise the past and break the hold of the Civil War legacy.

THE RICHMOND UNITY WALK

On June 18, 1993, black and white Richmonders came together
for an unprecedented walk through their city's racial history. In
ninety-five-degree heat some five hundred walkers from every
side of Richmond life, as well as people from other states and
countries, visited and marked sites along a two-mile route. Many
Richmonders, proud of their city's history as a birthplace of
American democracy, also wanted to recognize that two peoples,
Native Americans and African Americans, were being denied the
freedom and dignity the founders of the country had claimed to
cherish. As they walked together, they honored the dead and
acknowledged the pain suffered by all races, whether the Native
Americans who had first inhabited the area, the slaves who had
landed at Manchester Docks and been sold at Lumpkin's Jail, or
the soldiers who had fought and died for the Confederacy. Richmond Mayor Walter T. Kenney, who led the walk, said, "We did
not highlight the places in an effort to hand out guilt or vent
anger. We wanted to acknowledge their existence so that we
could close the door on the past and move ahead. This city will
never be the same again."

The premise of the occasion was that history's grip on the

future can be—and must be—loosened, and that this can only happen as the history is honestly faced and healing is genuinely sought.

The walk was initiated by Hope in the Cities, an organization that grew out of a grassroots effort to bring reconciliation over a forty-year period. From the beginning it involved black and white Richmonders who dared to cross the barriers by meeting in one another's homes, attending one another's civic clubs and associations, and undertaking community projects together. They owed their involvement to their work with Moral Re-Armament, which has a long record in this field. The walk was cosponsored by the city of Richmond and Richmond Hill, an urban retreat center. The Reverend Ben Campbell, the center's pastoral director whose vision inspired the walk, said, "Perhaps because racism started in its worst form in America, here on this ground, this is the place that the beginning of the end should take place."

The walk began with a Native American ceremony that included drumming, dancing, and prayer, followed by an invitation by Dakota elder David Larsen "to lift the veil of ignorance from our eyes and see we are all brothers and sisters." A *griot*, or storyteller, introduced an actor dressed as Patrick Henry, who declaimed outside St. John's Church the famous words that had been delivered in that church in 1775: "Is peace so dear and life so sweet, as to be purchased at the price of chains and slavery?" The *Richmond Times-Dispatch* wrote, "Moments later those words would be slashed by irony and the anguished shrieks of an actress grieving over the suicide of a fellow slave who hurled herself into a well after losing 22 children to slavery."

And so it went through the long afternoon as the roller-coaster of pride and shame challenged the participants. Perhaps because healing rather than blame was the object of the walk, minds and hearts seemed to be open to truths and insights in a way that other times may have been resisted or not even heard.

In Libby Park, hundreds paused to remember the site where Chief Powhatan's village had once stood. They looked down on the Manchester Docks, for a hundred years a principal port of entry for slaves. Earlier in the walk each participant had been handed a carnation. At this stop the flowers were gathered up and ferried down to the riverbank, where they were dropped in the water as a memorial to all the slaves who had landed and all who had perished in the "middle passage."

For the Reverend Tee Turner, an African American minister, the setting was emotionally powerful because of the statue of a Confederate soldier that towered above the crowd. He said, "When I saw the monument, I saw the pain that I have suffered as a black man. And then I began to look at it from a different perspective, and that was the perspective of grief." The whites had built the monument from their grief "and they need to be healed as well," the reverend said.

For many white Richmonders as well, the walk was an eye-opening and unforgettable experience. Ellen-Lee Meigs, who had grown up in the West End and never before visited the sites associated with slavery, said that participating in the Walk would end forever her attitude of "stinking superiority."

The Richmonders took this step believing that the negative power of a hidden history could be turned into "a positive force to begin to resolve painful racial division." They also believed that their city—in many ways a microcosm of America's urban centers—had a special part to play, not in spite of history but because of it. "It has helped me to reconcile and erase the line I drew between the North and the South," said Carolyn Leonard, coordinator of multicultural, multiethnic education in the public schools in Portland, Oregon, "to feel that I can embrace the United States as one nation made up of many diverse people who must work together."

At the end of the walk, as they entered the grounds of the state capitol, walkers were invited to write down on a piece of paper to be burned whatever might inhibit them from carrying forward an honest conversation about race, reconciliation, and responsibility. It was here that Dick Ruffin recorded the fresh insights outlined earlier in this chapter.

In February 1994 the city council adopted Mayor Kenney's resolution, which stated that through acknowledgement of its history "Richmond as the former capital of the Confederacy, has a distinctive moral mandate to take the lead in a quest for constructive race relations in this nation." On March 28, 1994, the council voted unanimously to set up a commission to establish the Richmond Unity Walk as a permanent national educational resource "as a contribution to the healing of Richmond's racial history, and as an inspiration to all the people of this metropolitan area and of other communities."

A video documenting the walk, "Healing the Heart of America," has been shown widely on television, and hundreds of copies have been distributed. The video is also being used as a resource and conversation starter in schools, colleges, and community groups. According to David Rusk, author of *Cities Without Suburbs,* the video "shows an important aspect of a trust-building process that can pave the way for successful metropolitan partnerships." In Chicago Alderman Richard F. Mell presented copies of the video to each member of the city council with a resolution that read: "If this type of courageous conversation can be done in Richmond, other cities including Chicago could begin honest conversations to heal historic wounds."

EXPANDING THE RICHMOND AGENDA

The idea of honest conversation is being put forward at all levels in the United States from the president on down. Sheldon Hackney, chair of the National Endowment for the Humanities, has proposed a national conversation in which we "grapple seriously with the meaning of American pluralism." One of his predecessors, William J. Bennett, speaking of the depth of the threat to the social and cultural life of America, said, "We need to have an honest, national conversation about these issues." In a speech at Virginia Commonwealth University January 20, 1994, Harvard's Cornel West said that the crisis in the country is a result of "our inability to speak candidly." Sanford Cloud, Jr., president of the

National Conference of Christians and Jews, has called on people "to get beyond the color and have a conversation."

Hope in the Cities is helping facilitate the honest conversations being called for. "Healing is the mission, honest conversation is the method," said Rob Corcoran, its national coordinator, who lives in Richmond. "Many conversations seek to enlighten and inform. Hope in the Cities also aims to transform."

This need for healing had become apparent in 1977, when African Americans gained a majority on the city council for the first time in the city's history and Henry L. Marsh III became Richmond's first black mayor. The old power structure was shaken and challenged. A period of confrontation and polarization ensued. Despite the change of leadership in the city administration, economic control was still firmly in the hands of the white business establishment, many members of which had little personal investment in the city. It was hard for African Americans to progress in other areas. A legacy of issues like school busing and white flight into the counties had particularly inflamed the divisiveness. A conviction was growing that something needed to be done at the grass roots to bring people together and support the vision of the new mayor that Richmond should become a "model for the nation."[1]

For both blacks and whites the decision to be part of a healing element in Richmond meant being willing to risk misunderstanding and rejection. Change did not happen overnight; in the words of Cleiland Donnan, it came "like onion skins—layer after layer." Donnan, a white business woman from an old Virginian family, ran a cotillion that had trained generations of West End teenagers in dance.

Over a fifteen-year period she reached out to African Americans, first professionally and then socially. The fears were palpable. "What will my friends think?" often went through her mind. She remembered vividly her anxieties as she waited for Winston and Janene Jones, an African American couple, to come to her home for lunch one spring day, and the first time she took one of her new black friends to her exclusive club in Richmond's West

End. Through her friendship with the Jones family, Donnan became involved in the community in a new and practical way, including working with Janene in her day-care center.

Over time Donnan faced up to what she called "my own false pride in my ancestors and all those beautiful tobacco plantations along the James River." She said that standing out, like a bolt of lightning, was the hurt and pain and suffering of slavery. "But, most of all, the seemingly small hurts stood out—my own arrogance, slights, my thinking that 'they,' the blacks in the East End, had their place and I deserved my place in the West End of town." Soon after this revelation, she had the chance to describe to an African American how she was brought up, to ask forgiveness for her "hurting ways," and to ask for help in becoming "part of the healing I knew was needed."

For community activists Collie and Audrey Burton,* who had been instrumental in the voter registration drive that had led to a black majority on the city council in 1977, overcoming prejudice and mistrust was no less difficult than for Donnan. Both tended to write off people like Howe Todd, a white assistant city manager, whom they associated with Richmond's white power structure. Yet when the Burtons began to meet such people informally in the homes of Cleiland Donnan and others connected with Hope in the Cities, they began to reflect more deeply about their relationships with and attitudes toward white people. Audrey said that the challenge given her by Moral Re-Armament, to scrutinize her own heart and motives in light of clear moral standards, enabled her to overcome the temptation to discount people like Howe: "Now I can be around anyone and it doesn't set off a time bomb."

Joyce Todd, Howe's wife and a former teacher in a private school, began to work at the Peter Paul Development Center, where John Coleman, its African American director, liked to say, "If you want to be a bridge, you have to be prepared to be

---

*Audrey Burton is profiled in Henderson, *All Her Paths Are Peace.*

walked upon." The Burtons, the Todds, and many others formed a growing and diverse network of people ranging from bankers to preachers who were interested in bridging the racial chasm.

PRACTICAL STEPS TOWARD DIALOGUE

By 1991 many people in Richmond had concluded that despite progress in many areas, the inability to talk publicly about issues of race, economics, and political jurisdiction was the region's most serious obstacle to progress. The Richmond area was faced with a declining tax base, an escalation of violent crime, and a complete breakdown of trust between the black-controlled city and the largely white county jurisdictions surrounding it. Numerous studies and enthusiastic "visioning" consistently failed to address the issue of how to build the relationship, create the trust, and generate the will necessary for real change.

It was at this point that Hope in the Cities took shape, bringing together people from all sections of the community in search of ways to address the underlying issues. At its heart was the idea that the participants would personally work through the issues together and, in doing so, fashion the trust on which to build.

As they met, they agreed that the city had more than enough organizations and programs; what was lacking was a serious attempt to address the lack of trust rooted in the racial issue, which was proving a stumbling block to all constructive initiatives. There was also a need for a group in the city that would be inclusive in its approach, free of the need to protect turf or claim credit for results achieved. As the public forums sponsored by Hope in the Cities became known as opportunities for unusual and constructive dialogue, city leaders became increasingly active.

Four principles emerged from this process of community building.

• Model, within the group that is attempting to bring healing, the change and the relationships that the group is asking of the wider community.

- Be inclusive. Take the risk of approaching as potential allies even those who are different or difficult to work with.
- Hold up a vision of what the community can be. Difficulties, if faced honestly, can become assets.
- Recognize that real change comes about when the hearts of people are changed. The energy and will for constructive change, including the political will, can only come through a transformation in the human spirit.[2]

These principles also became the basis of productive links with groups engaged in tackling similar issues elsewhere. People with helpful experience from other parts of the country or from other countries were invited to Richmond, and Richmonders, both black and white, traveled together to other cities. Working with individuals from Atlanta, Chicago, Los Angeles, the Twin Cities, and Portland, Oregon, the Richmond group produced a concept paper that focused on the need to deal with "the legacy of slavery" and proposed a conference that would have as its high point "a walk through history." They recognized that race in the United States, as one of them put it, was the most pervasive, guilt ridden, and least understood of human emotions, affecting taxes, housing patterns, communications and transportation systems, employment, and religion. As long as the issue of race was avoided, all would be damaged by it. If faced, however, it could be the start of a period of learning and growth that would give the country something to offer other nations.

A local sponsoring committee, which included the entire elected leadership of the region, senior corporate executives, and religious and community leaders, was formed to undergird the occasion. One of those constantly seeking ways to bring everyone to the table and to allow every voice to be heard was Dr. Paige Chargois, an African American Baptist minister. In the days leading up to the conference, she arranged for honest conversations among Richmond youth. She also orchestrated a dialogue between the members of the predominantly white Junior League and the Coalition of 100 Black Women. That week, a prayer breakfast organized by the mayor's office drew seven hundred participants.

The conference, "Healing the Heart of America—An Honest Conversation on Race, Reconciliation, and Responsibility," took place in June 1993. Whether it was because of the urgency in their own situations, a response to the concept of healing, or the courage and honesty of their Richmond hosts, hundreds of people from more than fifty U.S. urban areas and twenty other countries accepted the invitation of the mayor and the committee. The participants ranged from police chiefs to former gang members, from a Muslim imam to a Jewish rabbi, from the mayors of the Zimbabwean cities of Harare and Gweru to the deputy mayor of Roubaix, France, from community activists to ordinary men and women who wanted to learn how to get involved in helping their cities.

To Audrey Burton, one of the conference leaders, the process of planning the conference and the walk that was an integral part of it was itself an expression of honest conversation. Her involvement stemmed from the fact that people of European descent were bold enough to take to heart the expressions of hurt, fear, and anxiety they heard from African Americans and to begin a serious process of bringing the issues to the forefront for discussion. "Such an honest conversation on race has never before taken place in the United States on the spiritual level that characterized the Richmond process," she said. "Up until then race has been too often talked about on an intellectual level. The conference confirmed for me that rather than speak about racism, I am to speak about healing."

HEALING THE HEART OF AMERICA

The conference and walk were a step in the creation of a national network committed to healing the heart of America. In May 1994 Mayor Kenney was invited to give the keynote address at the sixth annual Brooklyn Unity Awards ceremony in hopes that the Richmond experience could be helpful in the highly charged atmosphere in Brooklyn following violence between blacks and Jews in the Crown Heights section. Speaking to two hundred community leaders on May 26, Mayor Kenney described that the process in Richmond "for moving past" and not getting stuck in the "blame game" was critical for real growth. "The mentality of victimhood or guilt-ridden shame," he said, "anchors us in inaction and diverts time and energy from the search for solutions. Regardless of past or present injustices, we are all responsible for our common future." He said that by bringing together individuals and groups that are engaged in similar activities, without the need to protect turf or claim credit for results achieved, Hope in the Cities had provided the arena for unselfish leadership and partnerships for building trust and hope.

One participant in the conference and walk, Bob Webb, former Washington bureau chief of the *Cincinnati Enquirer,* had worked on a newspaper in the South where he "used to be a conduit through my editorials and columns for forces fighting bitterly to preserve the status quo." When a new spirit was born in him, he began reaching out to African Americans for the first time. Linking up with others in Cincinnati who were engaged in this field of racial healing, he took the initiative with the mayor, the state treasurer, a rabbi, and a bishop to hold a Hope in the Cities forum. U.S. Appellate Court Judge Nathaniel R. Jones, who attended the forum, stated, "It is a lack of a sense of racial history that leaves people vulnerable to the demagogue." Former Ohio Governor John Gilligan said, "It simply will not do to ignore the continued existence of racist policies and practices in our society, in the hope that they will go away if we don't look at them." Episcopal Bishop Herbert Thompson, Jr., who had already held his own summit on racism, reminded participants, "We are in this for the long haul."

From Los Angeles to Philadelphia, from Hartford to Atlanta, men and women who were on the Richmond walk are today carrying forward the conversation in their cities. In Pittsburgh, for instance, a group of men and women, black and white, is determined to help dismantle "the vast racial imbalance at the heart of most churches, banks, corporations, and government agencies." Seven people from the Pittsburgh Leadership Foundation attended the Richmond conference. The foundation, which helped to launch Pittsburgh 2000, a bid to rouse the churches to address the city's needs, is regarded by many as one of the most effective urban initiatives by people of faith.

Chicago's response, which included a lunch and symposium, was sparked by a white lawyer, Margie Palmer. Mayor Richard Daley and seventeen aldermen joined the host committee for a symposium on race chaired by Margie and Alderman Richard F. Mell. Mell was one of the white faction who vehemently opposed Harold Washington, Chicago's first black mayor, thereby crippling the city government. Many people were astonished at the alderman's participation in the initiative. Speakers included Michigan Congressman Dick Chrysler and Jesse Jackson, Jr., now a congressman. Margie Palmer said, "At the end of the Civil War Lincoln had a vision to heal the nation. But he was cut down. Now we must pick up where he left off, to heal the nation."

For some months Hope in the Cities had been working on a framework of thought for the kind of bridge-building needed in the United States. After consultations in Chicago, a city that epitomizes the diversity of America, they decided to issue an invitation to citizens to join in a "renewed commitment to an American community based on justice, reconciliation and excellence." Described as A Call to Community, it was endorsed by many mayors, congressmen and -women, and religious and community leaders, including U.S. Senator Bill Bradley, and was placed in the *Congressional Record* of October 31, 1995, by Congressman Dick Chrysler. It was launched nationally on May 23, 1996, at the National Press Club in Washington, D.C.*

---

*Joining Hope in the Cities as partners in launching A Call to Community were The National Conference (formerly The National Conference of Christians and Jews), the YWCA of the United States, Study Circles Resource Center, The Faith and Politics Institute, and the Union Institute's Office for Social Responsibility. The diverse group of leaders at the press conference who expressed strong support for the Call included Congressmen Jesse Jackson, Jr., and Dick Chrysler; Paul Weyrich, President of the Free Congress Foundation; and Reverend B. Herbert Martin, a member of the Coordinating Committee of the Million Man March; Muslim American spokesperson, Imam W. Deen Mohammed; and Dr. Sidney Clearfield, Executive Vice President of B'nai B'rith International.

Bradley, in an earlier speech to the National Press Club on February 9, 1995, said that in cities across America where citizens are working together, words are the tools that build bridges between people. "The builders," he said, "are those in localities across America who are constructing bridges of cooperation and dialogue in face-to-face meetings with their supporters and their adversaries. Alarmed at the decline of civil society, they know how to understand the legitimate point of view of those with whom they disagree." Syndicated columnist William Raspberry, reflecting on the significance of the Million Man March and President Clinton's call for Americans to undertake the hard work of bridging racial division, wrote on October 23, 1995, "I've just seen a 'call to community' from a Richmond-based network that lays out just what is needed—at least for starters."[3]

CALL TO COMMUNITY

Call to Community, the fruit of the conversations and encounters around the country compiled by Hope in the Cities, lists seven points that contribute to partnership and responsibility:

• Listening carefully and respectfully to each other and to the whole community.

• Bringing people together, not in confrontation but in trust, to tackle the most urgent needs of the community.

• Searching for solutions, focusing on what is right rather than who is right.

• Building lasting relationships outside our comfort zone.

• Honoring each person, appealing to the best qualities in everyone, and refusing to stereotype the other group.

• Holding ourselves, communities, and institutions accountable in areas where change is needed.

• Recognizing that the energy for fundamental change requires a moral and spiritual transformation in the human spirit.

CONTINUING THE CONVERSATION IN RICHMOND

The conversation continues in the Richmond area. Central Virginia's public television station, Channel 23, for instance, initiated what it called a "frank and honest conversation on race relations" in May–June 1996. Seven weekly, half-hour, live programs provided an open dialogue on racial issues. "By acknowledging the realities of racism," said Executive Producer Marge Meyer, "we can hopefully move toward the recognition that character, not color, can emerge as the valid criterion for all people of Richmond." Those working with Hope in the Cities wrestle with how to fulfill the challenge of its mission statement to produce specific strategies for institutional change and how "to motivate individuals to change personal attitudes as well as the structures which perpetuate economic and racial separation."

With Richmond's homicide rate the second highest in the nation, Kenney's successor, Mayor Leonidas B. Young, a Baptist minister, called for a prayer service to heal the spirit of the city. Held on September 11, 1994, in Richmond's Cathedral of the Sacred Heart, it brought together Christians, Muslims, and Jews. Young said, "Any decisions or actions by City Council or the administration of the city are just pieces of paper without a foundation of commitment by people of spirit to come together for the uplifting of our city." This service is now an annual event.

SYMBOL OF A NEW ERA

One outward expression of the new spirit in Richmond was a July 1995 decision to erect a monument honoring international tennis champion Arthur Ashe, a Richmond native son. Ashe, who won the U.S. Open in 1968 and Wimbledon in 1975—the first black man to do so—as a child had been forbidden to play on the city's public courts in Byrd Park because he was black. Ashe, who died in 1993 of AIDS contracted from a blood transfusion, always said that his most oppressive burden was being black in the United States. In the last weeks before his death, he had followed with interest the plan for the Richmond Unity Walk.

The suggestion that a statue of Ashe be placed on Monument Avenue sparked hot debate. This gracious boulevard honors heroes of the Civil War. Whites had traditionally seen it as a monument to that war's heroes, whom they may or may not admire. Blacks, however, had seen it as a monument to men who had fought to keep them enslaved. Neither group was united on the appropriateness of the site for a monument honoring Ashe.

When the city council called a public hearing for July 18, 180 people signed up to speak. The packed chamber included the national media, who were anticipating a racial fight. Black and white participants spoke on both sides of the issue. Many views were expressed, but, thanks in large part to the tone set by Mayor Young at the outset, most people listened to each other respectfully.

In a statement on behalf of Hope in the Cities, Rob Corcoran said, "Arthur would be less concerned about where we put his statue than about the process by which we arrive at that decision. He would be pleased to see the city that once rejected him now facing its history with courage and honesty and opening the door to real change." He appealed to the council not to be diverted from the path of change and reconciliation: "Let us use this opportunity to develop a process by which we may embrace the triumphs and tragedies of our common history in a spirit of humility, repentance, and forgiveness."

After six hours of discussion, the council retired to a conference room to make its decision. Twenty minutes later they returned with a united decision to honor Ashe on Monument Avenue. "That our Planning Commission would unhesitatingly approve his statue for Monument Avenue is a testament to our progress, not a challenge to our heritage as Confederate capital," John W. Maloney wrote on July 11 in *Style Weekly*. "This is a city defining itself through its most public of symbols." At the groundbreaking ceremony Mayor Young said, "When you put spades in the ground and turn the dirt of the South, you will also be saying ashes to ashes and dust to dust to a history of racial strife." Columnist Bob Lipper wrote in the *Richmond Times-*

Dispatch on July 18, "Finally, Richmond has come to grips with its past and its demons."

A statue of the tennis star had been designed by sculptor Paul DiPasquale in consultation with the Ashe family. The idea was that it would stand in front of a yet-to-be-built Hard Road to Glory African American Sports Hall of Fame. This is the wish of Arthur's widow, Jeanne Moutoussamy-Ashe. DiPasquale's statue will, however, stand temporarily on Monument Avenue until the hall is built. Meanwhile, an international competition will be held for a design for the permanent Ashe statue on Monument Avenue. Joseph Seipel, chairman of the Department of Sculpture at Virginia Commonwealth University, believes this statue could be "a symbol of the new Richmond."

In the days after the decision, discussions around the city and media coverage and comment had, in the view of some Richmonders, a mellow quality not frequently seen in the city's public discussions. The Reverend Ben Campbell wrote that there was an unusual sense that something had happened. A city had come to a respectful consensus that something should be done in a certain way. Of course, there were many thoughts and feelings to the contrary, but even among dissenters there was not the usual darkness of loss. The course had integrity. "Perhaps it was the spirit of Arthur Ashe himself, a genuine heroic figure admired widely in Richmond and throughout the world," the reverend wrote. "Perhaps there was a suspicion that there were memories that really could be redeemed. Perhaps it was a hint that, with work and yielding, the future might hold more than continued despair and conflict."[4]

What made these understandings possible, he wanted to know. What made this meeting, which many thought would be a riot of ill will, end almost like a prayer meeting? What made even those disappointed in the decision feel that something good might have happened? What made eight council men and women appear to do something other than calculate political risk? What made those looking on do less than hope for failure? He answered, "It has been happening for some time; people just don't know it. Where racial brokenness is accepted in Richmond—not papered over—there are some good conversations taking place."[5]

Notes

1. Quoted in *New World News*, "Richmond—A model city?" January 7, 1978.

2. Hope in the Cities position paper, 1994.

3. Raspberry, A nation of poor listeners, *The Washington Post*, October 23, 1995.

4. "Monument," a *Richmond Hill Update*, August 1995.

5. Ibid.

14

Citizen-diplomats around the globe

[Would-be citizen-diplomats certainly need to be knowledgeable about any conflict in which they are involved. But they also need to be] knowledgeable about themselves and consciously seek to develop qualities of compassion, patience, humility, integrity and the capacity to listen.

AMBASSADOR JOHN W. MCDONALD, JR.
Founder, Institute for Multi-Track Diplomacy

WALKING THE TALK

John W. McDonald, Jr., who served the United States as ambassador under presidents Carter and Reagan before his retirement from the State Department in 1987, has had ample opportunity in his 40-year career to observe what works and what does not work. He has found that those people who are most effective are able to resist the temptation to offer solutions while encouraging those involved to take full responsibility; to stick with a problem because they care about the issue and want answers; and to seek nothing for themselves or their group. Such people, he says, "develop a capacity to listen not only to all parties in a dispute, but also for unexpected insights that may enable them to bring a needed factor to bear."

215

This chapter profiles some people who possess these qualities. Their experiences underline the important effect that personal decisions and motivations can have on society. By sharing their insights and experiences, they have been able to help others, sometimes in quite different lands or circumstances, to try new approaches. They are the kind of people you meet or hear from at the conferences at Caux. Most of them have spoken there. Like Mahatma Gandhi, they can say, "My life is its own message."

Cynicism feeds on the dishonesty of those in authority, and corruption is often more deadly than coups in the life of a nation. At the heart of any valid contribution to resolving conflict must be the integrity that inspires trust.

A CYPRUS CUSTOMS OFFICIAL MAKES RESTITUTION

Cypriot nationalist Spyros Stephou had just primed the bomb in the hold of the ship when a British patrol stopped by the ship's ladder and started a conversation.* Crouched by the ticking bomb, Stephou knew that if he were discovered he would face the death penalty; if he stayed he would be blown up with the ship. He managed to get out just moments before the ship was destroyed by the bomb. It was one of a hundred bombs he and his wife, Maroula, had smuggled into the port of Famagusta during his country's struggle for independence.

For the next forty years Stephou worked in the Cyprus Customs Service, retiring as deputy director. Because of his experience in dealing with corruption, today his services are much in demand in newly independent countries faced with setting up new institutions.

In the late 1950s, as a member of EOKA, the Cypriot independence movement, Stephou had been under orders from General

---

*Stephou's experiences are drawn from speeches he has given at Caux and at other conferences.

Grivas not to gamble, smoke, or drink for security reasons. But this warning had not deterred him. He says, "I was fighting with my wife against the British by day, and we were fighting against each other at night because of my gambling and drinking." When independence came in 1960, the fight against the British stopped; but the fights in Stephou's household continued.

In 1960 Stephou was invited to Caux. His first reaction when he heard people speaking about building a better world was that, if they really wanted that, they should change the British, in his view, the only obstacle. On returning home, Stephou realized that he had not brought his wife a present—not even a souvenir. "I knew I was not a good husband, but I never thought I was that bad," he says. His mind also went to their fellow fighters in the port. Although he and his colleagues had been united in the independence struggle, with freedom they had become enemies. "We were about to kill each other because we wanted the high positions the British had left."

Worried about the divisions in his home and in his nation, Stephou decided to make a fresh start. "I was honest with my wife, telling her everything I had done behind her back. I asked her to forgive me." Maroula was understanding; she had already known almost everything he confessed to her. She said she would back him in his new approach. This positive reaction from his wife encouraged Stephou to carry out what he felt was the most difficult part of his decision: to be honest with his boss in the port, risking imprisonment.

"One morning I knocked on the door of his office and when I entered, I threw on his desk three bags full of clothing and other articles and told him, 'These are things I have stolen from the Customs stores, sir. I have decided to bring them back to you. You can inform the director of customs and you can call the police if you want.'"

Stephou says that he never saw a man look as confused as his boss did at that moment. He was astonished not at the things Stephou had stolen but at the fact that he had brought them back. He said he would not report the matter to the police, and

217

he would report it to the director in a way that would not threaten Stephou's career. Stephou never heard about the incident again, and over the years he enjoyed seven promotions. Eventually, he became the only deputy director who had not earned a university degree. These courageous steps in honesty became the foundation stones of Stephou's work.

Stephou had many challenges, particularly after becoming deputy director. But his refusal to condone dishonesty—whether in a senior church official who was trying to pretend that furniture for his home was ecclesiastical material or in a relative who had failed to disclose nine cartons of dresses for his store—helped build trust among his officers.

When he was appointed district director in the port of Larnaca and responsible for the only airport in Cyprus at the time, one hundred kilos of heroin were passing through the port annually. The drug smugglers used every possible bribe to get him to turn a blind eye to the traffic. "I was often threatened I would lose my head if I did not turn it." Within two years, however, the illegal drug traffic through the port was stopped. The U.S. government offered him a scholarship in appreciation for his work. The British government decided to pay for the training of customs officers and offered four drug-sniffing dogs for use in the port and the airport.

Stephou likes to point out that Cyprus is only a hundred miles from three continents and is the meeting place of three religions: Christianity, Islam, and Judaism. Though the island is still divided and the Turkish army is still there, he believes that the work of reconciliation he and his friends are engaged in exemplifies how different religions, languages and cultures can work and prosper together on their small island. In reaching out to the Turkish community, he says, "We Greeks must overcome our superiority and dominating attitude."

AN ENGLISH JOURNALIST BLOWS THE WHISTLE ON HIMSELF

Graham Turner is a tough journalist, not afraid to cross swords with anyone on the great moral issues of the day.* Graham believes that anyone paid from the public purse who serves the public should come under fierce but fair media scrutiny. His paper, the London *Daily Mail*, describes him with some justification as "Britain's top investigative reporter." Those who say there is no connection between a person's private life and the way he or she performs on the job, Graham contends, "are talking nonsense." According to Graham, "How a person behaves privately is how a person is."

Graham believes that because journalists are outside the power structure, they have a clear responsibility to use honest methods of investigation and stick to the truth as it can be found. They serve as whistle-blowers in society, but "they had better be sure their own whistles are clean." If journalists are writing about politicians or actresses having affairs, for example, they had better not be doing the same themselves. How can a person be objective about the immoral behavior of leaders, he asks, when his or her own life is in a moral mess? "If you are corrupt, you had better leave your whistle at home."

Graham's views may not be acceptable to all his peers, but he is reinforcing them by the way he lives. He was a prime mover in setting up the International Communications Forum, a worldwide network of men and women in all branches of the communications field who want to be responsible not only for the quality of their work but also for its effect on society. He believes too that in view of the crises facing the world, people who work in the media have to offer solutions, not merely describe problems. It is their duty to offer hope and perspective for the world, elevating the noble as well as reporting the sordid. "How well we

---

*Turner has told his experiences at various events organized by the International Communications Forum.

perform that function," he says, "will have a profound effect on the direction of our civilization."

Graham, the first economics correspondent for BBC television, has not always held these convictions. Some years ago, he decided to write a book about money. Along the way, however, the subject changed because, as he wrote in the foreword, he had decided to live like a Christian again after having forsaken his faith in favor of making a name for himself in the world. In the book, *More Than Conquerors*, he wrote:

> It is perhaps worth saying that my change of direction involved paying a visit to the tax man to admit that the way I had been filling in my tax returns hadn't been all that might be expected of a serious-faced young man who was regularly appearing on television indicating that our economic masters were not behaving as they should!

The English journalist had been falsifying his expense accounts "with an expertise born of long practice." These accounts always included a monthly lunch with a gentleman described as "the senior economic adviser to the Treasury," a legitimate expense if the gentleman had only existed. The restitution to the British government and to his employer, the BBC, cost him £2,000. The revenue agent said, "We have no procedure for this." His BBC boss was embarrassed by the gesture. Because the boss had no idea where the returned money should go, it eventually ended up in the BBC War Memorial Fund.

Graham says that £2,000—probably £15,000 in today's currency—was a small price to pay for a clear conscience and increased effectiveness in his journalism. Incidentally, at that point Graham had three small children and had just gone freelance; he had no money to spare. Two months later he won a national journalism prize. The prize was £2,000.

GIVING EVERYONE A PLACE AT THE TABLE

Inclusion is a key word when it comes to resolving conflicts. The question Frank Buchman asked in 1946—"Where are the Germans?"—was important for the Germans. It was also important in demonstrating the concept for those from other countries. The readiness to include Germans and Japanese at Caux as equals so soon after World War II not only raised their morale but also helped motivate them to rebuild their nations on a different basis. Reaching out to people who are different is a vital step in the inclusion process. Chapter 13 on healing the heart of America indicated how some are doing this in the United States. In other countries too courageous individuals are doing the same.

AN INDIAN FROM EAST AFRICA MAKES A DIFFERENCE IN BRITAIN

"We have learned not just to react to events; in a multiracial city, you need to be two steps ahead." The speaker is Hari Shukla, who was head of the Race Equality Council of Tyne and Wear in England for nineteen years.[1] In this area of a million people, fifty-six languages are spoken; in some localities people from Asia, Africa, and the Caribbean and other minorities make up 60 percent of the population. With such racial diversity, unrest, even riots, would be expected. But Newcastle, where Shukla lives, has been relatively free of the racial disturbances that have plagued some other British cities. Shukla was decorated by Queen Elizabeth in 1984 for his contribution to racial harmony.

Some 2.4 million British citizens are from developing countries. A 1995 poll conducted for the *Guardian Weekly*, along with other surveys, indicates that racism remains a significant feature of British life and that black Britons are increasingly alienated. Another study by the Policy Studies Institute suggests that although black Britons have much in common with their white peers, both culturally and socially, "they found it difficult to lay claim to be British [because they felt] the majority of white Britons really believed that only white people could be British."[2]

Racial divisions are often allied closely to economic circumstances: Unemployment within the black community, according to government statistics, is twice as high as among whites. Britain's Home Office acknowledges that there may be as many as 130,000 racial incidents a year, with many of these landing in the laps of Race Equality Council officials like Shukla.

Shukla came to Britain in 1973 from East Africa. When he was appointed by the city, he was the only full-time community relations officer. By 1985 he had twelve full-time and thirty part-time staff. The previous Community Relations Council had folded due to the confrontational approach of his predecessor. "Right from the start," says Shukla, "I decided to follow a policy of cooperation and not to engage in confrontation. I also decided to be frank."

With Shukla's encouragement the various minorities began to cooperate, to form friendships, and to make a fuller contribution to the city. Asked to prepare curry for a thousand people to celebrate Chinese new year, Shukla enlisted the help of two police officers. The Sikhs offered the use of the kitchen attached to their temple. "So two Christians helped a Hindu, peeling potatoes and lifting heavy pots, to make curry in a Sikh temple for the Chinese new year," Shukla says.

In Newcastle representatives of the police, social services, and housing meet daily to review and anticipate events in the city. There is a five-language phone bank that residents can call to report police harassment, and they get a response in a language they understand.

"The name of the game is to listen," says the police officer in charge of community relations. "Too many organizations don't listen to what people want." He says the community is benefiting from a richness and diversity as individuals learn to understand different cultures. Children are growing up with a better understanding of the world because of the variety of people they come in contact with.

Shukla feels that the establishment of strong, positive relations between the police and the ethnic communities is a key to resolving problems. He believes daily communication is vital to maintain the confidence of minorities.

In the 1970s there was considerable hostility between the police and the ethnic communities. This animosity has been replaced with trust. In seventeen years there have been only about a dozen formal complaints. In 1979 one of Newcastle's mosques was firebombed by extreme right-wingers. Within an hour the chief of police, the leader of the City Council, the rabbi, and the bishop were all at the scene. It was they, not the Muslims, who spoke to the media and expressed outrage at the event. Police officers started a fund from their own pockets and presented the imam with a check for £500.

Outside events sometimes threaten the unity of the community. For instance, when Indira Gandhi was assassinated in India in 1984, Shukla and his colleagues called together the city's community leaders, including Hindus and Sikhs, and the authorities and managed to avert a clash at a memorial ceremony for the Indian prime minister. Later, members of all communities took part in a service of reconciliation in Newcastle's cathedral, with prayers for peace in India said in the language of each group. Similarly, during the Gulf War the city council called together the leaders of the Kuwaiti and Iraqi communities in the city. Some of the Kuwaitis were in financial difficulties because they could get no money from home. The Iraqi community was among those who decided to help pay the Kuwaitis' bills. Conflict was averted.

The most serious test came in 1992, when riots started among young unemployed people after two joyriders were killed in a car crash during a police chase. Although the ethnic communities were not involved, Shukla knew that those who instigate riots often look for added fuel. Fearing that an attack on members of an ethnic minority could provoke racial conflict, Shukla and his colleagues identified likely targets, such as restaurant owners who go home late at night. It took much detailed work to ensure that these people received police protection at vulnerable times, but Shukla believes that these efforts helped minimize racial conflict during the riots.

Shukla's media committee has taken imaginative initiatives. Every three months the committee invites newspaper editors and the heads of the TV stations to a working lunch to give the media executives firsthand knowledge of the different cultures in the community. Every two months the more junior newspaper and TV reporters are invited to a meeting with community leaders. Thus, when potentially divisive issues come up, the media people know the ethnic leaders personally.*

Although Shukla has retired from his post in Newcastle, he remains involved in a nationwide campaign to deal with many of the same issues he has tackled in his city for years. He is a member of a broad coalition, Hope in the Cities, which describes itself as "a partnership of people from different backgrounds whose aim is to make Britain a home for all who live in it." It is allied with the coalition of the same name in the United States. A former chief executive of Liverpool, Alfred Stocks, explained the belief that unites the members: "Without trust no matter how good the plans, they will not work; with trust you can do almost anything." When people accept change in themselves, they can become "catalysts of change in others."

---

*In 1993 while Prime Minister John Major was taking his turn as president of the European Community, British cities staged festivals. Newcastle's festival highlighted its multicultural society. A joint statement by the leaders of nine communities in the city stated:

We affirm our desire to promote respect and tolerance for the integrity of each others' beliefs, cultures and traditions. This desire arises not only from our common humanity, but also from our being people of faith and people of prayer. We recognize that as neighbors we have responsibilities to the community, the world and ourselves. We therefore urge all citizens both religious and nonreligious to put aside intolerance, prejudice and divisiveness to attain peaceful and fruitful co-existence in our area.

A MUMBAI WOMAN HELPS BRING PEACE TO A 'WAR ZONE'

"We have a network of people determined not to let our city go to pieces again, not to allow our police force to become so dehumanized that we could have another problem like 1992–93," says Sushobha Barve.[3] The city is Mumbai (formerly Bombay), and the problem she is referring to is the breakdown of law and order after the destruction of an ancient Muslim shrine, Babri Mosque, by Hindu militants. Sushobha, a Hindu, describes that destruction as "morally, ethically and legally totally wrong." It led to hundreds of deaths, bomb blasts on the scale of those that shook New York's World Trade Center in 1994, and a city numbed by fear. It catapulted her into action, even to the point of her risking her life by going to stay in one of the most polarized Muslim areas of the city.

Through Sushobha's determination to build bridges between the different religious groups, relationships of trust have been established, and confidence has begun to be restored. Realizing the importance of working with the police and creating trust between them and the citizens, she became involved in helping to set up peace meetings between communities and citizen-police committees attached to police stations. These committees are approved by the state government and the Mumbai police commissioner.

By the beginning of 1996 citizen-police committees were operating at twenty-four police stations. Week by week local representatives meet with the police, tackling grievances on issues ranging from removing impediments to employment to defusing tensions over the showing of a film deemed by some Muslims to be offensive to their religion.

The former police commissioner of what was then Bombay, Julio Ribeiro, wrote in the January 18, 1996, issue of the *Times of India*:

The biggest success has been recorded at Imamwada. . . . This area has been a flashpoint for communal strife in the recent past. Hindus and Muslims live in separate *chawls* (low-income dwellings), at stonethrowing distance of each other. Whenever a minor quarrel erupts, bottles and stones fly, acid is flung. Ms. Barve sat with these boys in the presence of police officers and got them to play with each other instead of fight. Table tennis, volleyball and cricket keep these young people busy. The local police also participate in the games. A reading room has been planned. The new leadership is more concerned with common problems affecting both Hindus and Muslims and has jointly approached police and municipal officers to solve nagging everyday problems such as water supply.

For some problems, says Sushobha, there are no answers. What has happened cannot be undone. But the divisions are made worse because no one has the time to listen to others. Describing how peace is coming to a "war zone," the *Sunday Times of India* quotes Sushobha: "The fact that people in high positions, including the police commissioner, were willing to give time to listen, without arguing, brought psychological relief."

She says that her experience has shown that even the most difficult issues can be tackled if the people on the spot are allowed to become involved in trying to answer them. Channels of communication have to be opened. She told the *New York Times* on November 19, 1993, "More rhetoric for communal harmony isn't enough. If we could make these citizen-police committees work, in the long run they would help the social fabric of the city." Indeed, she believes that unless there is a long-term plan to mend the social fabric of the city, there will be grave urban terrorism.

Sushobha has been prepared for this vital work by a number of crucial experiences. When she was in college, soon after the Indo-Pakistan War, she had her first encounter with a Muslim named Abida. One day Abida spoke of her relatives in Pakistan, and Sushobha suddenly found herself thinking that she could not trust the woman. She had the uncomfortable thought that she should apologize to Abida for the invisible wall that she had allowed to grow between them. This led to a reconciliation that, she says, "opened the windows of my heart and set me off on a road to build friendship with Muslims right across the length and breadth of India."

In 1984 she had an experience that she describes as a watershed in her life. It not only shook her physically and emotionally, but it made her realize that anyone could become a victim of violence in today's India. She was traveling by train with a woman friend, Sarla Kapadia, when Indian Prime Minister Indira Gandhi was assassinated by Sikhs. In Sushobha's compartment were two Sikh businessmen. A gang of young people entered her compartment, hunting for Sikhs. The two women tried unsuccessfully to hide and protect the two men, who were dragged out, beaten, and set on fire. Sushobha was manhandled by the youths. She felt that God had protected her from harm, but she agonized about what had happened to the Sikhs in the train and those around the country. She asked herself, "How are we going to repent and cleanse our sins? Is it possible to heal the wounds between Hindus and Sikhs?"

She decided to try. She felt that she should write letters to Sikhs—some known by her, some not. As a Hindu, she wrote, she wanted to apologize unconditionally for what her people had done. Khuswant Singh, a well-known writer and Sikh spokesman, was one of those to whom she wrote. He replied, "I was in tears as I read your letter. As long as we have people like you around, we will survive as a nation."

Sushobha told a conference in India soon after, "The essential is men and women who are willing and dare to break the chain of hate and revenge."

After discovering that the two Sikhs she had met on the train had survived the ordeal she was able to meet them. From that time on she became single-minded in her efforts. She went to Pakistan to build bridges with people there. She went to Bangladesh to show solidarity following catastrophic floods and a cyclone. In 1989 she traveled to Bihar in Eastern India after a thousand people were killed in clashes between Hindus and

Muslims. And in 1992 she was mentally prepared to respond to the violence following the destruction of the Babri Mosque.

Another challenge faced her in Asia's largest slum, Dharavi in Mumbai, which had also been wracked by rioting. For a month she had been going there, spending twelve to fourteen hours daily, experiencing the tiny, dimly lit, one-room houses, open gutters, and common public toilets. She spent a lot of time listening to people recount their difficulties but always returned to her own home at night.

A Dharavi woman said to Sushobha, "You go away every evening to the safety of your home. What right have you to tell us to stay? You don't know what it means to be in a burning slum. You don't have to face the pelting stones and the fire."

Sushobha suddenly realized that she had no moral right to tell people to be fearless, to stay put and face the attackers, if she was not prepared to stay with them through the night. From that flowed her decision to move into the area to the consternation of many of her colleagues.

She often found the work there very frustrating and at such moments was overcome with a sense of utter hopelessness and fear. In the slum she kept her calm, but at home she wept uncontrollably. "Prayer, daily time of silence and the warmth and simple trust reposed in me by the slum dwellers kept me going," she says.

Through those days she came to realize that a peacemaker had to find her way into people's hearts and win their trust and confidence. "Sincere words alone don't do it," she says. "One needs to practically share their burdens. Justice is an important part of peacemaking. A society that does not have justice cannot have long-term stability."

She realized too that it was easier to be compassionate toward victims but tougher to open her heart to aggressors and to those whose political philosophy she did not share. She had the thought that she must pray for compassion for the aggressor, which meant praying for her own people, with whose actions she disagreed.

Sushobha believes that it is important in crisis situations to keep one's heart open to all sides and that whatever the historical wrongs, the majority community has the greatest responsibility to maintain peace and harmony. "If the minorities feel insecure and afraid and suffer from a sense of grievance, the majority must reflect on what in their attitude has caused [the minorities] to have such feelings," she says.

The Mumbai paper, *Communalism Combat*, wrote in August/September, 1994:

> A social activist, a retired supercop and the police commissioner of [then-] Bombay have together taken an initiative to re-open communication between hurt, angry, mistrusting Muslims and the city's police force. . . . Consciously avoiding any fanfare or publicity, a beginning has been made in an effort to heal wounds that run very deep. . . . Not everyone is satisfied with the explanations, prepared to forget the past and look to the future without some clearcut guarantees in advance. But in a few parts of the city, despite initial reservations, some Muslims have decided that the exercise should be given a decent try.

A NIGERIAN EMIR SHELTERS IBOS

The emir of Kano, the political and spiritual head of ten million Muslims in northern Nigeria, has been on the throne more than thirty years and is regarded as one of the best traditional rulers in his country.[4] He has been chairman of the Emir's Conference of Nigeria, is a former ambassador to Senegal, and has served as chancellor of Nsukka, Ibadan, and Maiduguri Universities. As a young man he was chief of police in Kano and saw with his own eyes the corruption and misuse of power by authorities. He intervened on the side of the poor and oppressed.

The emir's main preoccupation for many years has been to work for the unity of Nigeria's various tribes. The largest tribes in Nigeria are the Muslim Hausas in the north and the Yorubas and Ibos from the predominantly Christian south. The emir also cares about the environment "given to us by God to enjoy, protect and preserve for generations to come." For twenty-five years he has spearheaded campaigns to counter the spread of the Sahara Desert southward.

Various incidents over the years testify to the emir's influence. In 1976, for instance, the head of state, Murtala Mohammed, who was a Muslim from Kano, was assassinated. Radio Cotonou asserted in a broadcast in the Hausa language to northern Nigeria that Christians in the south had assassinated the head of state because he was a Muslim and that Muslims were going to retaliate. Ibos in the north began packing as they had during the civil war.

That evening the emir went on the radio and appealed for calm. "What has happened is not a religious affair," he said. "It must have been the work of misguided officials. Do not take the law into your own hands, let Allah do his will." This appeal, in Hausa, was aired several times. That night too another ruler, the sultan of Sokoto, repeated the same plea nationally over Radio Nigeria. Nothing more was heard of the troubles. A week or two later the new Nigerian head of state came to Kano to express condolences on the death of his predecessor and to thank the emir for his action to calm the people.

In 1987 religious riots in Kafanchan spread to Kaduna and Zaria. Some 150 Christian churches in Kaduna and many mosques in the area were burned. Many Christians fled from the north. There was "a real possibility of a religious war," according to the British Catholic weekly, *The Tablet*. Some of the anti-Christian instigators came to Kano. The emir immediately came out of his palace to meet them and hear their complaints.

"This is not the way," he told them firmly. "Take the lawful way." The popular Nigerian magazine, *Newswatch*, commented later that, but for the emir's timely intervention, riots would have spread to Kano and from there to the rest of the country.

Only a month after the riots, Anglican Bishop S.I. Kale traveled from Lagos to join the emir at a conference in Kano on the theme, "New Horizons for Africa." At the conference the emir insisted on seating Bishop Kale on his right and the Anglican

Bishop of Kano, B.B. Ayam, on his left. "We must unite, Christians and Muslims," he said, "to fight the enemies that endanger the unity of our country: corruption and division with mistrust."

Speaking at a conference in India in 1989, the emir described how peace and trust had been restored between Hausas and Ibos after the 1967–70 civil war. "We were instrumental in arranging the final resolution of the conflict," said the emir, "by holding secret meetings with some of our friends with whom we were able to maintain our personal friendship throughout this conflict."

Before the war began the emir had saved hundreds of Ibos by hiding them in his palace. Afterward, he said, "It pleased God to enable us to help heal the wounds and scars of the war by arranging the return of their property as well as all proceeds realized from rents in their absence. The Ibos showed a magnanimous spirit of clemency and gratitude to our people."

It was his "unshakable belief," the emir said, that the way out of international and intracommunal conflicts is "for those of us who are privileged to be national or community leaders to be true to our conscience, admit our errors to ourselves, concede the rights of those on the other side and resolve to live in peace, fellowship and concord with our brethren."

GETTING BEYOND BITTERNESS

In 1987 Gordon Wilson lay under the rubble of a bomb blast in Enniskillen, Northern Ireland, holding the hand of his twenty-year-old daughter as she died. Her last words to him were, "Daddy, I love you very much." On TV the next day Gordon said, "Marie's last words were of love. It would be no way for me to remember her by having words of hatred in my mouth." Through his demeanor he struck a blow for a new Ireland that still reverberates.

Whether in Northern Ireland, northeast India, or on the Pacific island of Fiji, the willingness to move beyond personal antipathies is contributing to the hope that in the next millennium humankind will find new ways of living together in peace.

AN INDIAN SEPARATIST BECOMES A CATALYST FOR UNITY

Northeast India is a sensitive, strategic area. It was there that the Japanese advance was halted in World War II and that Chinese troops entered India in 1962. Divisions of the Indian army are stationed there permanently. Its 90,000 square miles are connected to the rest of the country by a narrow railway track, a thin road, and a fragile pipeline. Some part of the population are tribal people, living mostly in the hills. A large number are Christians. The Assamese and Bengalis, Hindu and Muslim, live in the plains.

The people of the hills and plains have a history of violent confrontation. In the 1960s the people of the Khasi and Garo hills, then part of Assam, were agitating for their own state. At the end of 1967 *Weekend Review* stated, "It is too late for a rapprochement—a hill/valley compromise is now no longer possible." In 1968 the *Indian Express* carried an editorial asking, "Will Assam be a second Vietnam?"

Yet on April 2, 1970, 100,000 people gathered peacefully on the parade ground of Shillong for the inauguration of a new hill state, Meghalaya (Abode of the Clouds). Prime Minister Indira Gandhi told the crowd that the creation of the state showed that "even the most intractable human problems can be solved amicably."

This time the *Indian Express* commented, "The birth of the 'Abode of the Clouds' seems to have generated a climate of goodwill which few could have believed possible even a few months ago."

A new spirit was evident between the peoples of the hills and of the plains. A few weeks earlier B.K. Nehru, the governor of Assam and Nagaland, had told the Assam legislature, "Seldom have such far-reaching constitutional changes been brought about with so much goodwill and understanding."

There was little doubt in the minds of even his political opponents that Stanley Nichols-Roy was one of the catalysts for that new spirit.[5] He was sworn in that day as a cabinet minister.

232

Stanley Nichols-Roy was a dynamic, broad-shouldered man whom a Shillong paper had once described as "a human steamroller." His father, the Reverend J.J.M. Nichols-Roy, had been a leader of the Khasi people, had served in the Assam cabinet, and had been in the Constituent Assembly that had produced India's constitution.

In 1960 Stanley was appointed General Secretary of the All Party Hill Leader's Conference, newly formed to fight for a separate state for the hill areas of Assam. In 1967 extremists in his own party were attacking him for not threatening to resort to violence if statehood was withheld. People outside the party were saying that he was destroying India's unity by demanding a separate state.

It was a discouraged Stanley who attended a dinner in Delhi composed of people who were planning to go to a conference at Asia Plateau, a center of reconciliation set up by Rajmohan Gandhi. They described to him how situations had been transformed and bitter people had been reconciled with their enemies at Asia Plateau and Caux. A German woman spoke of the experience at Caux of Irène Laure and of the reconciliation between France and Germany. "I said to myself at that moment," Stanley commented later, "that this could be the solution for our situation." Intrigued by what he had heard about Asia Plateau, he decided to go there and took with him a party of thirty-two from the northeast of India.

At Asia Plateau Stanley met political figures from many countries. He also met Indians from the northeast who were dedicated to a different kind of politics than he was and who told him how their effectiveness had increased following their decisions to put things right in their own lives. Stanley's horizons were enlarged. He decided to do three things: to be honest with his wife about what had been going on when he was on tour; to straighten out his relationship with Chief Minister B.P. Chaliha, leader of the plains people, whom he disliked; and to stop thinking only of a separate state. He said, "I want now to care for all the people of India and for the peoples of the world in the way I have cared for my Khasi people."

Stanley returned to Shillong with a sense of hope. His wife, Helen, said, "I knew it was a new Stanley as he walked into our home. I was so happy after a talk with him that when I was driving through Shillong next morning, I found myself waving to complete strangers."

The governor's wife, Shobha Nehru, later told a friend that it was Stanley's honesty with his wife that convinced her friends that Stanley could be trusted. Chief Minister Chaliha said, "You know, that man Nichols-Roy is different. He used to be hard. He used to be stubborn. I am so impressed with his change that I am now prepared to work unitedly with him."

This is what Chaliha did. Chaliha opened his home to further the process of reconciliation. Political figures from other countries, like Irène Laure, were invited to speak about their experiences.

Other political leaders of the hill people also attended conferences at Asia Plateau. One was Hoover Hynniewta, who had been the first to articulate the demand for a hill state. By then he hated not only the chief minister but also Stanley. Jealous of Stanley's leadership, Hoover had turned to violence. He apologized publicly to Stanley for his hatred. On his return from Asia Plateau, he went straight to the chief minister to apologize and ask to start a new relationship.

The change in Stanley and others on both sides of the northeast dispute gave hope to many, including policy makers in New Delhi. The Indian government came forward with a proposal for the creation of the State of Meghalaya, to be autonomous in all but a few matters (which were to be managed jointly by Assam and Meghalaya). The offer was less than what the hill people had asked for and yet considerably more than what the plains people had said they would reject. To the astonishment of political commentators, both sides accepted the proposal. The All Party Hill Leader's Conference announced, "We resolve to give the plan a fair trial."

So it was that the new state came into being. Stanley said:

I am very grateful to God, to our people, both in the hills and in the plains, who had the good sense to arrive at a consensus and agreement. I am told by those who run national affairs that the resolution of this question received more support from all political parties than any other issue since independence. It only indicates that politics can be played in a different way. When we see that demands are generally accompanied by burning of buses, breaking of heads, killing, it is not easy to keep a group of people, traditionally warlike, to peaceful means. But the heritage of faith in our part of the country, plus something more in the last two years, has had a part to play in this settlement.

The joyous inaugural event was an unusual one for politicians. Everyone seemed to be giving everyone else the credit. Meghalaya Chief Minister Williamson Sangma praised the wisdom and foresight of political leaders in Delhi and Assam, who had made it possible for the Assam Reorganization Act to be passed in record time. He said, "We can set an example for the rest of the country of how to work together in spite of differences of language, culture and creed."

In the years that have followed Meghalaya has had its ups and downs. But Stanley Nichols-Roy, whether in government or out, continued to work diligently until his death in 1994, to maintain that new spirit and to share with people around the world what had made it possible.

AN ERITREAN UNDERGROUND FIGHTER
REACHES OUT TO ENEMIES

It is just as well that the Ethiopian authorities did not know the extent of Abeba Tesfagiorgis's involvement in Eritrea's underground struggle for independence when they abducted her from her office in 1975 and threw her in a six-by-five-foot cell with five other women.[6] In 1961 Eritrea, then in a loose federation with Ethiopia, had been annexed by that country, touching off a struggle for independence. Despite the six months she had spent in prison, the imprisonment of her husband and her father, and the threat of execution, Abeba would not divulge information about others. She even forgave the man who had betrayed her to the authorities.

After graduating from college, Abeba had gone to work in 1961 for Ethiopian Airlines in Asmara, the Eritrean capital, and was a member of the underground group at the airline company. She wrote two novels to address the social evils in her country and, as cofounder of the Eritrean YWCA, helped develop classes for women and organized conferences. She also founded the Relief and Rehabilitation Association of Eritrea and got permission to distribute grain, milk, and blankets to farmers. Alarmed at the way the program was bringing people together and creating a sense of community, the government shut it down, and Abeba had to operate clandestinely. In 1975 she was arrested.

Released because nothing could be proved against her, she went to Ethiopia. Then, as the situation worsened she and her husband went to the United States. Their two older daughters stayed behind to fight in the underground.

In 1991 the Eritrean freedom fighters finally prevailed over the Ethiopian forces, bringing an end to the war. During the thirty-year conflict 50,000 people were killed, hundreds were tortured, and nearly a third of the population of three million was forced to flee. Every Eritrean family suffered losses.

After independence Abeba decided to write a book about her people's struggle. Published in 1992, *A Painful Season and a Stubborn Hope* chronicles the sacrifice and suffering of the women of the independence struggle as well as their incredible readiness to forgive.

Abeba returned from exile in the United States in 1992 to help found the Center for Human Rights and Development in Asmara. She does not hate the Ethiopians who imprisoned her, believing that the war was often as much of a nightmare for the Ethiopian guards as it was for their prisoners. She thinks that those same qualities of selflessness, commitment, and caring that helped win the war despite every kind of difficulty are needed if Eritrea is to reap the fruit of its hard-won independence and give hope to the rest of Africa.

In July 1993 Abeba was asked to give the keynote address at a symposium on regional cooperation in the horn of Africa, held in Addis Ababa. She challenged the politicians and government representatives to use their education not to boost their egos, but to serve others. At this symposium she also told the group:

> Let accountability be first to our conscience. It is not only the government who should be held responsible, but the people as well. Mengistu did not pull the trigger that killed the Ethiopian youth during the Red terror. He used people who deadened their consciences.

Speaking at Caux in 1994, Abeba said, "Reconciliation and healing takes time but you win as an individual, as a family, as a nation."

AN IRISH NATIONALIST IS NOT HELD BACK BY TORTURE

The featured speaker at a 1994 meeting in Glasgow, Scotland, on the theme "From Ireland with Hope" was Paddy Joe (P.J.) McClean from Northern Ireland, who had been interned for four years in the 1950s and then again in 1971 for his struggle against British rule.[7]

When P.J. was arrested in 1971, he had been chairman of the Civil Rights Association, which had always stood for nonviolence. But after internment without a trial, he lost faith in the instruments of the state. He was elected secretary of the Internees Camp Council by the thousand prisoners in the Long Kesh Camp. In detention, during the "deep interrogation" that P.J. and others underwent—days when he experienced what he describes as twenty-four forms of torture—he lost more than fifty pounds. "I thought that the Government could never afford to release me alive," he says. The week of torture was only stopped when, through a sympathetic Protestant warder, word was gotten to Ireland's William Cardinal Conway, who went immedi-

237

ately to Britain to see Prime Minister Edward Heath. When P.J.'s case came to court, the government offered no evidence against him but kept him in prison. "No person I ever met," P.J. told his Scottish audience in 1994, "ever came through that sort of experience without hate."

P.J. and the others took the British government to the International Court of Human Rights in Strasbourg, France, and each won a compensatory award of £14,000.

In his years in detention P.J. had plenty of time to think. As a school principal and chairman of a nonviolent civil rights association, he had seen how much was expected of his leadership. With the craving for peace he saw on all sides, he took a fresh look at the hatred in his life. It was not long before he realized that his hatred was not going to answer the violence and injustice. Instead, it was doing him a lot of harm and blocking his effective communication with the young prisoners.

"My years of involvement in nonviolent protest and my previous life's experience in dealing with younger people in schools, clubs and family had told me that hatred was no foundation on which to build any sort of future," he told the Glasgow audience.

P.J. went through a period, first, of depression and then, of self-examination, which he likens to the stages of mourning: anger, blaming others, and threatening revenge, followed by acceptance of the situation, adjustment, and starting the journey again from there. P.J. continued his story:

> I began to see how to turn the whole situation around and how to set about building a society that really worked. Although my own personal hatred of what had happened to me constantly prompted feelings of rage and a strong desire for revenge, I knew in my heart that was a wrong approach either to living of life or in finding any sort of solution to problems. The only option for me was to cast off this baggage and in doing so communicate with others so that they could identify and do likewise.

P.J. believes that he could not have rid himself of his hatred were it not for the fact that he had won redress from the British government. With the money awarded to him, he went back to his hometown and bought the former police station, which had just come on the market, and made it his home. His friends teased him for having become "institutionalized."

Like many nationalists, P.J. used to believe that "a united Ireland," with the British driven off the island, would solve all problems. For years the Protestants in Northern Ireland, out of fear of losing their British identity, had built a virtual one-party state, by gerrymandering constituencies. There was discrimination in housing and employment, denying people's equal rights. But, he says, he had come to recognize that other people had rights as well, even those Protestants who did not want a united Ireland. It was important to create a level playing field "so that Catholics and Protestants and people of no religion could feel an equal part of society and have a fair chance to move forward."

P.J. says that neither Catholics nor Protestants, neither Irish nor British, are free of guilt for having allowed grievances to grow and fester. "Society as a whole has paid dearly because unfairness created alienation, and alienation became a breeding ground for terror. Even if the British government is not free of guilt," he says, "it is not responsible if I do not work for what is right, rid of any baggage of bitterness and grievance." While restitution for the past may be necessary, wrongs committed by others, he believes, must never be used as an excuse to remain sunk in a spirit of blame.

His country had all the rights needed to produce a settlement within a democratic framework. From everyday conversation it was clear that all people were ready for change. The fact that tens of thousands took to the streets during the 1995 visit of President Clinton indicated that they were welcoming the end of armed conflict and celebrating the peace. P.J. says that everyone, especially political leaders, had to grow away from the old habits of negative knee-jerk reactions and shooting down ideas just because of their source. "A cease-fire in the head," he says, "is every bit as necessary as the cease-fire on the streets."

Peter Hannon, also from Northern Ireland but from the Protestant establishment, writes in his book, *Whose Side Is God On?*:

> P.J.'s sense of outreach and initiative is remarkable. He sits down readily with those from all sides of the community, Unionists and Sinn Fein, the Orange Order and the police—to work to build bridges across barriers of different political conviction. He has his own firm convictions—and we by no means always agree—but his readiness to listen and to learn is a constant challenge to me.

P.J. represents his political party, the Democratic Left, at the Forum of Peace and Reconciliation that has been meeting weekly in Dublin Castle since 1994. The forum was set up by the Irish government as a means of bringing together representatives of the political parties in Ireland to listen to each other. He hopes that in time they will become accustomed to each other's viewpoints and will work together toward accommodation of those views. He finds the forum "a great educator and reconciler." In many ways it is a repeat of his experiences in the camp council in Long Kesh, "but at a more sophisticated and realistic level of debate." Of course, he points out, "We can go home at night after the forum."

A FIJIAN CHIEF APOLOGIZES FOR RACISM

Ratu Meli Vesikula radiates the self-assurance that comes from being born to a chief's family in Fiji and having achieved the rank of regimental sergeant major in the British Army.[8] But he is, he says, in a phase of change and healing in his life, an experience he would like his country to share.

"Fiji—the way the world should be" was the proud boast of the island's tourist brochures, until 1987, when in what he calls "one act of madness" the harmony was shattered by a coup that overthrew the elected government. There was violence in the streets, and Fiji papers ran headlines like "Suva—city of fear."

After twenty-three years' service in the British army, for which he was decorated by Queen Elizabeth, Ratu Meli had returned home. As a member of a family of hereditary chiefs, he felt it was his duty to use his training to benefit the country. "I loved my country," he says, "and recognized the need for economic, political and social change." He went to work in provincial administration, thinking that changes would be achieved by the normal parliamentary process, not with guns.

The coup was proclaimed "in the name of the indigenous people." Out of touch with events in the capital, Ratu Meli had readily accepted this justification and was soon enlisted as a leader of the Taukei nationalist movement, whose slogan was, "Fiji for the Fijians." The Indians they were attacking made up 48 percent of Fiji's population.

"I advocated violence, instigated violence, talked of sending Indians away from Fiji," he says. "I was in the thick of things." As spokesman for the Taukei movement, he even read a statement threatening to put Indians in the *lovo* (a Fijian oven). He became a cabinet minister in the interim government. When removed from the post, he led a breakaway and even more extremist faction.

It took Ratu Meli five months to realize that the coup had not been mounted to benefit the indigenous people but instead to restore people to power who "had broken the country's moral backbone." For the chief this realization was a period of "personal revolution":

> The change that took place within me involved the awakening of my spirit. I had come to realize that the "us" and "them" attitude I held was divisive and damaging. Once played upon by the use of race, it awakened prejudice within me and generated fear, hatred and greed. My group and I had become a powerfully divisive and damaging force in the land.

During this time of turmoil Ratu Meli met the Reverend Josefata Davui, who helped him through a phase of change and healing that made real what had been a nominal Christian faith.

"One of the first things my radical Christian friend said to me was that violence would never bring anything good for Fiji, that there was a better way."

For many months they met together daily for prayer, Bible reading, and fasting. "I began to look at my country differently," he says. "I saw a Fiji that included everyone, a multi-ethnic nation free of prejudice, hate and division and encompassed in love, where everyone felt included and strove to reach their full potential for the nation. For the first time I found in the effort to bring our people together a purpose for my life."

At a conference in Sydney, Australia, in 1989, he told of his new attitudes. "Two-and-a-half years ago," he said, "I was preaching violence and fear to the people of Fiji. But a complete transformation has taken place in my life, thanks to a lot of people who cared."

Suresh Khatri, from Suva, then spoke, saying, "I respond, as a Fiji Indian and a Hindu, to Ratu Meli, saying these words because to Fiji he has represented hope in the fact that man can change. This is a factor which is not often taken into account in politics."

Ratu Meli returned to Fiji with a realization: "God has no favorite race. We are all his children, standing equal in his sight. I began listening to God and found new ideas were put into my heart."

After apologizing to a man he had treated unfairly a few years earlier and to his wife, Elizabeth, for years of unjust treatment, "the thought came to me as sharp as an arrow that I must apologize publicly to the Indian leaders and leaders of other races for the way I had treated them." This he did through the English and Hindi press. "They were victimized and made scapegoats," he says. His apologies resulted in his being persecuted, arrested, jailed, sued, and labeled a betrayer of his own people.

New awareness about what had been happening in his country gripped him so tightly that he wanted to take on single-handedly those who had led the coup. But instead he learned to forgive. "In forgiveness everybody wins," he says.

In 1990 he cohosted a conference in Fiji to bring together people of different views and recommence a dialogue that had been lacking since the coup. At the conference at the University of the South Pacific in Suva, Ratu Meli said:

> I want to turn to my brothers and sisters from the Indian community. I would like to apologize for all the hasty words and actions I carried out three years ago. I ask you to forgive me for all those unkind words and unkind deeds I did.

Indians responded and took his hand. Y.P. Reddy, the head of a construction company that had been badly hurt by the coup, said, "There is a great change. He is sincere. He and I and all of us can work together for the betterment of Fiji."

In his effort to build bridges, Ratu Meli had earlier visited the deposed prime minister, Dr. Timoci Bavadra. "My coming was a shock for him and his friends," Ratu Meli says, "but he had his arms outstretched. It was a great day."

Ratu Meli has continued to work for understanding in Fiji, offering a hand of friendship even to those he feels led the country astray. He has shared his experiences too with others whose countries are threatened by ethnic conflict, from Canada to Cameroon and from India to New Zealand. "Emptied of bitterness," he says, "I became available for God to use me."

A further stage in his change of attitude occurred during a visit to South Africa, where he stayed with an Indian family for the first time. "I was looked after in a way I had never been looked after before. It melted my heart. There are good people everywhere."

In 1991 Ratu Meli had had a dream of paradise, where children of all colors played together without discrimination. It was so vivid that when he woke up he had the strong sense that he should take the message to South Africa. He bought a ticket, confident that the money would be forthcoming; it soon was—through a business friend.

While in Southern Africa, at a meeting of Commonwealth heads of government in Harare, Zimbabwe, Ratu Meli met Nelson Mandela. The Fijian said to him, "Nelson, I've come because I've a story to tell you. The story of my change and forgiveness and reconciliation and the effect on Fijians and the story of my dream where there was no discrimination and hate."

For twenty minutes he told the South African what had happened to him. Then Mandela put his arm around Ratu Meli and said, "My brother Ratu from Fiji. I thank you for coming all this way. I want you to know that I also have the vision for my country."

Ratu Meli says that three years later, when he watched the South African independence celebrations on TV, he remembered his dream. "This time it was not children. It was the citizens of South Africa. I closed my eyes and said, 'I have seen paradise.'"

The chief welcomes what has been achieved in Fiji since the 1992 general elections and "a proper working of the rule of law." He points to the cessation of violence, end of ethnic hatred, and prolonged period of peaceful coexistence as an inspiring story. He expects there may be setbacks along the way. He says that it is a long-term process but that "no amount of political maneuvering will succeed in breaking the will and aspiration for what is best for our country."

Ratu Meli believes that the will to put differences aside is alive in the hearts of his people. "When I think back to 1987–88," he says, "I shudder to think what terrible fate would have befallen my people had I not found a change of heart and been freed of fear, greed, and hate."

FOLLOWING AN INNER COMPASS

For many people the spur to action has been rooted in faith. Some speak of God's will. Others may refer to Allah or, as Mahatma Gandhi called it, his inner voice. Others may simply want to call it conscience. Writing in the August 4, 1988, issue of *The Times* (London), British writer Bernard Levin said:

Call it God, call it soul, call it spirit, call it the subconscious, call it a packet of prawn-flavored potato crisps, for all I care; it tells the truth. Reason later finds arguments to back up the truth (or, too frequently, to deny it), but that extraordinary and inexplicable moral gyroscope which we all have in us will bring us back into balance if we will only let it.*

Whatever the source, there sometimes comes to the human spirit a prompting or even a certainty that sheds light on some unexpected truth, spurs a courageous act, or leads an individual to a dedicated life. The stories that follow illustrate the belief expressed by former British ambassador A.R.K. Mackenzie that, "if we are willing to accept the discipline of humbly listening each day for the whispers of the Almighty, we can get the unexpected thought which will solve deadlocks."

A SUDANESE GENERAL HELPS END A CIVIL WAR

General Joseph Lagu says he is still a shepherd boy at heart. But he has also been a guerrilla leader and vice president of his country, the Sudan.[9] In 1971 he made a decision that has become, as *Religion, the Missing Dimension of Statecraft* affirms, "a poignant example of how a personal spiritual commitment at the principal-actor level can influence the outcome of a conflict." At that time he was the military and political leader of the guerrilla movement in the south in the first civil war between Muslim-dominated north Sudan and the largely Christian south. He had been fighting for eight years.

On December 6, 1971, the general was confronted with a dilemma. He received a message that a Sudan Airways plane had crashlanded in an area controlled by his guerrillas. There were twenty-nine survivors, mostly Muslims from the north. Only two weeks earlier the Sudanese army, whose policy at that time was never to take prisoners, had killed a number of Christian wor-

---

*Reprinted with permission of *The Times*.

shippers in a church. There was considerable pressure on the general to take revenge.

"Let us sleep over it," Lagu told his officers. He describes what followed:

> I had a sleepless night on a stretcher. "Christ, if you were here, what would you tell me?" I asked myself. The story of His having compassion on the hungry multitudes came to mind. He didn't want to send them away hungry. He would want me to have compassion. "But these are enemies," I thought. Then another conversation came to mind. How many times were we to forgive our brother? "Seventy times seven."

Lagu remembered something his chaplain had said to him in 1953: "The thought that comes in the cool of the morning or the evening may be a vision of God." He said to himself, "God may be giving you guidance. God Almighty has been talking to you."

The next morning the general called together his staff, most of whom shared the conviction that all the prisoners should be killed or held for ransom:

> I have already made a decision which some of you will not like. But you'll appreciate it is me not you who will stand before God to answer for a bad decision. I have decided to let them go unconditionally.
>
> "Are you mad?" they asked.
>
> "We are fighting the government not the northerners," he responded.

He reminded his staff that in 1955, on the eve of independence, Christian southerners in the Equatorial Corps had mutinied and killed their officers and any other northerners they could catch. "It gave a bad picture of the South Sudanese," he said. "I want to show the North and the rest of the world we are different. When these people go to the North they will be our ambassadors."

That is indeed what happened. As the general told a conference in Cameroon in 1994:

> They spoke well of the conduct of our men and the cause for which we were fighting, and their stories were well publicized. This caused embarrassment to the government who came under serious pressure to start serious negotiations with our movement. This resulted in the Addis Ababa agreement that ended seventeen years of conflict between the South and the North. The lesson I learned from the crisis is that it is rewarding to do what you believe to be right before God, as the silent voice tells you.

After the settlement Lagu was appointed inspector general of the Sudanese army and later became the country's vice president. But for refusing to be a "yes man," he fell out of favor with the president, Gaafar Nimeiri. Nimeiri was himself overthrown in a coup in 1985. After being briefly imprisoned and evicted from his home, Lagu went to England. He has since served as his country's ambassador to the United Nations. Now as a roving ambassador for his country, he offers his services to help bring peace.

In 1994 Lagu stood on the podium at Caux with another Sudanese general and ambassador, General Mohamed Zein elAbdeen, a Muslim and a northerner. They are both committed to working together for peace in their country. Lagu is ready to overcome his hate, and elAbdeen is ready to acknowledge mistakes made by northerners. He says:

> We generals are living in one room, very friendly. He starts in the morning reading his Bible, I read the Qur'ān. I have got something which we can share together because we believe in the same God. A just and lasting peace can only be achieved through a process of reconciliation, compromise and confidence-building.

A SOMALI AMBASSADOR FORGIVES HIS TORMENTOR

As the Somali ambassador to the United States and a son-in-law of his country's president, Dr. Yusuf Omar Al-Azhari led what he calls "a golden life."[10] But one day, "the hour of accountability" as he says, caught up with him. His father-in-law was assassinated, and a military junta took over the country. He was picked up at 3 o'clock in the morning, handcuffed, blindfolded, and put in a cell nine feet by twelve feet. Al-Azhari was to remain in that cell—in solitary confinement, with nothing to read, no one to talk to, and no one to listen to—for six years.

For the first months of his imprisonment, he was tortured daily. He was consumed by hatred and afraid that he would have a stroke or become insane or die. "My brain was trying to burst," he says. Then one night, he recalls, he knelt down at eight in the evening, soaked with tears, and asked for guidance from the Creator. When he finally got up from his knees, it was four o'clock in the morning. "Eight hours had passed as if it were eight minutes," he says. "I never had a better eight hours of prayer in my life."

His inner voice told him, "Be honest to yourself and those around you, and you will be the happiest person on earth. Don't limit yourself to earthly matters only, go beyond that."

From that day on, fear had no place in his life. It was, he says, "as if I had found a new identity." He was freed of hate, despair, depression, and the desire for earthly greed and enjoyment only. The next day the guards found a new person, calm, brotherly, and submissive. They couldn't torture him as before. "How could you have changed overnight?" they asked him.

Al-Azhari decided to accept prison life instead of fighting against it, dividing his hours into time for physical exercise and time to conduct debates with himself about his past. He spent hours thinking back over the wrongs he had done in his life and also reviewing the good things. Six years in prison gave him a unique training for life. "When I look at the scars I carry," he says, "they don't remind me of the evil things done to me. I see beyond them."

In January 1991 the Supreme Revolutionary Council, which had taken over the country, was finally deposed. The commander-in-chief of the armed forces, Major General Mohammed Siad Barre, fled to Nigeria, where he was given asylum. Emerging from prison, Al-Azhari went to search for his family and found them living in a hut in Mogadishu. When his wife saw him standing at the door, she fainted. She had been told that he had been killed trying to escape.

"Can you forgive a man who has done all that?" Al-Azhari asked at a 1996 conference in South Africa whose theme was "Healing the Past, Building the Future." "Can you forgive a man who has killed your father-in-law and put you in a cell where you could become a vegetable or mad or even dead and who has never asked for forgiveness? That's a big challenge."

One day he was overwhelmed by the feeling that he should forgive this man who had caused him so much misery. It took him two years. He says, "I asked for guidance and found I could no longer resist the need to forgive."

But how could he get a ticket to Nigeria? Al-Azhari had no money: His bank account had been confiscated and his land auctioned off. Three days later he was asked to represent his country at a conference of the Organization of African Unity to take place in West Africa and was thus able to visit the eighty-seven-year-old former dictator. He tells what happened at their meeting:

I went all the way there just to tell him, while he was still alive, that I forgave him. I could see tears flowing down his cheeks. I thanked God for letting me fill the heart of such a man with remorse. He said to me, "Thank you. You have cured me. I can sleep tonight knowing that people like you exist in Somalia."

Today Ambassador Al-Azhari is working unofficially to bring peace and reconciliation to his country, a country without a government, a judicial system, police, or schools and where at least 40 percent of the children die before reaching ten years of age. He is sustained by his prison experience. "Love had been planted in my heart," he says, "and I vowed there to serve my fellow countrymen and women, poor and rich, to reconcile and settle their differences with harmony, love, and forgiveness."

AN ARAB DIPLOMAT UNITES THE UN

In July 1958 there was a crisis in the Middle East: A revolution took place in Iraq. Neighboring Lebanon and Jordan felt threatened by the Iraqi conflict. At the invitation of President Camille Chamoun and King Hussein, U.S. marines landed in Lebanon and British troops in Jordan. Meanwhile the Soviet Union was moving armor south to reinforce Syria. At the height of the Cold War, the world was brought to the brink of a third world war.

By August 20 *The Times* of London was calling the situation "the most urgent and baffling problem in the world." The newspaper said that "any real possibility of an agreed settlement in the Arab world" had disappeared. Yet the very next day it would run the headline "Arab states find peace formula," and on August 22, "Unanimous UN vote for Arab plan." The paper editorialized: "Overnight an almost magical transformation came over the scene where until yesterday the General Assembly . . . could not see how to extricate itself from the maze." Even Israel had voted favorably.

Much of the credit was given to Abdel Khalek Hassouna, secretary-general of the Arab League.[11] Resting in his home in Cairo, having just returned from an exhausting trip to Japan, he was suddenly conscious of a feeling that he was urgently needed at the United Nations. Hassouna flew to New York and worked to bridge the gulf of bitter division between the two main groupings of Arab opinion behind which the great powers had aligned in hostile confrontation. The *Washington Post* said that the surprise revival of Arab unity was hatched in the Hotel Pierre in a series of meetings called by Hassouna.

Some scoffed when Hassouna first called in the top diplomats of ten Arab countries. But all came. Hassouna sought to raise the discussions above the question of who was right and who was wrong. He painstakingly put forward another criterion: the objective search for what was right. He believed that the Qur'ān opened the door of hope to the hearts of the faithful in amity with friends. He liked to quote Sura 60:7: "It may be that Allah will ordain love between you and those of them with whom you are at enmity. Allah is mighty, and Allah is forgiving, merciful."

A resolution was finally agreed on. Because the Arabs were united, every other country supported it as well. The *New York Herald Tribune* headlined its lead editorial, "Statesmanship from the Arab nations." UN Secretary-General Dag Hammarskjöld described the resolution as one of the strongest ever adopted by the United Nations. The *Washington Post* said on August 24, 1958, that the resolution was "courteously phrased, with no hint of condemnation" and called it "a triumph for Hassouna." The crisis was over.

One newspaper account attributed the resolution to "fast diplomatic footwork." To Hassouna it was more than that, although *The Times* called him "an expert in swift action in equalizing disputes and finding points on which two parties agree." Hassouna had been schooled in the Qur'ān as a boy and as a young man had studied at the universities of Cairo and Cambridge. He had gained wide diplomatic expertise through his service with the Egyptian Foreign Ministry and his four successive five-year terms with the Arab League. "He showed himself to be a servant of peace in an age of strife," according to Arabist Charis Waddy, "and saw in the precepts of Islam the hope of a just solution to the many conflicts and problems that confronted him."

Hassouna believed that there should be a consistent motivation toward peace in the mind of a faithful Muslim. He gave the resolution of the 1958 Lebanon crisis as an example of such motivation. The riches of the Qur'ān and the life of the prophet Muhammad were a living part of his search for contemporary

251

solutions. He saw his experience during those days as an example of God's direction in a difficult situation.

Hassouna said that had he not cultivated that habit of expecting guidance, he doubted whether he would have gone to New York. "As I returned to my room that night [after the conflict had been resolved]," he said, "I could think of nothing, do nothing but thank God."*

A U.S. SUBMARINER LAUNCHES A DIFFERENT KIND OF MISSILE

For seven years in the 1960s, at the height of the Cold War, Douglas Johnston served underwater, in Polaris submarines probing the defenses of the Soviet Union. A graduate of the U.S. Naval Academy, he had become at twenty-seven the youngest officer ever to qualify for command of a nuclear submarine.

Johnston would have described himself in those days as a hawk. If a nuclear attack was launched against the United States, he was ready to press the trigger that would initiate a retaliatory nuclear strike. He later served in the Pentagon as director of policy, planning, and management in the Office of the Secretary of Defense. Then he went on to teach at Harvard, where he set up the first executive program in national and international security for top-ranking military and diplomatic officials at the John F. Kennedy School of Government.

Times have changed and so has he. Today Johnston is executive vice president of the Center for Strategic and International Studies (CSIS), a think tank based in Washington D.C., where he chairs the program on preventive diplomacy. In this capacity

---

*During World War II Hassouna had learned that an attitude of listening to thoughts that come when attuned to God in prayer could bring inspired guidance into even the most difficult affairs of modern life. In 1942 as Governor of Alexandria, when General Rommel's Afrika Korps was pushing eastward along the Mediterranean coast, he drew on this experience in broadcasts that stabilized a situation of panic.

Johnston is particularly focused on the role of spiritually motivated people in resolving national and international conflicts. "We need a new paradigm," he told London's *Financial Times* in August 1995. "We can no longer base our security on a competition in armaments. It must be on the strength of national and international relationships."

Johnston believes that with the decline of the East-West confrontation and most of its regional manifestations, few conflicts of the future will be rooted in ideology. Instead, most will derive from clashes of communal identity, whether on the basis of race, ethnicity, nationality, or religion.

Johnston is the principal author and co-editor of his organization's *Religion, the Missing Dimension of Statecraft*. The book, which has a foreword by former President Jimmy Carter, contains seven case studies conducted by the center and, according to a review that appeared in the *New York Times* on July 9, 1994, "holds lessons not only for government officials but also for religious leaders willing to take initiatives for peace." *Foreign Affairs* said in its July/August 1994 issue that the book "brings badly needed balance into the discussion of religion and international affairs."

The research project at CSIS that resulted in the publication of *Religion, the Missing Dimension of Statecraft*, took seven years and $364,000 of funding to complete. Johnston assembled a highly qualified multidisciplinary project team whose range of knowledge spanned theology, political science, psychology, military strategy, sociology, foreign policy, and religious studies.

Johnston writes in the book's introduction that the focus is on individuals operating from a religious or spiritual basis because this aspect has been particularly neglected in the study of international relations:

Such persons are often better equipped to reach people at the level of the individual and the subnational group than are most political leaders who walk the corridors of power. They are also better attuned to dealing with basic moral issues and spiritual

253

needs, at times extending beyond the boundaries of their own faith traditions.

Johnston was brought up by parents who were non-church-going Baptists. On his nuclear submarine he volunteered to be the Protestant lay leader who took the Sunday morning service. But he says, "I would usually play poker all night Saturday and proceed right from there to give my sermon." His experience of real faith came later through dealing with a difficult situation in his life. "It's out of adversity that you turn to God for some sort of help," he says. These days, Johnston says, he feels his faith very strongly. He sometimes goes on weekend retreats to Catholic monasteries, where he finds the atmosphere especially holy. And for more than twenty years the former naval officer has been involved with the national prayer breakfast movement. It is through this movement that Johnston became aware of the effective work being done by people of faith in resolving conflicts between disaffected factions, sometimes even stopping wars.

In 1995, during the week marking the fiftieth anniversary of VE Day, Johnston was a speaker at the Royal Institute of International Affairs in London. He told a distinguished audience that although spiritual factors will play an increasing role in resolving political conflict, political theory has not caught up with this reality. Insensitivity to spiritual influences on politics, Johnson said, has led to "uninformed foreign policy choices," not least toward Iran and Lebanon. "I am absolutely convinced we did not fully comprehend the dynamics that were taking place," he said.

On July 16, 1995, He told an interviewer from the *National Catholic Register:*

It is my hope that religion and spirituality will become more widely appreciated as important factors in mediation. Though the book treats case studies on an international level, it's not difficult to extrapolate those same principles relating to trust and credibility down to the local level. It is not as though religion should become a tool of statecraft, it is just that the positive role of religion should be recognized and reinforced as the situation permits.

Johnston notes that spiritual peacemakers have helped to heal differences sufficiently frequently and effectively that they should command the attention and support of those who seek new approaches to the current world disorder. In a commentary that appeared in the *Washington Post* on April 16, 1995, he wrote:

Religious communities should bring their considerable, but largely underutilized, assets to bear in the task of peacemaking, and policy makers should encourage and reinforce, but not seek to own, such efforts wherever possible.

Notes

1. Shukla has described these events in many speeches. He was also profiled in *For a Change*, November 1988.

2. Statistics from *Guardian Weekly*, March 26, 1995.

3. Sushobha Barve is profiled in Henderson, *All Her Paths Are Peace*.

4. This discussion is based on speeches in Caux and at Asia Plateau, India. Isaac Amata and Hugh Elliott also provided information. The emir was profiled in Ukoku, *For a Change*, July, 1991.

5. The material on Stanley Nichols-Roy was published earlier in Henderson, *From India With Hope*.

6. Abeba Tesfagiorgis is profiled in Henderson, *All Her Paths Are Peace*.

7. This discussion is based on a cassette recording of the speech in Glasgow, communications to the author, and an article by P.J. McClean in the *Sunday World* (Belfast) on January 7, 1996.

8. Based on speeches by Ratu Meli Vesikula at various conferences and an interview conducted by the author in Caux in 1955.

9. This discussion is based on interviews with General Lagu. He was also profiled in an article by Henderson, "The Conciliator," *The Sun*, Baltimore, September 3, 1988.

10. This discussion is based on speeches at a conference in Bloemfontein, South Africa, April 4–8, 1996.

11. Much of Hassouna's story appears in Waddy's *The Muslim Mind*.

Remaking the World: Frank Buchman and Moral Re-Armament

MRA is a way of life. Its goal is global
transformation that is carried forward
by people of different convictions
and faiths who seek God's inspiration
for individual and common action.
As agents of change, they work
for new motives and relationships
at all levels of society,
beginning in their own lives.

MRA STATEMENT
Cyprus, November 1993

A VISIONARY AT WORK

In 1921 an American Lutheran minister from Pennsylvania, Frank Buchman, defined his aim as "a program of life issuing in personal, social, racial, national, and supernational change."[1] He never wavered in that intention, and by the time he died in 1961 his commitment had achieved extraordinary changes in individuals and nations. He had been decorated by many governments for his work of reconciliation; he was nominated for the Nobel peace prize, he was made the subject of a *Time* magazine cover, and he had served as inspiration of the Oxford Group, Alcoholics Anonymous, and Moral Re-Armament.

The term Moral Re-Armament dates from 1938. As the prospect of war loomed on the horizon and rearming was a priority for the nations of Europe, Buchman called for moral and spiritual rearmament as a complement to military rearmament. The concept caught on and was soon known as MRA. MRA was an extension of the work of the Oxford Group that Buchman had initiated in the thirties and whose origins went back even earlier. (A description of the Oxford Group appears later in this appendix.)

During his lifetime Buchman was never far from controversy. His efforts to redirect or "change" Hitler and those around him led to accusations of pro-Nazism. His labors to develop an ideological alternative to communism earned him opposition from the Kremlin. His commitment to faith and his strong emphasis on moral standards evoked hostility in those to whom such concepts were anathema.

THE BASIS OF A LIFE'S COMMITMENT

Like many inspirational figures in history and founders of orders, Buchman could point to a defining moment in his life: an experience at a church in Keswick in the north of England in 1908. This experience drew a line under the early part of his life, which had been productive but exhausting. Buchman had graduated from Muhlenberg College in 1899 and Mount Airy Theological Seminary three years later. Accused of ambition by a fellow student, he decided on the day he was ordained to start a new church in Overbrook, a Philadelphia suburb. He worked so hard at this undertaking that he became exhausted and had to rest. Traveling in Europe, he studied the Christian hospice work in Germany and Switzerland. On his return he founded a Christian hospice for orphans and destitute boys in Philadelphia.

Buchman had also been impressed by the work of Toynbee Hall, a settlement house in the East End of London, and a little later started a similar settlement in one of Philadelphia's poorest areas. However, because of clashes with his six-member board over its unwillingness to provide what Buchman felt was enough money for food for the children, he resigned. Exhausted once more and with much turmoil of spirit, he went abroad again.

This second overseas trip included a visit to the English Keswick Convention, an annual gathering of evangelical Christians. One Sunday he heard Jessie Penn-Lewis preach. She made the sufferings of Christ come alive for him in a way that years of church attendance and seminary lectures had not. For the first time he saw the great gulf that existed between him and the six board members and realized that his work had become his idol. "I thought of those six men back in Philadelphia who I felt had wronged me. They probably had, but I'd got so mixed up in the wrong that I was the seventh wrong man. Right in my conviction, I was wrong in harboring ill-will. I wanted my own way and my feelings were hurt."

That same day he wrote and apologized to the men, asking for their forgiveness. From that moment Buchman was a free man and also found a new effectiveness in helping others. Ninety years later those central ingredients of his experience—restitution and forgiveness—are seen in the heart of the work of those who followed him.

In 1909 Buchman was asked to become YMCA secretary at State College, Pennsylvania. (The YMCAs at that time dominated the religious life of most American campuses.) According to YMCA leader John R. Mott, Penn State was "the most Godless university in the country." It was there that Buchman developed the principles of his life's work. In so doing over a seven-year period, he not only helped to turn that campus around but also contributed to a spiritual awakening at Yale and other U.S. universities. The Yale University publication, *The Week,* wrote of Buchman's work, "This new evangelism of the twentieth century is transforming our colleges."

At Penn State, Buchman adopted the discipline (learned from visiting preacher F.B. Meyer) of taking time from five to six every morning, before the telephone started ringing, to prepare himself for the day and to ask God what He wanted done. He was encouraged by Professor Henry Wright of Yale to pursue "two-way prayer," listening as well as talking to God and writing down the thoughts he received. This concept of seeking guidance from God became the central pillar of his life and work. At this same time Buchman also confirmed his sense that a life of faith should be a disciplined life—that the reference point for behavior and action should not be conventional or comparative standards but something more rigorous and unchanging. From a book by Robert Speer, *The Principles of Jesus,* he derived the principles of absolute honesty, purity, unselfishness, and love as measuring rods for daily living. To him there was a direct correlation between clarity on morals and the ability to discern guidance from God.

LESSONS FROM ASIA

In 1915 Buchman left Penn State; he had been invited to India to help prepare a large-scale spiritual campaign. His main responsibility was to train Christian workers, but he also addressed large crowds of up to 60,000 people, an experience that convinced him that personal work, or "life-changing," was far more effective than mass meetings, which he likened to "dropping eye medicine from a third-story window."

In 1916 Buchman got a part-time job as Extension Lecturer in Personal Evangelism at Hartford Theological Seminary. This post allowed him time to travel, and for the next three years he spent many months in China, where he got to know Sun Yat-sen, regarded as the founder of modern China. Buchman's direct assault on the narrowness of some foreign missionary work and on Chinese corruption, concubinage, and opium-smoking produced dramatic results, both in getting Chinese leaders to take Christianity seriously and in provoking opposition from some church leaders. Sun Yat-sen said, "Buchman is the only man who tells me the truth about myself."

Buchman's biographer, Garth Lean, summarizing the lessons Buchman had learned till then, wrote:

During the years at Overbrook and the hospice, he had begun to understand human nature more thoroughly—and also to discover that God was reliable, that in a life of "faith and prayer" practical needs were met.

At Penn State he had found that people could change radically and that, through such change in individuals, the tone of an institution could be altered.

In China he had come to believe that what was true for a university could prove true for a nation.

Whereas Buchman spoke of Penn State as "the laboratory" in which he tested principles, he saw China as "the proving ground of the power to turn nations Godwards." Buchman always regarded his spiritual discoveries as having universal application. After his experience in the little church in Keswick, he never again considered that any other human being, however corrupt, was beyond the reach of the grace that had healed his own hate and pride.

Buchman's lectures at the Hartford Seminary, according to one of his students, Edward Perry, "were totally unlike any others in that sedate institution." His method

> mostly consisted of stories of people whose lives had been changed by God's power working through him. It was fascinating, up to date, real. His picture of a real ministry was not a matter of eloquent sermons and well-organized parish activities, but of meeting people's deepest needs one by one.

At this time Buchman already was seeing the long-term answer for the world's problems in a radical reawakening of faith. "I was convinced after my time in Asia that God meant me to bring a moral and spiritual awakening to every country in the world, and I personally felt called to give my whole time to that work."

He believed that a new leadership needed to come from the students at the universities, so he set up conferences to enlist and train them. Henry van Dusen of Union Theological Seminary was to comment on one fruit of Buchman's work later, when he wrote in 1934 that "of the fifty ablest Ministers on the Atlantic seaboard today, somewhere near half were directed into their vocation through his influence at that time."

EXPANSION TO AN INTERNATIONAL STAGE

In 1921 Buchman, attending a conference on disarmament in Washington, D.C., at the invitation of a British general who was interested in his work, became convinced that pacts and leagues alone would not outlaw war. He felt that the transforming power that he had seen at work in individuals needed to be brought to nations. Now in his forties, he resigned from his position at the Hartford Seminary. He had no base and no income except for a monthly payment of fifty dollars from a family insurance policy. He never again held any paid position.

Over the next years Buchman's priority was choosing and training new leadership, particularly from among the universities of the United States and Britain. Each year saw his work expand, involving him in further extensive travel. After one trip to South America where he observed the inroads being made by communism, he suggested to some young men that they should plan as thoroughly as the communists to bring a Christian revolution to their leaders.

The response to his work grew, and each summer between 1930 and 1937 he arranged meetings at one or more colleges in Oxford, where thousands of people would take up temporary residence to learn about his ideas. In 1933 five thousand guests turned up for at least one part of an event that filled six colleges and lasted seventeen days. Almost a thousand were clergy, including twelve bishops. A team of four hundred guests met with Buchman at 7:30 each morning. In 1934 three hundred Canadians and Americans crossed the Atlantic for the house party. In 1935 six thousand people attended, and meetings were held around the country. This work became known as the Oxford Group. Malcolm Muggeridge, summarizing the decade, wrote that the group had generated the only religious revival of the period.

Although the greatest response came from the educated and privileged classes, which had a strong sense of service, the group philosophy also appealed to working people and the unemployed. Oxford students went on campaigns in the East End of London, and East Londoners, including leaders of the unemployed, began to join the Oxford Group missions.

The progress in Buchman's work could be seen not only in its effect in numbers enrolled but in its profound effect on individuals, whether it was C.F. Andrews, one of Mahatma Gandhi's closest colleagues; Eric Liddell, whose life was commemorated in the movie, *Chariots of Fire*; or Paul Tournier, the eminent Swiss psychiatrist who wrote, "I owe him everything, all the spiritual adventure which has been my life." It could also be measured in dozens of what nowadays could be called spin-offs, like Alcoholics Anonymous* and the Reverend Sam Shoemaker's Faith-At-Work movement. Alcoholics Anonymous's "Big Book" contains Bill Wilson's codification of the Oxford Group's life-changing principles, which have become famous as the "Twelve Steps."

In 1993 the Roman Catholic Bishop Emeritus of Leeds, William Gordon Wheeler, looking back sixty years, said that the Oxford Group had taken Oxford by storm:

Against a background of the hunger marchers and general malaise in the country, the spiritual quality of the Group motivated some of the finest young men and women of that genera-

---

*Visionary though he may have been, even Buchman might have been surprised at the value others placed on Alcoholics Anonymous (AA) and its continuing relevance. Author Scott Peck believes that the greatest positive event of the twentieth century was when Bill W. and Dr. Bob convened the first AA meeting in 1935. He wrote in *Further Along the Road Less Traveled*, "It was not only the beginning of the self-help movement and the beginning of the integration of science and spirituality at a grassroots level, but also the beginning of the community movement." The origins of AA in the Oxford Group are described in Hunter, *It Started Right There*.

tion. . . . The simple challenge of the four absolutes and the fact of guidance set many free. . . . That spiritual movement of the Holy Spirit which was active here in my day is still at it, effectively, in the work of reconciliation and Moral Re-Armament, against the current breakdown of social relations where alcoholism, violence and consumerism threaten to tear God out of the human heart.[2]

SCANDINAVIA

In Scandinavia too there was a widespread response to the Oxford Group. From a Swedish socialist author, Harry Blomberg, Buchman had gotten the concept of "moral rearmament." He saw it as an apt description of what he was trying to do. Moral Re-Armament, or MRA for short, was launched in 1938 in Britain in the East End of London and in the United States at mass meetings in the Hollywood Bowl and at Madison Square Garden. In a speech at Visby, Sweden, Buchman made it clear that it was more than a change of name of the Oxford Group; it was a call to go beyond revival to revolution and renaissance. He called on people not only to change themselves and learn how to change others but "to reach the millions and save a crumbling civilization."

Although his efforts many years before to redirect China had seemed to be unsuccessful, Buchman still believed in the power of changed individuals, particularly well-placed individuals, to affect policies, and even relations, between nations. "Are we beginning to see that not only individuals but cities and nations may be different?" Buchman asked in 1935.

There were developments through his work in Europe during the thirties that encouraged him in this approach. For instance, a dispute over Greenland fisheries involving Denmark and Norway had come before the Permanent Court of International Justice in The Hague. The court had decided in favor of Denmark. This decision angered one of Norway's leading journalists, Freddy Ramm, the only newspaperman to fly with explorer Roald Amundsen over the North Pole. Ramm's intense hatred of the

Danes was reflected in his columns, as he tried to incite his countrymen and countrywomen against their neighbor. When the Oxford Group came to Norway, Freddy Ramm, ever the curious reporter, came to its first conference in 1934. He became so engrossed by what he heard that he did not open the bottle of whiskey he had brought with him. He was captured by the idea of what an individual could do in the world if he started making the changes he wanted in the world within himself. "The ice melted in my heart," Ramm said, "and a new unknown feeling began to grow, a love of people unfettered by what they could give me." As he began to face up to the things that were wrong in his own life, he realized that he needed to make restitution to the Danes for his hatred and for what he had done to turn his people against them.

Shortly afterward Ramm was one of the advertised speakers at a major meeting in Odense, Denmark. The Danish audience knew who he was. He simply described what had happened to him and apologized. He ended by asking the audience to stand and join him in singing the Danish national anthem. The audience rose and spontaneously started singing the Norwegian national anthem. The Danish daily, *Dagens Nyheder*, carried Ramm's words:

> The main thing I am here to tell you is that my greatest fault was the hatred of the Danes. My mind was poisoned with that hatred. I used my pen as well as I could in the service of my hatred and justified myself as an idealist. Then I met the Oxford Group with its challenging way of life. Now I am here to put things right with my old enemies.

Five years later World War II started, and the Nordic lands were invaded. Every day through his column Ramm found imaginative ways of maintaining the morale of his people. The Germans had him deported to Germany. In Germany he became ill, and the Germans decided to transport him back home. But the ordeal had been too much for him, and he died at Odense station.

Norwegian Bishop Arne Fjellbu, speaking at the end of the war, said that the coming of the Oxford Group to Norway was an intervention of providence in history. "I wish to state publicly," he said, "that the foundations of united Resistance of Norwegian churchmen to Nazism was laid by the Oxford Group's work."

As well as making individual efforts in the 1930s, Scandinavian politicians joined together to create the "Oslo states," a bold but unsuccessful effort by the smaller countries to unite to avert war. The editor of *The Spectator,* Wilson Harris, noted that the cooperation of Norwegian and Finnish political leaders at the League of Nations was due to their association with the Oxford Group.

THE NETHERLANDS AND BELGIUM

Another who worked with them was Dutch Foreign Minister J.A.E. Patijn, who had gone with Buchman to Sweden to prepare the Visby assembly. He, like Ramm, had been able to affect relations between countries. There had been a seventy-year-old river conflict between the ports of Antwerp in Belgium and Rotterdam in the Netherlands. The World Court handed down a verdict in favor of Belgium. The delight of the Belgian press was irksome to the Dutch, not least to Patijn, who was then the Dutch ambassador to Brussels. He was slated to speak at a banquet in Brussels and, though normally quiet and courteous, he had prepared some biting phrases in retaliation for the press attack.

Patijn's wife, Elsie, who had undergone the kind of change Ramm had experienced, suggested to her husband that God might give him wisdom as to the kind of speech he should make. He brushed the suggestion aside. But, he said later, as he was dressing for dinner, something said to him, "Forget your pride. This is your chance. Seize it." To everyone's astonishment he complimented his host country on the court decision, which, he said, paved the way for better friendship in the future. The next day the Belgian press adopted a new tone, and bitter comments ceased. The Dutch press followed suit. "The fact that I was able to make such a speech," he said later, "was only because of my deep conviction that it was much more in accord with God's will than the speech which I had previously wished to make."

The following year Patijn was made foreign minister. Interviewed about the new attitude he seemed to be bringing to the task, he said,

> When I have an important decision to make, I have learned to think it over during a quiet time of listening to God. After our quiet time each morning, my wife and I talk over the guidance God has given us. This gives me a feeling of greater objectivity. I have found in this way the greatest help in the solution of personal and family difficulties, and in my work as foreign minister.

GERMANY

All through the thirties the situation in Germany was much on Buchman's mind, and many of his campaigns were designed to influence its leaders. His work within Germany soon drew the vigorous opposition of Nazi leadership and was banned by the Gestapo. Outside Germany he was sometimes misunderstood or criticized for his efforts. A *Manchester Guardian* correspondent repeatedly asked him, "Have you changed Hitler yet?"

In September 1939 Germany invaded Poland. Buchman's efforts to prevent war had been in vain. But his work, particularly in the Scandinavian countries, as Bishop Fjellbu would later confirm, helped stiffen the resistance to the Nazis. In Denmark, for instance, those associated with the Oxford Group took a variety of initiatives. Valdemar Hvidt, a High Court advocate, started LAB, the National Movement to Combat Unemployment. This development, according to the Danish prime minister, not only dramatically reduced the unemployment figures but also became the strongest unifying factor in the country; it incidentally deprived the German occupation authorities of a case for transporting unemployed workers to Germany.[3]

Richard Möller Pedersen, a theology graduate, and Troels Oldenburg, a lawyer, helped establish teamwork among various youth organizations, which brought the popular front against Nazism to life. Colonel H.A.V. Hansen became the channel for uniting politicians and the people with army officers under a single command in the resistance movement.[4]

The Reverend Howard Blake, an American clergyman working in Denmark at the time, says that many of the initiatives went back to a meeting called by a prominent shipowner, Christian Harhoff, who was active in an earlier six-week Oxford Group campaign. When the Germans suddenly invaded Denmark, he realized that there would be a strict prohibition of meetings by the occupying forces. So he phoned all those with whom he had worked, or who had spoken publicly at occasions, and invited them to his home that very night. "Out of that meeting," wrote Blake, "came initiatives that greatly helped to unite divided groups to stand and act together in the first difficult years of the occupation."[5]

In 1943 the Oxford Group people in Denmark were active, with others, in helping Jews to safety. Keld Jorgensen, one of those later responsible for Moral Re-Armament in Denmark, wrote, "It was actually during a night, when we had to hide in a forest from the Germans with 250 Jews, that I decided to accept the challenge I had met through the people in the Oxford Group. The next night we got all 250 men, women, and children safe to Sweden."[6]

PREPARING THE UNITED STATES FOR WAR

With most of his committed personnel involved in the war effort in different countries and travel almost impossible, Buchman worked with those still available in the United States. His focus became the preparation of the United States for the war effort: the building of morale and efforts to break industrial bottlenecks. This period also saw the development, with the enlistment of talented people from the entertainment industry, of drama as a way of communicating ideas. Their work included a patriotic revue, *You Can Defend America*, which came with a handbook and a foreword by General John J. Pershing, and the industrial drama, *The Forgotten Factor*, written by Alan Thornhill. Then-Senator Harry Truman said of these plays and the teams of people traveling with them, "Where others have stood back and criticized, they have rolled up their sleeves and gone to work. They have already achieved remarkable results in bringing teamwork into industry, on the principle not of 'who's right' but of 'what's right.'"

A conference and training center for Moral Re-Armament was established on Mackinac Island, Michigan.

POSTWAR EFFORTS

When the war ended in 1945, MRA entered a new phase. Ever since the outbreak of the war Buchman and his colleagues, even those on the world's battlefronts, had been thinking about how to rebuild the postwar world. To assist in this task, some of Buchman's colleagues in the U.S. armed forces were given speedy discharges on the intervention of Secretary of State George Marshall.

In April 1945 Buchman and a team were in San Francisco, where members of the new United Nations were trying to get agreement on the UN structure. A difficult issue facing them was the fate of non-self-governing territories, for which a trusteeship status was being worked out. The British delegation was finding General Carlos Romulo, who was chairing the delegation of the Philippines, particularly difficult. A performance of *The Forgotten Factor* was on the official program. The play was introduced by General Romulo and A.R.K. Mackenzie, a member of the British delegation. Romulo told fellow delegates that what they would see on stage was "something that can be transferred to our conference rooms."

Garth Lean wrote of Romulo, "After seeing *The Forgotten Factor* he completely changed the tone of his next speech on trustee-

268

ship. When he had finished speaking, he passed a note to Mackenzie with the words on it 'the forgotten factor?' "

Alistair Cooke reported that, as the conference dragged on, journalists had been listing the unsolved issues:

> The list last night was formidable, but now to the astonishment of delegates and press alike, it would seem that Dr. Evatt [Australian minister of external affairs] has undergone a personality change and General Romulo has unaccountably fallen in love with the British.

On the initiative of the Swiss, a center of reconciliation was established a year later in Caux, Switzerland.* In 1952 a team of two hundred people involved in five stage productions and led by Buchman, spent many months in India. The following year another team traveled with plays throughout Africa. Other missions went to Southeast Asia and South America. Buchman was working more and more toward indigenous leadership in countries. Buchman had always envisaged MRA not as an organization you joined or as a home for any single spiritual idea, but as a good road on which people of all faiths could travel together. Those years saw spiritual leaders and people from the Buddhist, Hindu, and Muslim faiths coming to Caux and to Mackinac.

The experience gleaned in industry during the war was to prove helpful in ending industrial deadlock. In the early fifties newspaper headlines proclaimed MRA's role in solving strikes at United Airlines and National Airlines. At the same time musical productions out of the Mackinac center brought the ideas of MRA to millions. They drew on the expertise of Hollywood. One play, *The Vanishing Island* by Peter Howard and Cecil Broadhurst, portrayed in satirical style the weaknesses in East and West and the need for "a superior ideology." It traveled around the world and was part of an effort to develop an ideological answer to commu-

---

*The effect of Caux in postwar Europe is detailed in section 1, chapter 2.

nism. It drew considerable opposition from both communists, who saw it as undercutting class warfare, and from some in the democracies, who objected to their weaknesses being exposed.

In 1959 the booklet, *Ideology and Coexistence,* was sent to millions of homes in America and other countries. It was an attempt to clarify the ideological struggle, but its forthright analysis of the nature and aims of communism contributed to the image that MRA was just a vehicle of anticommunism.

EFFORTS TO END RACIAL DIVISIONS

In the fifties another important strand of MRA's work was woven when black leaders began coming to the conference center at Mackinac. Then in 1955 an international conference was held in Washington, D.C. More than a thousand people from forty-one countries attended. A new dimension of racial unity was one of the themes. Among the blacks present from the United States was Mary McLeod Bethune, the seventeenth child of a family of former slaves, founder of Bethune Cookman College, and a former adviser on minority affairs to President Franklin Roosevelt. She said on that occasion:

> There are sixteen million people like me in America who have been dreaming, praying, working, toiling, sacrificing, forgiving for an hour like this. Only a basic change of heart in men and women of all races can handle the present integration program in the U.S. Laws and law enforcement alone can never do it. The task of morally rearming the nation is the greatest job to which any of us can apply our energies and talents. To be part of this great uniting force of our age is the crowning experience of my life.

Sitting in a wheelchair near the front was Mrs. William P. Wood of Richmond, Virginia, whose parents had been slave owners. She asked if she might speak. Rising from her chair, Mrs. Wood apologized for the racial prejudice she had felt. She said to

Mrs. Bethune, "I am glad to take this opportunity to shake hands publicly with someone of your race, because I helped to build racial bitterness. I have decided to commit the rest of my life to building bridges between the two races."

This moving encounter became the centerpiece of a musical show, *The Crowning Experience,* created at the Mackinac center by Alan Thornhill and Cecil Broadhurst. It was based on the life of Mrs. Bethune; her role was played by American mezzo-soprano Muriel Smith and that of Mrs. Wood by British actress Phyllis Konstam. The impetus for the creation of the musical was an explosion of violence in Little Rock, Arkansas, in the autumn of 1957 over the integration of black and white schoolchildren.

In June 1958 *The Crowning Experience* opened in Atlanta. Thirty years later the *Atlanta Daily World* described what happened. The issue then, wrote the paper, was desegregation. The play began with two performances in the civic auditorium, one of the few places open to black and white people at the same time:

Sixty plain clothes policemen mingled with the crowd, prepared for an explosion. The Jewish owner of the Tower Theater "came in trepidation and left in exultation." He approached the Moral Re-Armament cast and offered them his theater without any color bar for as long as they could fill it. The play ran for five months, without incident—except the precedent of interracial audiences pouring through the doors.

The paper quoted pioneer black attorney, Colonel A.T. Walden, who said, "Atlanta will never be the same again. The atmosphere throughout the city, the shops and buses [at that time just being desegregated] changed, and was the talk of the town." And when John F. Kennedy became president, he sent for Walden to learn the story behind the change of atmosphere.

That summer *The Crowning Experience* broke attendance records when it played at the National Theater in Washington, D.C. In September 1958, Drew Pearson described its effect in Atlanta in his syndicated column, "Behind what happened in

Georgia is an even more amazing story of how dedicated people from all walks of life are organizing to find a solution to a problem that our political leaders have been unable to resolve—the explosive challenge of Little Rock."

A group of Africans from different countries who were in the United States to help with the MRA program had taken their film *Freedom* to Little Rock. Among those who saw it was Mrs. L.C. "Daisy" Bates, president of the National Association for the Advancement of Colored People, who had risked her life taking black children to a white school. She went with a party made up of both races to the Mackinac center. There she decided to visit the governor of Arkansas, Orval Faubus; unknown to her, he had also seen *Freedom*. The interview and handshake between the two was described by a CBS radio commentator who was summing up the principal events of 1959 as "possibly the most significant news event of the year which marks the end of a hundred years' civil war in the United States of America." An editorial in the Hearst chain of papers just before Christmas commented, "Usually Moral Re-Armament works quietly in furtherance of its purpose but sometimes its efforts culminate in drama. . . . Well, this story couldn't have come at a better season, could it?"[7]

The story behind this event was told by the African American weekly, the *Pittsburgh Courier,* under the headline, "Bates stresses role MRA played in 'miracle' of Little Rock." The paper quoted Mrs. Bates's husband as saying,

This week Mrs. Bates, a strong foe of Governor Faubus, met the Governor for more than two hours. It was her experience with MRA that gave her the courage to ask for this appointment. It was probably something of Moral Re-Armament in him which made him accept. It is hard to evaluate now, but it may be a turning point. If we instill MRA into the people of Little Rock, it will turn the city from chaos into happiness.

Six years later Mrs. Bates said that when it came to school integration, better jobs for blacks, and desegregation of restaurants and hotels, Arkansas had made more progress than any other state.

MRA AFTER BUCHMAN

Buchman's biographer, Garth Lean, wrote:

> Buchman, because of age and increasing ill-health, was not always able to participate in these adventures, but no one doubted who was behind the initiatives. In 1958 the National Association of Colored Women's Clubs, at their convention in Detroit, awarded him a permanent trophy as "the greatest humanitarian of them all."

The initiatives in the field of race relations and industry were dealt a setback when in 1961 Buchman died at age 83. Despite good intentions he had not prepared adequately for his succession. There was no process for resolving differences, partly because there was a certain naiveté among his followers, who could not imagine that serious differences could divide such a closely knit fellowship.

During the 1950s there had been phenomenal growth in the work of MRA in terms of both outreach to the world and numbers of people who had made themselves available to work with Buchman, full-time and unpaid. But the trade-off was that inadequate time was sometimes given to helping full-time workers find their right place and talk through areas of dissatisfaction. The task at hand sometimes took precedence over the best development of the individual worker.

There were clashes of view among Buchman's colleagues. There had always been a tension between those in MRA who put priority on changing the world and those who emphasized changing people. In Buchman's mind the two were meant to go hand in hand. Those most passionate to reach the wider public focused their efforts on creating plays, films, advertisements, and the like to get the MRA philosophy to the public. They thought of MRA as democracy's inspired ideology, the ideological answer to communism and fascism. And their efforts were taken seriously by the communist leadership, which often credited them with more influence than they had and regularly attacked MRA in radio broadcasts and in the press. Some others, concerned that something of faith might be lost in activity and the emphasis on ideology, tended to dwell more on personal sanctity and salvation.

Although the selflessness and flexibility of this committed team meant that they could do remarkable things, such as moving large numbers of people at short notice to situations in need of help, some people suffered from the pressure of feeling that they had to conform to the behavior expected of them. In their zeal individuals were at times excessively responsive to direction and correction from the small group of people around Buchman. A rigidity of control emerged, and a certain harshness characterized some relationships. An unintended consequence was that many people, especially those with a weak sense of self, were deeply wounded. Younger leaders were not always encouraged to give direction to a work that had spread to thirty or forty countries. They chafed for change in the way decisions were made and in the content and packaging of the message.

Some people feel that Buchman, particularly after suffering a stroke in 1942, did not see issues and people as clearly as he once had. Buchman foresaw some of the generational difficulties in the handover of his work but could not forestall them. In 1960, shortly before his death, he said, "When I am gone the work will be run by a cabinet of like-minded friends around the world. But you are not ready for that yet. First there will be one man."

For a time Buchman's mantle fell, as he had wished, to Peter Howard, a talented British journalist who had a vibrant faith and had written many books and plays for MRA, who had the confidence of the MRA teams around the world, and who was able to keep MRA united despite its diversity and pulls in different directions. But Howard died unexpectedly four years later at the age of fifty-six.

With Buchman no longer around, and the maturity and spiritual insight of Howard suddenly removed, some saw it as the moment to withdraw from full-time work; others sought the chance to try their wings. Unresolved difficulties, which had been kept quiet by workers' loyalty and their sense that they were having an important impact on world events, came out into the open. Strong and sometimes harmful words were exchanged.

A split was precipitated as a younger group of Americans who had a passion to change the thinking and living of their generation decided to give primary emphasis to reaching young people. They broke free of some of the rigidities of Buchman's last years and, tapping the idealism of the Kennedy generation, they experimented with new structures and methods. They dropped MRA's traditional focus on applying faith in all spheres of human activity. They launched musical shows called "sing-outs," a pictorial magazine called *Pace,* and a liberal arts college at the conference center at Mackinac designed to rally young people around a positive vision.

Many MRA adherents around the world, especially those most impatient to follow Buchman's admonition to "reach the millions," were impressed by the apparent success of these new methods and followed their lead. Others resisted. Communications largely broke off. There was almost paralysis; there were occasional newspaper predictions of collapse. Although the magazine and college soon incurred huge debts and folded, the "sing-outs" evolved into the U.S.-based program of "Up With People," which cut its links with MRA and incorporated separately. Today "Up With People" still gives a global educational experience to several hundred young people each year through training programs and opportunities for service.

The period after Buchman's death was as painful to MRA people as it was unexpected. Large parts of MRA's work had been deeply disturbed by the exclusive emphasis on youth. "Up With People" was seen as a departure from the focus on life-changing and a watering down of the basic principles of spiritual guidance and moral standards on which MRA had been based. Led by the

British arm of MRA and with a degree of self-righteousness that became clear to them only in hindsight, many underscored the necessity for personal change and genuine spiritual experience as the keys to creating new societies. In the 1960s they continued to work for healing and reconciliation in families, communities, and industry, and between races, religions, classes, and nations. Solid work was accomplished through the Westminster Theatre in the United Kingdom; at a new conference center, Asia Plateau, at Panchgani, India; at Caux; and in countries less affected by what had happened in the United States. These efforts, however, sometimes lacked the vision and boldness that had characterized Buchman's earlier work.

These divisions had shaken the confidence of those committed to MRA. Reconciliation and forgiveness, defining characteristics of MRA, were missing at a crucial moment in MRA's own life. Confidence and trust were reestablished over time. The cabinet Buchman had hoped for slowly became a reality, and MRA emerged on a healthier basis—less strident and more humble, less judgmental of other people and more inclusive of those with similar aims. To this day its committed people say that as MRA tries to contribute to healing the past in the world, it also needs to keep working at building bridges to those who went a different direction in the 1960s.

MRA's work in the United States—which had suffered a hiatus that was deeply regretted by those who felt that MRA could have given helpful input to U.S. crises in the 1960s and 1970s—was slowly rebuilt. But Mackinac and the other centers had been sold to support "Up With People" or pay debts or because they were no longer being used. The work in areas like race relations, for instance, was reestablished with regional centers. Its current program, "Hope in the Cities" (discussed in section four, chapter 13), was launched in 1995. During that same year a center for reconciliation was opened in New York City near the headquarters of the United Nations where MRA is accredited as a nongovernmental organization (NGO).

Leadership in many areas in the United States and around the world now comes from men and women too young to have known Buchman or even Howard. To an extraordinary extent MRA has managed to remain faithful to the methods and approach of its founder, taking to heart the lessons learned from mistakes made, without becoming institutionalized (as many organizations in similar situations have done). Formal organization is still kept to a minimum. Coordination is achieved through extensive consultations between MRA's committed people at national and international levels. Leadership is open to people of all backgrounds. Actions are often undertaken in association with people and groups with related concerns. In the 1980s, through careful, step-by-step preparation, a consultative process was put in place to facilitate decision-making on a global basis. It involves the variety of people associated with MRA around the world and has won the confidence of most oldtimers and newcomers alike.

In 1996 MRA's assembly center at Caux celebrated its fiftieth anniversary. In the 1980s and early 1990s new programs were developed at the center:

• The Caux Round Table (discussed in section three, chapter 12), which works to heighten common understanding among world business leaders from Europe, Japan, North America, and other areas so that they may better cooperate in addressing global challenges.

• The International Communications Forum, drawing together men and women in all areas of communication and entertainment who want to take responsibility for the effect of their work on society.

• Creators of Peace, a worldwide link-up of women who conducted a workshop at the Fourth World Conference on Women in Beijing in 1995.

• Annual Dialogues on the Preservation of Creation, which address environmental concerns.

• Caux Anniversary Lectures by varied personalities.

• The Caux Scholars Program, an academic program for university students, who benefit from the presence of people at Caux who have practical experience in conflict resolution.

At an international consultation in Cyprus in November 1993, worldwide goals for MRA internationally were agreed on as follows:

- Heal the wounds of history that sustain cycles of revenge, especially where cultures and civilizations meet.
- Strengthen the moral and spiritual dimensions of democracy by challenging selfish interests and corruption.
- Help individuals and families to counter the climate of blame and selfishness with a culture of care and personal responsibility.
- Foster ethical commitment in corporations and the professions to create jobs and to correct economic and environmental imbalance.
- Rebuild a sense of community and hope in cities and tackle the causes of racial and communal discrimination.
- Forge networks among people from different cultures and faiths based on a shared commitment to work for reconciliation, justice, and peace.

Notes

1. The material in this chapter is taken largely from Lean's authoritative biography of Frank Buchman, *On the Tail of a Comet.*

2. Evensong, University College, Oxford, England, January 31, 1993.

3. Described in full in Nissin and Poulsen, *På Dansk Friheds Grund.*

4. Ibid.

5. Blake, *Way to Go.*

6. Letter to author, November 6, 1995.

7. *MRA Information Service,* January 9, 1960.

BIBLIOGRAPHY

Adenauer, Konrad. *Briefe 1949–1951*. Berlin: Wolf H. Jobst Siedler Verlag, 1983.

Alcoholics Anonymous. New York: Alcoholics Anonymous World Services Inc., 1976.

Ashe, Arthur. *Days of Grace*. New York: Alfred Knopf, 1993.

Austin, H.W. *Frank Buchman As I Knew Him*. London: Grosvenor, 1975.

Bernard, Stephane. *The Franco-Moroccan Conflict, 1943–1956*. New Haven and London: Yale University Press, 1968.

Blake, Howard. *Way To Go*. Merrifield, VA: Pooh Stix Press, 1992.

Buchman, Frank. *Remaking the World*. London: Blandford Press, 1961.

Campbell, Paul. *A Dose of Your Own Medicine*. Ottawa: Grosvenor, 1992.

Campbell, Paul, and Peter Howard. *America Needs An Ideology*. London: Frederick Muller, 1957.

Carmichael, Robert. *Robert Carmichael par lui-même*. Belley, France: Les Editions de Caux, 1975.

Cassidy, Michael. *A Witness For Ever*. London: Hodder and Stoughton, 1995.

Chavanne, Frédéric. "Où aimerais-tu que je change?" N.p. 1995.

deWatteville-Berckheim, Diane. *Le fil conducteur*. Colmar, France: Editions Alsatia, 1993.

Elliott, Hugh. *Darkness and Dawn in Zimbabwe* (pamphlet). London: Grosvenor, 1978.

———. *Dawn in Zimbabwe* (pamphlet). London: Grosvenor, 1980.

Entwistle, Basil. *Japan's Decisive Decade*. London: Grosvenor, 1985.

279

Esterhuyse, Willie. *Apartheid Must Die.* Cape Town: Tafelberg, 1981.

Faure, Edgar. *Si tel doit être mon destin ce soir.* Paris: Librairie Plon, 1984.

Friends of Moral Re-Armament. *Which Way Cambodia?* Phnom Penh: Friends of Moral Re-Armament, 1993.

Gandhi, Rajmohan. *The Good Boatman.* New Delhi: Viking, 1995.

Gareis, Hansjörg. *Das Beste kommt noch.* Schorndorf: N.p., 1994.

Graham, John. "Sit Down, Young Stranger." N.p., 1995.

Grandval, Gilbert. *Ma mission au Maroc.* Paris: Librairie Plon, 1956.

Hale, Reginald. *The Fight to Serve.* Ottawa: privately printed, 1994.

Hamlin, Bryan. *Forgiveness in International Affairs* (pamphlet). London: Grosvenor, 1992.

Hannon, Peter. *Southern Africa: What Kind of Change?* Johannesburg: Grosvenor, 1977.

———. *Whose Side Is God On?* Belfast: N.p., 1995.

Henden, Jon, Erling Förland, and Sven Fraenki. *Education for Tomorrow's World.* London: Grosvenor, 1970.

Henderson, Michael. *All Her Paths Are Peace.* Hartford, CT: Kumarian, 1994.

———. *A Different Accent.* Richmond, VA: Grosvenor, 1985.

———. *Experiment with Untruth.* Delhi: Macmillan, 1977; South Asian Books, 1978.

———. *From India With Hope.* London: Grosvenor, 1972.

———. *On History's Coattails.* Richmond, VA: Grosvenor, 1988.

———. *Hope For a Change.* Salem, OR: Grosvenor, 1991.

———. *Moral Re-Armament . . . A Factor in World Affairs* (pamphlet). Newberg, OR: Barclay Press, 1981.

Hovelsen, Leif. *Out of the Evil Night.* London: Blandford, 1949.

———. *The Flying Norseman.* Ishpeming, MI: National Ski Hall of Fame Press, 1983.

Howard, Peter. *The World Rebuilt.* New York: Duell, Sloane and Pearce, 1951.

Hunter, Willard. *It Started Right There.* Salem: Grosvenor, 1994.

Ideology and Coexistence (pamphlet). New York: Moral Re-Armament, 1959.

Jarlert, Anders. *The Oxford Group, Revivalism and the Churches in Northern Europe, 1930–1945.* Lund: Lund University Press, 1995.

Johnston, Douglas and Cynthia Sampson. Eds., *Religion, the Missing Dimension of Statecraft.* New York: Oxford University Press, 1994.

July, Pierre. *Une république pour un roi.* Paris: Editions Fayard, n.d.

Lean, Garth. *On the Tail of a Comet* (published in the United Kingdom as *Frank Buchman—A Life*). Colorado Springs: Helmers and Howard, 1988.

———. *Rebirth of a Nation?* Poole, Dorset: Blandford, 1976.

Lean, Mary. *Bread, Bricks and Belief.* Hartford, CT: Kumarian, 1995.

Marcel, Gabriel. *Fresh Hope for the World.* London: Longmans, 1960.

———. *Plus décisif que la violence.* Paris: Librairie Plon, 1971.

Micaud, Charles A. *Tunisia—the Politics of Modernisation.* New York and London: Praeger, 1964.

Monnet, Jean. *Mémoires.* Paris: Fayard, 1976.

Montville, Joseph. Editor, *Conflict and Peacemaking in Multiethnic Societies.* Lexington, MA: Lexington, 1989.

———. Coeditor, *The Psychodynamics of International Relationships.* Lexington, MA: Lexington, 1990.

Mottu, Philippe. *The Story of Caux.* London: Grosvenor, 1969.

Mowat, Robin. *Decline and Renewal.* Oxford: New Cherwell, 1991.

———. *Modern Prophetic Voices.* Oxford: New Cherwell, 1994.

Nissin, Henrik, and Henning Poulsen. *På Dansk Friheds Grund.* Glydendal: Foundations for Danish Freedom, 1963.

Peck, Scott. *Further Along the Road Less Traveled.* New York: Simon and Schuster, 1983.

Petersen, Peter. *Sind wir noch zu retten?* Stuttgart and Bonn: Burg Verlag, 1985.

281

Philips, Frederik. *45 Years with Philips*. London: Blandford, 1978.

Piguet, Charles, and Michel Sentis. *The World at the Turning*. London: Grosvenor, 1982.

Piguet, Jacqueline. *For the Love of Tomorrow*. London: Grosvenor, 1986.

Pribram, John G. *Horizons of Hope*. Tulsa, OK: H.P. Publishing, 1991.

Price, David J. "The Moral Re-Armament Movement and Postwar European Recovery." London University, 1979.

Rusk, David. *Cities Without Suburbs*. Washington, DC: Woodrow Wilson Center Press, 1993.

Shriver, Donald W., Jr. *An Ethic for Enemies*. New York: Oxford University Press, 1995.

Smith, Alec. *Now I Call Him Brother*. London: Marshalls, 1984.

Smith, Arnold. *Stitches in Time*. London: Andre Deutsch, 1981.

Sparks, Allister. *Tomorrow Is Another Country*. New York: Hill and Wang, 1995.

Speer, Robert. *The Principles of Jesus*. Fleming, NJ: Revell, 1902.

Spoerri, Theophil. *Dynamic Out of Silence*. London: Grosvenor, 1976.

Tesfagiorgis, Abeba. *A Painful Season and a Stubborn Hope*. Trenton, NJ: Red Sea Press, 1992.

Theroux, Paul. *The Kingdom by the Sea*. Boston: Houghton and Mifflin, 1983.

Turner, Graham. *More Than Conquerors*. London: Hodder and Stoughton, 1976.

Twitchell, Kenaston. *Regeneration in the Ruhr*. Princeton, NJ: Princeton University Press, 1981.

Vock, Franz Johann. "Zur Bedeutung der Moral für die Politik: Eine Untersuchung der Arbeit der Moralischen Aufrüstung an drei Fallbeispielen," Salzburg University, 1989.

von Herwarth, Hans. *Against Two Evils: 1931–45*. London: Collins, 1981.

Waddy, Charis. *The Muslim Mind*. London and New York: Longman, 1976.

INDEX OF PEOPLE

NOTE.   As listed by full or last name.

Index

Index